HEALING RELATIONSHIPS

LEN KOFLER
(with assistance from Prof. Petruska Clarkson)

Healing Relationships

A Practical Guide for
Christian Counsellors and Carers

ST PAULS

ST PAULS Publishing
187 Battersea Bridge Road, London SW11 3AS, UK

Copyright © ST PAULS UK 2007

ISBN 978-0-85439-739-6

Set by Tukan DTP, Stubbington, Fareham, UK
Printed in Malta by Progress Press Company Limited

ST PAULS is an activity of the priests and brothers
of the Society of St Paul who proclaim the Gospel
through the media of social communication.

Contents

Preface   9

Chapter One: Overview of Kofler's personality model and the
five therapeutic relationships: a Christian point of view   15
  1. Introduction to Kofler's personality model   15
  2. The five therapeutic relationships   21
  3. The goals of psycho-spiritual therapy, in adherence to the
     five relationships   25
  4. The importance of relationship   26
  5. Exercises   29

Chapter Two: The transpersonal relationship – the beginning
and end of the therapeutic process   30
  1. The nature of the transpersonal relationship   30
  2. Exercise   32
  3. Current reluctance in the therapeutic world to accept the
     transpersonal relationship   35
  4. Yoga therapy and spirituality   36
  5. Kenosis as the basis of counselling – an attitude and a skill 36
  6. Exercise   42
  7. Further exploration of the transpersonal relationship 42
  8. How can we facilitate the healing process?   48
  9. Four stages of spiritual unfolding   49
 10. The use of the Bible in counselling   53
 11. Exercises   58
 12. Two case studies of the transpersonal relationship   59

Chapter Three: The working alliance   64
  1. The nature of the working alliance   64
  2. The place of the working alliance in Kofler's personality
     model   65
  3. The skills necessary to establish a working alliance 67
  4. Empathy   68
  5. Exercise   70
  6. The importance of the working alliance   70
  7. Descriptions and conditions of the working alliance 72
  8. A clear contract helps to avoid potential problems 75
  9. Exercise   81
 10. The historical development of the concept of the
     working alliance   81
 11. Establishing the working alliance   84

12. Exercise   91
13. Management of the working alliance   92
14. The influence of expectations on the working alliance   94
15. Threats to the working alliance   96
16. Exercise   98
17. Two case studies for the working alliance   98

Chapter Four: The transference relationship: the client's perspective

perspective   103
 1. A description of transference   103
 2. Freud's position with regard to transference   107
 3. Exercise   110
 4. Freud's development of the concept of transference   110
 5. Carl Rogers and transference   112
 6. The re-experiencing therapy of Merton Gill and transference   113
 7. Past experience and present reality   115
 8. The counsellor and transference   117
 9. The all-pervasive nature of transference   117
10. Transferential relationship   119
11. Resistance to transference   120
12. Some transference-inviting questions   122
13. The importance of transference for learning   122
14. Some common transference patterns in therapy   124
15. Transference and idolatry   125
16. Exercise   127
17. Managing the transference relationship   127
18. God-representation   131
19. Exercises   138
20. Two case studies of transference   139

Chapter Five: The countertransference relationship: the counsellor's perspective

counsellor's perspective   145
 1. Working on oneself   145
 2. Freud, post-Freudians and countertransference   146
 3. A potential countertransference   147
 4. Exercise   147
 5. What is countertransference?   148
 6. Patterns from the past disturbing the here-and-now reality   151
 7. Unfinished relationship   153
 8. What are some of the effects of countertransference?   154
 9. How can we manage and use countertransference?   161
10. Failures in the transference and countertransference
    relationship   162

11. Exercise   163
12. How can we assess the effectiveness of transference and countertransference?   164
13. Summary of transference and countertransference   166
14. Exercise   167
15. A case study of countertransference   167

Chapter Six: The developmentally needed or reparative relationship   169
1. Christianity and the Cross   169
2. What is the developmentally needed or reparative relationship?   170
3. Regression and reparative work   171
4. How is this relationship beneficial?   174
5. Diagnosis   176
6. Establishment of the relationship   180
7. Discipline and the developmentally needed relationship   182
8. Reparative relationship linked with the developmentally needed relationship or trauma   184
9. Be careful what you do as a counsellor!   185
10. The heart of the developmentally needed or reparative relationship   188
11. Management and maintenance of the reparative relationship   191
12. Jesus' death and God's forgiveness – a reparative experience   193
13. Practical measures   194
14. Exercises   195
15. Anger and reparative experience   197
16. Exercise   199
17. God's reparative relationship   199
18. The reparative effect of laughter   200
19. Criteria for evaluating the effectiveness of the reparative relationship   202
20. Exercise   205
21. Three case studies of the reparative and the developmentally needed relationship   205

Chapter Seven: The person-to-person or I–You relationship   211
1. What is the person-to-person relationship?   211
2. The destructive use of the person-to-person relationship   212
3. The constructive use of the person-to-person relationship   213
4. Discernment in the use of the person-to-person relationship   215
5. Self-disclosure   216
6. I–You relationship and object relationship   218

7. Further aspects of the I–You relationship 221
8. How to establish the person-to-person relationship 223
9. How to manage the person-to-person relationship 224
10. When do we use the person-to-person relationship? 226
11. Distinction between person-to-person and
    countertransference responses 228
12. Failures as opportunities for breakthrough 234
13. Criteria for evaluating effectivene of the person-to-person
    relationship 235
14. Exercise 236
15. Two case studies: of the I–You relationship 237

Chapter Eight: Relatedness to self 240
1. Low self-esteem 240
2. Improving our self-esteem 242
3. The destructive critic 243
4. How do I gain control over the internal destructive critic? 243
5. Exercises 249
6. Body image and self-concept development 250
7. The influence of culture and subculture on self-esteem 253
8. The influence of family on self-esteem 253
9. Support network 254
10. Exercise 255
11. Self-reliance and God-reliance 255
12. Training yourself for self-reliance and God-reliance 256
13. Exercise over several weeks 257
14. How can parents, teachers, counsellors and formators help
    those in their charge to develop a healthy self-concept? 263
15. What are some signs of positive self-esteem in people? 264
16. How to improve the self-concept step by step 264
17. Exercise 266
18. We are made in the image and likeness of God 267

Conclusion 269
1. Summary 269
2. Recent work on the spiritual dimension of counselling 272

Glossary 275

Bibliography 278

Index 284

Preface

Why did I decide to write this book on psycho-spiritual counselling from a Christian perspective? My experience of working with the formation of clergy and religious at the Institute of St Anselm has led me to ask some searching questions about the place of spirituality in counselling, How can we be more helpful to those clients whose religious belief system is central to their lives? How can we use their spiritual resources in the process of counselling? Do we not limit the healing process, if we just use traditional psychotherapeutic approaches, which do not take the spiritual dimension into consideration? Why do we hesitate to use the language of spirituality and the religious framework from which it is derived, when these are meaningful for so many clients? Surely the client's religious belief system and spiritual convictions need to become a focal point for integration? It is questions like these that have motivated me to write a counselling book based on Christian thinking.

My work as a counsellor and Director of the Institute has made me increasingly aware of the profound importance of relationship in the process of healing. Out of this experience I have formed my own understanding of what it means to be a human being, and from this understanding has evolved a personality model that is both integrative and holistic. I have, therefore, chosen to base this book on my own personality model, in conjunction with the comprehensive definitions afforded by Dr Clarkson's "five therapeutic relationships".

The book is meant to be a training manual for Christian counsellors; while much of what it has to say pertains to all forms of counselling, it does not deal specifically with group therapy. It is primarily about the therapeutic relationship that exists between the counsellor and the individual client. My intention has been to keep the book simple, yet profound. It is not intended to be a scientific or academic work; it is meant to be, first and foremost, a practical guide for people who want to familiarise themselves with counselling skills and approaches, from a Christian perspective. I am fully aware that exploring the inter-connectedness between psychology and spirituality is no simple task, but it is an essential one. This book seeks to give some early indicators as to the future direction that this exploration might take; it is intended to help those who work in a counselling, formation or pastoral setting.

Although Healing Relationships is written primarily for trainee counsellors and carers who share its Christian perspective, no such limits can be set for those clients whom the counsellor or carer will eventually encounter. This is not a book where the student can expect to find answers to questions relating to other Faiths or to secular perspectives. Nonetheless, it is vitally important that the trainee counsellor should be able, as far as can be reasonably expected, to communicate with a client in a linguistic register that is relevant to the client, and which shows respect for that client's background, no matter what it may be. You do not have to be a Muslim to counsel a devout Muslim, but it will not help the therapeutic process if the counsellor is found woefully ignorant of Islam. If the client comes from an almost entirely secular background, it will probably do more harm than good to refer frequently to the Cross or the power of prayer. It is a question of appropriateness and common sense. For some clients, who are apparently not open to the language of religion or spirituality, Christ is encountered first and foremost in the therapeutic relationship itself.

Method and objectives

Underlying the book's philosophy is an integrative approach to counselling. Every counsellor will have a preference for one particular approach or another, usually derived from his or her own history. It is easier to teach just one approach. When we first started work at the Institute, we had many discussions about espousing a single approach, perhaps transactional analysis or the person-centred approach. However, in the end we opted for the more difficult route of integrative counselling. Among the staff were people from varied counselling and analytical backgrounds, but it was generally agreed that there was a danger in teaching the single approach: a person who has studied according to a narrowly defined discipline tends to find it hard to think beyond it. Narrowness of vision can result, so can a certain form of extremism. Since all counselling approaches have much to offer, we decided to offer instruction in all of them during our courses, and to allow the trainee counsellor to discover his or her own preferences and priorities. We knew that such an integrative approach would present problems, particularly that of "cherry-picking", but we thought that the breadth of our method would be a great advantage. We have not regretted our decision. In any case, counselling, as we never tire of saying, is about the therapeutic relationship.

The organisation of the book's material is straightforward. Each chapter has a main title, and several sub-headings, which are listed beneath the title. These sub-headings are numbered, so that the passages to which they refer can be easily located. The first chapter provides an overview of the book's contents. Chapters four to seven deal with the five therapeutic relationships as seen from a Christian point of view (Transference and Countertransference being divided for convenience into two chapters). At appropriate intervals summaries of important points are presented, so as to be readily available to the reader. These are revision aids, not intended for "fast track" reading.

A varied diet of Exercises is offered to the reader, in the hope that these will strengthen his/her grasp of what the author is saying or teaching. These exercises should not become burdensome. Any written answers should be in note form, so that modifications can be easily made. When you encounter a real problem in answering a question, it would be as well to discuss it with your supervisor.

The central chapters all end with case studies, to embody and clarify the nature of each specific therapeutic relationship. One study is usually of a priest or religious. The second is of a layperson, who may or may not belong to a definite Faith family.

Chapter eight deals with the counsellor's own predicaments and selfhood, and tries to help the trainee to coordinate the work of therapy with his/her own spiritual journey. The final chapter, the conclusion, is a summary of the book's content and approach, and offers some concluding thoughts; it also swiftly surveys some recent publications that deal with the spiritual dimension in counselling.

The use of language in the book needs a brief explanation. The words "client" and "patient", and "counselling" and "psychotherapy" will be used interchangeably. Humanistic psychologists prefer the term "client", to get away from the medical model prevalent in older psychoanalytic usage; however, at the Institute of St Anselm we use a variety of therapies and terminologies, selecting those most appropriate for each client/patient. A glossary is included in the appendix to assist the reader who is unfamiliar with some of the counselling terminology used in the text. Biblical quotations are taken from the Jerusalem Bible.

Although the gender of a counsellor undoubtedly has some impact on the therapeutic relationship, this does not, we believe, impinge on matters related to skills and scientific method. The conventional forms s/he, him/her and him/ herself have therefore been generally used. Although this is occasionally cumbersome, it is at least impartial, and serves to remind us that gender is no restriction, whoever the client is. It also makes it easier to draw distinctions between the sexes, where this is necessary. The anonymity of those who have so generously shared their most private thoughts and feelings is protected throughout. The case studies I have chosen vary widely, to give the reader as broad as possible an experience of the ways in which God works through psychology and psychotherapy.

It is important to remember that many of the clients seen by a Christian therapist are not Christians. It is our ethical responsibility to work with them within the parameters of their own values and belief systems. We use Christian terminology with those who speak that language, and secular psychological terminology with others. It is a question of appropriateness. However, because the subject of the book is Christian in its emphasis, and because St Anselm's is a Christian Institute, the language of the work will generally assume a Christian character. Because our experience at St Anselm's has religion at the heart of it, I am aware that there is a tendency in the book to draw on encounters from within that environment. However, all of us also have wide experience of counselling within secular society, and it is hoped that you will find the cross-currents stimulating and thought-provoking.

Writing this book will have been worthwhile if you, the reader, are inspired to live life more fully. This can only be achieved by leaving the safety of comfortable habits and thought patterns, so as to search for the richer land God has planned for you. It is a process of conversion and reconciliation.

Over the years, many participants of the Institute of St Anselm have asked me to put my ideas on paper. This book was partly inspired by these requests. I want to thank all the clients who have shared their lives with me. Through their courage and hard work, I have been privileged to experience the fascinating and awesome grandeur of the creature made "a little less than a god", whom God himself has crowned with glory and praise (Psalm 8:5). Doing therapy feels like reaching inside another person and finding the heart of God.

My deepest appreciation goes to my mentor and friend Petruska Clarkson, R.I.P., who shared her wisdom and professional expertise with me for many years, making this book possible. My profoundest thanks go to Thalia Slin, who was always ready to help in any way in producing this manuscript. My gratitude goes also to Laura Wells, who assisted with the typing of the original MS. Many thanks go to Marion Daly, Eileen Plunket, Derek Clark, Louise Cuming, and all those who have commented on the text, to Jeremy Rowe for preparing the text for publication, and to Thérèse Garman for her many suggestions for clarifying the text. My wish is that all past participants of the Institute of St Anselm and many others may profit from this book on their journey to the promised land, and in becoming better carers, leaders, formators, pastoral workers, growth-facilitators, priests or religious, counsellors or psychotherapists.

Len Kofler,
Director of St Anselm's Institute

Overview of Kofler's personality model and the five therapeutic relationships: a Christian point of view

1. Introduction to Kofler's personality model 2. The five therapeutic relationships
3. The goals of psycho-spiritual therapy
4. The importance of relationship 5. Exercises.

1. Introduction to Kofler's personality model

Anyone who deals professionally with people has a frame of reference for what a human being is; this may be implicit or explicit. For all of us, whether pastoral helper, leader, formator, counsellor or therapist, this frame of reference is relevant whenever we are dealing with or trying to help a particular individual. In this book I use my own personal model, which is a holistic, integrative personality model. Through my research into personality models used by psychotherapists and members of other helping professions, I have found that the human personality is most usefully identified under four categories, which are revealed through four corresponding methods of revealing it: spiritual self (transpersonal approaches), the conscious self (cognitive approaches), the unconscious self (psychodynamic approaches) and embodiment (bodywork and bio-energetics). The spiritual self, the conscious self, and the unconscious self ideally form a unity. In reality, they are very often disjointed and even behave as if independent of one another. This is why many therapeutic approaches take just one isolated "self" or dimension of the person and focus on it, developing highly sophisticated techniques and tools within this discrete discipline for the purpose of healing, while unfortunately disregarding the other related "selves". The isolation of a single "self" is not constructive, because all the "selves" are necessarily inter-related.

All three "selves" are embodied. The body is a central element of being human. Therefore, if a client comes for therapy, my first question is: "Have you seen your doctor? What does he/she say with regard to the problem you have mentioned?" If there is a physical cause for the disease, all therapy might be to no avail. For instance, a student once came to me for counselling, complaining that he was not feeling well. He had seen the doctor, who had told him that there was nothing wrong with him physically. He was a very bright student, who attended all the required lectures, and studied for hours on end in the library. I asked him gently, "Do you ever go for a walk?" His reply was "No". Even when he had to deliver a letter to the post office, which was only twenty minutes away, he took the car. He decided to go for regular walks, and his condition quickly improved!

The "spiritual self", the "conscious self", and the "unconscious self" form a little trinity. This trinity is embodied, and it is embodiment that enables a unity that echoes that of the Blessed Trinity. In Genesis 1 and 2 we read that God made us in His image and likeness; that He made us male and female. He made us a perfect whole, with three dimensions – spiritual, conscious and unconscious – integrated in and through embodiment. In Genesis 3 we read of man's disobedience that leads to shame, embarrassment, a shifting of blame, and a guilty fear of the Lord God. Adam blamed Eve, who in turn blamed the serpent. With the fall, the image of God in man was wounded, and every aspect of our being was affected, and consequently suffered. We experience this "fallenness" in every part of our being: thinking, feeling, doing, creativity, intuition, worship, relating to others, and indeed in simply being. Ephesians spells out this woundedness:

> Intellectually they are in the dark, and they are estranged from the life of God, without knowledge because they have shut their hearts to it. Their sense of right and wrong once dulled, they have abandoned themselves to sexuality and eagerly pursue a career of indecency of every kind. (Eph 4:18-19)

In his Epistle to the Romans Paul asks desperately: "Who will rescue me from this body doomed to death?" (Rom 7:24) These and many more passages in both the Old and New Testaments, together with our own personal experience, remind us what it means to live in this wounded image of God's likeness. For it is within this wounded being that our three selves are incarnated.

The conscious self or "middle self" is our conscious mind. It is that part of us which is "awake", and of which we are aware. It is the part of us by which we reason, think, and make decisions – the conscious mind of modern psychology.

The unconscious self or "lower self" in my Personality Model is similar to the Jungian concept of the unconscious. It performs millions of important functions within the body and mind, every second of the day and these are recorded by the unconscious, which is the memory centre of the personality. All feelings experienced in the present, or when we were young, are stored within this memory centre of the lower, unconscious self. The lower self forgets nothing; its job is to store things up.

Finally, what is the spiritual self or "higher self"? It is the most enlightened aspect of our nature, through which we communicate with God. It is a part of us, and yet at the same time, because of our fallenness, it sometimes seems to be beyond our human reach. The spiritual self is where the Blessed Trinity dwells. It is the holy ground of awe in us. This is the space in us where God can be reached through an inner illumination. True prayer and meditation take place here. Yet it is not so much a level, as an all-pervasive spirit; it has been called the "breath of life" a phrase translated from the Hebrew "ruah". It is the "spiritual self" that engages in communication with the indwelling Blessed Trinity. This is the part to which we must turn in order to become more fully self-actualised, self-fulfilled, integrated and mature. Once we grow to realise more fully our original God-likeness, we become more powerful in Him. We gain a new life of power and happiness; we know we have a greater, more perfect and more powerful part of ourselves than we usually experience in everyday living. We can turn to our higher self and learn to trust it as a great source of comfort and inspiration. No more do we have to struggle with trying to reach a remote God in the heavens who will listen to our small problems. God is dwelling within us, in our spiritual dimension. He longs to help us in our difficulties. This higher or spiritual self, empowered by the indwelling power of God, has the power to solve our problems and to heal us.

Through the indwelling God we are linked with all other higher selves and connected to them. This truth is beautifully expressed in the doctrine of the Communion of the Saints, but also in quantum physics. We are all interconnected. This inter-connection enables us to seek the co-operation of other "higher selves", provided that the co-operation does not conflict with the interest of the others who are concerned.

Sometimes we are just not "tuned in", outside our awareness, and so do not allow access to the "higher self", which will never intervene in one's own affairs unless its help is specifically invited to do so. It may weep for us in our troubles, since it is with us in everything; but it will not step in to help unless specifically asked. The prayer of petition exemplifies this phenomenon: the middle or conscious self has to prepare itself as an intermediary, so that the lower or unconscious self may receive what has been asked for. In other words, we need to learn to communicate with our higher self. We attempt to do this, above all, by "tuning in", by prayer. For myself, I have found in recent years that contemplative prayer has set me once more in touch with the "higher self", when it was becoming distant. We have to make a constant effort to get in touch with the "higher self", the abode of the indwelling God in us. If we do this, and keep on making the effort, a new life of happiness, love and peace will be ours. We have to be in tune with the "higher self" in order to be in tune with God. This higher self is still part of us; we have not lost it, even if we have stopped communicating with it over the years in a meaningful way. Until now, the words of Genesis, affirming that we are made in the image and likeness of God, may not have meant that much to us, yet in the truth of these words lie our power and strength, and they hold the key to performing miracles. However, before we can draw on the power of the higher self, we need to have faith in it. In their book *SQ: Spiritual Intelligence* (2000), Danah Zohar and Ian Marshall discuss at length how we can develop this gift.

In this "trinity of selves" which exists within us, there is an inter-relatedness which is wholesome, and which maintains the essential unity of one self within the human person, in spite of the fact that the three "selves" have different functions. God is at work in us through the higher self, whether we know it or not, whether we are aware of it or not. In a simple and yet highly complicated way, the lower self is also active in us without our knowledge and awareness. However, original sinfulness has brought about an imbalance of interaction. That means that we often make decisions and act on them without using the "higher self" or spiritual intelligence, and without connecting ourselves in that way with the Holy Spirit. Because of this, we make wrong decisions and act in wrong ways, sometimes with awareness of what we are doing, and at other times without that awareness. In this way we harm ourselves. Some people live their lives in such a way that the lower self dominates them far too much. They constantly react to situations rather than respond to them. This has become habitual behaviour for them. The "middle self" and the "higher self" do not get a chance to balance the controlling "lower self". Another imbalance of interaction exists when people function as if they were no more than a conscious mind. Their conscious mind with all its faculties may have been developed enormously. They try to sort out every problem in an intellectual way, neglecting the "lower self" (the "feeling self"), or the "higher self", or both, until their emotional and spiritual life is starving. A third imbalance of interaction between the three "selves" can come about by spiritualising everything and neglecting the "middle self" and the "lower self". If a problem arises, such a person will try to sort it out by saying prayers of petition and doing nothing else; I once dealt with a priest who was involved in homosexual activity by frequenting public toilets. He said to me: "I keep on praying that God may take away this desire from me", as if the prayer required no self-denial on his part.

By over-emphasising any of the three "selves", the human being becomes pathological. We can see, then, that a proper balance of interaction is needed if a healthy unity of the three embodied "selves" is to be achieved.

19

Trusting firmly in this personality model, the counsellor is now in a position to ask him/herself, "Which dimension of the human being needs addressing in this client before me? Do I need to do bodywork, or do I need to deal with the unconscious? Do I need to make a link with his/her spiritual dimension or with his/her conscious self?"

At this point it is necessary to reiterate that this is a matter of prioritising. In fact, all the "selves" are inter-related, and so none of them can be completely eliminated from the investigation of a client's problem; but one dimension or "self" will need more immediate attention than the others. The personality model is like a simple map to show me which aspect or aspects of the client need attention at a particular moment in my therapeutic work. The more I develop my own spiritual intelligence, the quicker and more constructively will I be able to determine what is needed at any given moment in my therapy, formation or pastoral work.

Diagram of Kofler's personality model

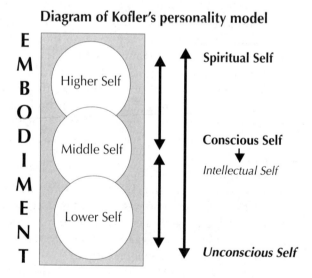

2. The five therapeutic relationships

Reflecting on the Mystery of the Blessed Trinity, it becomes clear that God is perfect relatedness. Our relationship with God has been the central theme in all religious traditions. Our human relationships "de facto" include our relationship with God, although sometimes we are not consciously aware of it. From Clarkson's studies, based on twenty years of research into the various therapy approaches, it is clear that five kinds of human relationship can be established (1995, 6-21), and that the final one of these five to be considered, the transpersonal relationship, is spiritual in its very nature. These five relationships provide an integrative psycho-spiritual framework for therapy, indeed for any pastoral relationship; they permeate all the approaches of counselling (although not all of the five are acknowledged by all the approaches). Five kinds of discourse about the therapeutic relationship are, therefore, potentially possible, whichever approach to psychotherapy or counselling is espoused; these five relationships can also be found in community life, in education, in pastoral work and charities, in fact wherever help is offered and received. All five relationships may occasionally be present in a single therapeutic session; some of them always are. So let us consider these five therapeutic relationships one by one:

i. The working alliance

When we want to offer help to anybody, we need to establish an agreement with them as to how help might be given and accepted. This we call the working alliance. Both therapist and client are involved in this process of establishing a working alliance. When we employ the services of a builder, we do not allow him to come into our house and make alterations without a detailed contract. If we go to the doctor, we tell him where we ache, so that he may prescribe medication or find some other way of dealing with the ache. In the same way, if we want psycho-spiritual therapy, we go to a psycho-spiritual therapist to share our concerns and to ask for help in finding solutions and healing. So that the process may have an ordered framework, we establish the number of sessions, the room where they will take place, the fees, and so on. This is the practical basis of a contract that will empower the counsellor to use counselling skills so as to facilitate the establishment of trust, respect, empathy and unconditional love. It forms the foundation for the working alliance and the beginning of a professional relationship.

God's love provides the model for the working alliance. It is our source of inspiration and constant encouragement, as we grow in our love for our clients, our parishioners, or members of our community. We know that we shall never fully achieve this unconditional love. Sometimes anger, resentment, envy, jealousy or other emotions may block it; nevertheless, the ideal towards which we aim is this kind of love. We are always trying to be better at loving.

A clear working alliance is important for both individual and group therapy and for work in any pastoral setting. A good working alliance is the basis of all therapeutic, pastoral or educational work. Without a good working alliance, many mistakes can be made. Ninety-five percent of counselling problems arise from a faulty working alliance, where expectations, boundaries or responsibilities have not been clearly defined. Over and above this task of defining the process, the contract for a working alliance requires that therapist and client agree to continue to work together, even when the going gets rough, or when one or the other does not want to continue, although in a few cases referral may be the better option. The contract of persistence usually constitutes the lynchpin of the working alliance.

ii. Transferential and countertransferential relationship

This can also be called the unfinished, biased or incomplete relationship. Sometimes, controversially, Clarkson uses the word "distorted". Transference in its widest sense describes the human tendency to carry past experiences into the present. These experiences may be in the form of expectations, wishes, feelings or other behaviour patterns. Psychoanalysts use the term *transference* to describe what may happen in the relationship between client and analyst during treatment, for example where the analyst is seen and experienced as a father by the client. The term *countertransference* refers to the reactions of the analyst with regard to the transference of the patient. The analyst may become a father who cares for the client, or may react in a punitive way in the manner of a sterner parent. This relationship is differentiated from the working alliance, although it can enter the alliance at some stage.

Transference and countertransference are human experiences which can also happen between analyst and patient outside the treatment session. They can be part of any relationship, for example in community living between a superior and members of the community, or even between different members of the community. In the seminary it is likely to occur between staff and students, and in pastoral work between the parish priest or pastoral worker and their parishioners. One day, a priest came to me complaining that his bishop would not provide money for him to undertake a further year of study at the Institute. He said, "He is my father, and therefore he should give me the money to stay on for another year".

iii. Developmentally needed and reparative relationships

There are areas in most people which have not been developed, and which need to be developed. We call this the *developmentally needed* relationship. Maybe we find it difficult to trust anyone, because we never developed basic trust. Or perhaps we never developed autonomy, and so we cling unhealthily to someone else. We may never have developed a clear identity, and do not really know who we are. In all these cases, the personality needs to be engaged with and built up, and the origin of the problem addressed. These are the tasks of the *developmentally needed* relationship.

The developmentally needed relationship refers to a particular developmental period. No matter what comes up in the therapy session, the client appears to go back to that period of his/her life, that stuck place, that fixation point, that point of developmental arrest. The developmental needs of the client were not met or not met sufficiently at the time, and so they keep recurring, and blocking progress.

By way of contrast, the *reparative* relationship refers to a traumatic childhood event, such as the loss of a parent or sexual abuse; it can also refer to the strain induced by rejection or deprivation, or to the trauma created by a catastrophe such as starvation or becoming a refugee. In these cases, the personality has been traumatised by some external influence; its weakness does not stem from an internal precariousness. The injury is "repaired" by attending to it with care in safe therapeutic environment, where the pain can be understood and given a fresh perspective, within which the healing can begin.

iv. Person to person relationship

This could be given other names: the "dialogic relationship" or "I–You" relationship. This is not the relationship with the Transcendent. It is the relationship with the other human being, in the *space* of which the "I–Thou" relationship with God can become apparent. This relationship is not that of an expert with an inferior, or even that of a consultant with a client. It is essentially a relationship between two people, who treat each other as equals, even though it is still guided by professional principles.

v. Transpersonal relationship

This term can be somewhat confusing at first. Transpersonal does not mean impersonal. Impersonal is a negation of the personal, whereas Transpersonal means "personal plus" – the personal is transcended.

Clarkson uses *transpersonal* to describe our relationship with things, which don't fall into any of the categories already mentioned. These things may be concerned with the spirit, or the soul, or with God or with complexity, chaos, quantum physics, or the many kinds of things, mysterious and awesome, which lie beyond human understanding. We say that this

24

relationship is indescribable, because it is experienced beyond the boundary of words; yet we still feel the need to attempt to describe it. This paradox will be explored in chapter two.

3. The goals of psycho-spiritual therapy, in adherence to the five relationships

i. To widen consciousness

This is achieved by bringing unconscious material into consciousness so that we can take more responsibility for our life. For example, it is unconscious material that causes people to be unaware of the impact their actions have on other individuals. This goal is particularly pertinent to transference and countertransference, but is present in all five relationships.

ii. To help us to live more in the here and now as an adult rather than regress to the hurt child

In this way our relationships will be much more mature than the relationships which we have when we regress. We will not always achieve this, but we will become aware when we regress, and will be able to do something about it. Again, regression can occur within any of the five relationships, but it is, perhaps, most obvious during transference.

iii. To help us develop a more mature, adult spirituality

God can be a transferential object for us – a substitute for our parents. We may never give God a chance to be God in our relationship, because we constantly transfer personal past experiences on to Him. Balance can be found by focusing on the transpersonal relationship.

iv. To use spiritual resources in our process of healing and integration

Faith and sound psychology can be a tremendous force for healing, when they act in conjunction with one another.

25

v. To overcome past "stuckness" and repair hurts of past experiences

We do this through the developmentally needed and reparative relationship. Human beings are not static, but dynamic, in a process of constant development from the moment of conception until death. They pass through stages of development during which they have to negotiate certain developmental tasks. Erikson (1992, 54-81) outlines this process of development very clearly If the developmental stages are not fully achieved, a personality deficit remains, which will cause problems at later stages. The individual does have the opportunity later in life to make up for these deficits, and this is where counselling is frequently effective.

4. The importance of relationship

Relationship is the most important aspect of any human being's life. Hardened criminals will rather be executed than be in solitary confinement. To be placed in solitary confinement is the ultimate punishment for human beings. Have any of you ever been sent to Coventry? It is a horrible English expression which means that people behave as if they don't know you. It's a terrible experience. In some cultures it's a notion that is sometimes used in a practice like voodoo, where a curse is placed on somebody, and nobody is allowed to speak to them. Eventually they die from the effects of isolation from human community. Clearly, human relationship is the most important thing for any human being. But, essential as it is, it is also where destruction happens. We would rather live in a bad relationship or a destructive relationship, than be cut off from our interaction with other people. Therefore, as counsellors, formators and helpers, the way in which we relate to those in our charge is most important. Relationship is also the most powerful tool for good we can possibly have. But it is not *just* a tool that we use; it has to be more than that, because in relationship, we ourselves are the instruments of healing.

Relationship defines what is between us. It's not me and you, it's not one plus one, it is what is between us. Relationship pervades everything; it pervades this book, it pervades the way we look at flowers. Can you imagine how many relationships have brought you to the present moment? So relationship is utterly pervasive, and at the same time it is quite a mysterious thing. I don't know if anyone can easily define relationship. I certainly can't.

What does relationship mean? When do I have a relationship with somebody and when not? I have mentioned the potential for damage, because it is when we love someone, or when we are in a binding relationship, that we can really hurt people. We sometimes hear of a stepfather who has been accused of abusing his children. Those young children were in his care and needed relationship with him, but not the type of relationship that he engendered.

So relationship contains the seeds for all the most terrible and damaging things human beings can do to each other. We know that statistically you are more likely to be killed by a member of your own family than by a stranger. That's how dangerous relationships are. Where does sexual abuse happen? It happens in the closest family relationships. At the same time, we can say that the therapeutic relationship is the true locus, the heart, of all therapeutic efforts. It is the heart of formation work. It is the heart of pastoral work. It is the heart of community living.

Psychotherapy and counselling are just one hundred years old; this is an eye blink in the history of humankind. Counsellors and psychotherapists have become – and I am not the only one to refer to them as – "new priests", because they hear confessions – not sacramentally, of course – and make people feel better, and they keep their clients' secrets. They offer them understanding, though they cannot offer absolution. So it is something that has only come about in the past hundred years, with people's breakdown of relationship with the Church, and the breakdown of extended families in our culture. When people lived in communities, the notion of going to speak to a stranger about what was wrong with your friend or your husband hardly existed. You would speak to people in your family, or you would speak to local people involved in your culture.

All relationships have therapeutic potential. Is there anybody who has not been helped by a friend? There is some contention about how relationships with counsellors differ from ordinary friendships. This is because it is difficult to define the healing that can happen with a good friend – or even a hairdresser. Think how many stories a hairdresser listens to. A good hairdresser makes people feel better; the clients relax and give the hairdresser their confidence and their secrets. When the clients leave, their self-esteem has been restored. So hairdressers hear an enormous amount, and often unknowingly apply a kind of therapy – as do bartenders! Can you imagine how much counselling bartenders undertake? There are people in such jobs who will accept, who will listen, who will give unconditional positive regard, contain and keep secrets, and help people get in touch with the healing inside themselves. They differ from counsellors, in that they are not contracted to behave as they do. It is also undeniable that the hairdresser or barman will sometimes collude with the customer, and that may make matters worse. As counsellors and therapists, we are trained professionally to carry out the tasks of listening, responding and behaving in particular ways, but in its essence our work of receiving a client's confidences and relating to him or her is not so far removed from that of these gifted people.

As in all close relationships, when we work as psycho-therapists and counsellors, we can either exacerbate what was wrong in the early relationships, or we can be a force for healing. We can be destructive or constructive.

Relationship is the key to helping those who are lost, abandoned or forsaken, to rejoin the family of humankind. The final thing I want to say at this point is that all approaches to therapy or counselling use relationship. Counselling is the intentional and professional use of relationship for the purpose of healing the client.

5. Exercises

1. Write some notes on the following:
a. Comment on the importance of relationships as indicated above.
b. What does the Christian Mystery of the Blessed Trinity say about relationships?
c. What are the essential dimensions of Kofler's Personality Model?
d. Enumerate the five therapeutic relationships of the Clarkson model.
e. Give two examples of each therapeutic relationship.
f. Compare a good relationship and a destructive relationship, which you have experienced in your life.
g. What are some of the important aspects of a good relationship?

2. Now address this personal task:
Reflect for a few minutes on which dimensions of Kofler's Personality Model need more attention in your own life.
a. What decisions might you need to take, to give these dimensions the necessary attention?
b. Devise a plan for taking these decisions, outlining how they might constructively affect your understanding of relationship.

CHAPTER TWO

The transpersonal relationship – the beginning and end of the therapeutic process

1. The nature of the transpersonal relationship 2. Exercise 3. Current reluctance in the therapeutic world to accept the transpersonal relationship 4. Yoga therapy and spirituality 5. Kenosis as the basis of counselling – an attitude and a skill 6. Exercise 7. Further exploration of the transpersonal relationship 8. How can we facilitate the healing process? 9. Four stages of spiritual unfolding. 10. The use of the Bible in counselling 11. Exercises 12. Two case studies of the transpersonal relationship

1. The nature of the transpersonal relationship

According to our Christian belief we come from God and we return to God. Thus our long-term therapeutic process is seen as beginning with God in the transpersonal relationship and ending with God, although God's presence is recognised throughout the process. Even the short-term therapeutic process can be seen as beginning and finishing with the transpersonal relationship. The transpersonal relationship is the relationship that is all pervasive; it unites us with God and all the resources in the universe. Through God we are linked with the whole of creation. We are part of the universe. It is the relationship which ultimately gives meaning to our existence. As we mature as persons, we become more aware of the cosmic dimension of our existence and of our cosmic participation. The transpersonal relationship is the relationship that will never end.

The transpersonal relationship helps us to contain and transcend the woundedness that we experience. It is our most basic relationship, without which we wouldn't exist. Part of our therapeutic journey, particularly in the second half of life, is to learn to come to terms with this fact, accepting this is the beginning of the deeper healing process. Some people fight all their life facts and events in their history, which they cannot change. For example, they struggle against the fact that their parents were poor or didn't have time for their children, that their mother died when they were young, and so on. It is our attitude towards these unchangeable events, which needs to change. Instead of fighting, we have to learn to accept such facts and events as part of our journey.

Being aware that God called me into existence out of his love, and wants me to share his happiness, provides a haven from which I can face my woundedness safely, because, as Christians, we know that Jesus suffered too, though he was innocent, and that He redeemed us through his suffering. Thus we are called in our daily life to a similar experience of suffering – dying and rising to new life – the Paschal Mystery experience, which is the essence of the therapeutic process. We need to let go of certain wishes and desires, which belong to the past such as: "If only I had good parents my life would be different" or "If only this had not happened to me, I would be much better off now". These are facts, which we cannot change. However, we can change our attitude towards them.

SUMMARY:

The transpersonal relationship is:
- the most basic relationship
- the all pervasive relationship
- the never ending relationship

The transpersonal relationship reveals that:
- we are created by God
- God loves us
- we are united with the universe
- we are called to a cosmic participation
- there is ultimate meaning in life

The transpersonal relationship helps us to:
- contain our woundedness
- transcend our woundedness
- accept unchangeable events and facts in our life
- make meaning of the Paschal Mystery experience in our life.

———

Anthropology shows us how, from the earliest times, prayer, religious ritual, meditation, silence and space regularly preceded any important human undertaking. People invoked the presence and help of the gods. They were convinced of their limitations and the need of the help of the gods or higher beings. When we counsel a client we need to come from the "right" place within ourselves. In Transactional Analysis language ("TA") this means that we must "speak from the adult", while in Christian language it means that we must speak from the "spiritual self". It is the place in us where we are deeply connected with God, the Healer. This is a good place from which to begin our counselling process. We need to use our spiritual intelligence. It is, therefore, important that we find a minute or two to recollect ourselves before a counselling session.

For a believer, the transpersonal relationship in individual counselling is a relationship of three: God, client and counsellor. This awareness will help the counsellor to have the kind of respect, acceptance and patience with the client, which is needed for a growth-producing relationship. The Spirit of God will lead us in the exploration of what the client brings to the session. The Holy Spirit will also guide us to explore the unique personhood and spirituality to which the client is called by God. There may be moments in the session when the counsellor and the client sit in awe and prayer. The client and counsellor may decide to start and/or finish with a prayer or moment of silence. All our growth and healing manifests God's glory, and so it follows that all counselling which produces growth is spiritual.

2. Exercise

Write short notes on the following. What is the function within transpersonal relationship of:

a. prayer   b. religious ritual
c. meditation   d. silence
e. space   f. the counselling process?

The counselling relationship is a relationship of three

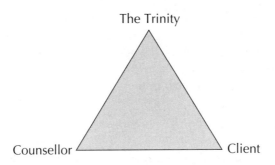

The Trinity

Counsellor   Client

Therapeutic work needs to be built upon the transpersonal relationship. This relationship supports and nourishes all other relationships. It helps us to transcend many things in our life which we otherwise might never be able to transcend. For instance, even though I have worked constructively on my anger, I may well become conscious of more anger invading my heart, as I reflect upon the injustices in the world. I may keep on generating anger by clinging to these injustices and hurts. Similarly, I may refuse to relate to my neighbour, husband, wife, son, daughter or members of the community, because they have hurt me. However, the awareness that we are interrelated and interconnected, that we all belong to God's family, that God forgives us, and that we are called to forgive ourselves and others, may help me to let go of my pain and hurt, and to work through my anger towards renewed relationships with others. This continual awareness is provided and nurtured by the transpersonal relationship.

When I find myself involved in a deeply negative transference or countertransference relationship, this realisation of "interconnectedness" may help me to relate to the person in front of me as adult to adult. The transpersonal relationship provides me with many resources which I will need as I enter more deeply into the therapeutic process. The thought that God created me and loves me, even when I am experiencing myself as "worthless", as if "I should not exist" as "bad", will help me face my feelings; I shall be able to look at them, and allow them to become a conscious part of myself, even though I may not feel loveable and may not be ready to accept the Good News of God's love for me. Later on in the therapeutic process, the transpersonal relationship will help me to hold on to the good aspects of myself as well as the less good aspects. It helps me to accept and hold the polarities of good and bad in me.

SUMMARY:

Therapeutic work needs the transpersonal relationship to:
- nourish all other relationships
- help us to transcend hurts
- motivate us to deal with negative transferences and countertransferences
- provide us with many resources
- help us to accept and hold the polarities of good and evil within us

———

Transpersonal Relationship is a matter of experience rather than analysis. Occasionally, the counsellor may feel that there is an opportunity to discuss the transpersonal relationship, and that talking will open a spiritual avenue; sometimes, when the client is obviously suffering a great deal, the transpersonal relationship may be induced through invoking the name of Jesus, as the one who suffered for us. When a person has Faith, suffering will have a special meaning; pain has to be accepted, not rejected, and this acceptance is itself a passage to the transpersonal relationship. If the counsellor is able to reflect the client's experience accurately, this may reinforce Faith. At the core of the transpersonal relationship, as always in counselling, is love.

3. Current reluctance in the therapeutic world to accept the transpersonal relationship

It is strange that although psychotherapists have to deal with all kinds of problems such as sexuality, aggression, dependency and lack of responsibility, for many the exploration of spiritual concerns still remains a taboo subject. However, over the past decade, there have been many indications that this has begun to change. Non-Christian disciplines can help us here. Mystics from all kinds of backgrounds meet in this matter of transpersonal relationship. Here we find a common denominator. This is a basis for the meeting of different members of a religion: each worshipping in their own way, just being with the divine. The transpersonal relationship is the basis for dialogue between various Christian denominations, between various religions and between religion and the scientific world.

Swami Ajaya (1985, 282) a clinical psychologist and swami, lamented the resistance to spirituality in therapy. "Yet strangely enough", he lamented, "the open exploration of spiritual concerns still remains taboo for the majority of psychotherapists."

We need to determine whether, as therapists, we are inclined to give in to this resistance. Are we closed or open to the transpersonal relationship and the concepts behind it? On the one hand, there are clients and therapists who have no awareness, or no named awareness, of the spiritual dimension of the relationship. Others may resist any intrusion of the spiritual, the transcendental, or the numinous into their own experience. They are in a state of resistance to the sublime. They may deny or resent the possibility that extra-rational factors may impinge on their conscious life. Some clients say that when they have shared and wanted to deal with spiritual concerns, the psychotherapist has been unable to work with them. The spiritual dimension, Ajaya says, is inherent in Yoga therapy.

4. Yoga therapy and spirituality

During a course of Yoga therapy, the client learns to overcome conflict, to go beyond his limitations and to experience a wider unity. Identification with the ego is transcended. Consciousness of the Self, which is seen as the most comprehensive centre of integration, begins to dawn. According to yoga therapy, our spiritual evolution takes place in three stages. Of the seven chakras (basic energy centres in the body) the three highest lead us to ever-wider experiences of spiritual growth.

The fifth chakra, "vishuddha" leads the ego to surrender its authority to a universal nurturing centre of love and wisdom. We still remain identified with the ego, but the centre of our interest is now some aspect of universal consciousness. This becomes the object of our devotion. At the sixth chakra, "ajna", our ego with its limited perspective finds further dis-involvement. We become neutral observers of life's melodramas and we experience an underlying unity of being. At the seventh chakra, "sahasrara", we pass beyond involvement with forms. We realise our highest state, which is unitary consciousness. Clearly, the Yoga therapist is using, or opening up to, the transpersonal relationship, and is inviting the client to follow the same path of enlightenment. We can learn much about the spiritual side of counselling from the concepts of Yoga.

5. Kenosis as the basis of counselling – an attitude and a skill

The word *Kenosis* comes from the Greek language and means *emptying oneself.* As a counsellor, I have to empty myself to allow God to work through me, to become a channel of grace. I have to empty myself of all my prejudices, judgements, feelings and thoughts, so that I can be fully present to the client. In this way, God's grace can work through me. Kenosis is one of the ways in which we can be sure of being really present to the client. At the beginning of each counselling session, I take some space to empty myself and be ready for God's grace, and for the client. I empty myself of any preoccupation I may have with theory or skills, and of any prior knowledge which I may have about the client, so that I can be fully present to what s/he brings to me. In the presence of God I am a receiver of insights and inspirations. In the presence of the client I am receptive to *reactive counter-transferences*, of what is going on in the client's unconscious in the here and now, and of the many insights which I can gain through them. I am also receptive to *projective identification*, which is a pre-verbal way of communicating (DuPont, 1984). I will want to make sure that my *proactive countertransferences* (my own unfinished business) do not interfere with the counselling process; this too is Kenosis.

DEFINITIONS:

What is reactive countertransference?

This is what I pick up through my unconscious from the unconscious self of the client, so that I become aware of it in the here and now. By means of this process I may be able to reveal to the client what is going on in his unconscious.

What is projective identification?

We see projective identification as Ogden does (1979), as a process which has three phases. Let us take the prime example of a baby:

a. The first is a fantasy stage. During this stage the baby imagines that s/he can split off an unwanted or endangered part of himself and push it outward into the mother.

b. The second is the induction stage. The baby behaves in such a way that the mother, the intended recipient of the endangered part, is made to experience the same feelings as those which the baby wishes to remove and destroy.

c. The third is the metabolisation stage. During this final stage, the recipient inwardly processes the projection and returns it in a modified form to the baby.

For example, a baby experiencing discomfort from an impulse or feeling such as fear or anxiety wants to get rid of the anxiety or fear. Unconsciously, he imagines that he can evacuate it and deposit it with his mother. He cries, struggles and whines in such a way that he evokes within his mother feelings akin to his own unwanted feelings. The mother absorbs, and then returns these unwanted feelings in a modified form. The baby can cope with this metabolisation. Finally, the mother might cuddle the baby and gently laugh at his temper.

Projective identification for adults follows much the same route. The client fantasises about pushing off some unwanted aspect of the self on to the therapist. Induction follows, with the counsellor being "asked" to feel the same as the client. In the metabolisation stage, the counsellor processes the projection, and returns it in a modified form to the client, who can then see the unwanted obstacle from a clearer perspective.

What is proactive countertransference?
This is the counsellor's reaction to the client, coming from unfinished business in the counsellor's own life story. This can and often does interfere with the counselling process.

We shall now apply the meaning of Kenosis to the counselling process in further detail. We begin with two principles, which may at first appear to be in conflict with one another, but which in fact balance each other:

1. Just as the Word of God, though emptied, did not cease to be the Word, so the counsellor cannot cease being what she or he is. Often the counsellor has to leave his/her own social environment and enter another social environment, e.g. a different social class. To some extent, the counsellor has to leave his/her own culture in order to be able to enter the culture of the client. Although this may mean that temporarily the counsellor leaves behind his/her own culture and language, this does not mean that the self of the counsellor is diminished; one does not have to be a Maori because one is counselling a Maori. In this process, the counsellor has to accept his/her limitations; only through acceptance will s/he travel far along the road to detachment.

2. The counsellor has to go beyond or transcend his/her own culture and mentality so as to be open as far as possible to the culture and mentality of the client with whom s/he is working. Whatever in us is able to awaken others to a new way of life is gain for them. The simple fact that the counselling is done by someone who belongs to a different culture, often adds a singular value to the client.

Let us now look at some of the concrete ways in which Kenosis can work for a counsellor. For some – and this is quite common at St Anselm's, where the community is international, kenosis may need to occur as the result of a language barrier confronted during their studies. Others may find it in the impossibility of entering into any kind of deeper relationship; they may need a lot of counselling themselves. The barrier that prevents the forming of a relationship between client and counsellor may be a purely personal problem. It can also be the result of basically different cultural attitudes. Kenosis will place the counsellor in the receptive attitude that is needed so as to understand the client. Kenosis rids the counsellor of pride in his own culture. On the other hand, he must not give unconditional admiration to the culture of the client, which must also be transcended. Every culture has its weak points. It, too, has to pass through conversion if it is to receive healing.

The culture of the client will enrich the counsellor, if s/he gets to know and appreciate it, as far as possible. As s/he draws closer to the client, the counsellor will feel himself/ herself more and more in harmony with the world of the client, its nature and its culture. As a supervisor, I have often observed that, where there is a distance between counsellor and client at the beginning of the counselling process, it gradually vanishes, until towards the end the relationship is very close. The process enables deep human relationships to develop. In the person of the Christian counsellor, Christ once more eliminates the distance separating God from human beings. We may call this process adaptation or inculturation.

At the Institute, one of our obvious barriers is that of language, since many of the student counsellors have English as their second language. They come from all over the world. They are required to have reached an acceptable standard of written and spoken English, but that does not mean that they understand all the nuances of this difficult language! Kenosis will help us when we are faced with the ordeal of counselling clients with language problems, where extreme difficulty in communication may lead to feelings of utter frustration and discouragement. If we want to be transformed in depth through the pain of being with a client who has language problems, there is no alternative to perseverance. Otherwise, our words remain mere tools, which we use to communicate ideas that do not connect with the client at any depth. When confronted by language difficulties of any kind – and this by no means pertains only to foreigners – the counsellor must empty him/herself of the internal demand for instant and clear verbal communication

We need to keep in mind the reasons for these different kinds and forms of Kenosis. The reason is that we hold this message very dearly: God loves us, and we are called to love others, our clients.

Perfect Kenosis has been attained on the Cross. No counsellor's spirituality can escape this fact. The cross remains the central mystery of human life. We come through death to resurrection: life reveals itself to us in the very midst of death. This is the Paschal Mystery experience, which we have to undergo constantly if we want to become effective counsellors. As the counsellor enters deeply into the mystery of death, s/he can only save people by manifesting in her/his life and in the counselling process itself, the secret of hope. Counsellors often lose heart when they see how ineffectual their efforts appear to be, but we must bear in mind that we do not know exactly where our work is really effective. When Christ died on the Cross, he reached the extreme point of Kenosis, and at the same time he drew all people to himself. When we feel crucified in the counselling session, we may draw the client to ourselves unexpectedly. This is the mystery of suffering. By embracing this understanding, the therapist can ground his/herself psychologically and spiritually. At the level of embodiment, it is also possible to ground oneself, by putting one's feet down appropriately, by breathing deeply, or by sitting comfortably. In this way the therapist will be able to be fully present to the Spirit as well as to the client, and become a channel of transformation.

SUMMARY:

Some aspects of the function of kenosis for the counsellor:

- Space and silence at the beginning of the session.
- Emptying oneself of prejudices, information, extreme negative or positive emotions.
- Emptying oneself of the preoccupation with skills, theory, and proactive countertransference; becoming receptive to the inspiration and guidance of the Spirit, and to reactive countertransference and its insights.

———

6. Exercise

Write a few lines in answer to the following. What are:

- Reactive countertransference?
- Proactive countertransference?
- Projective identification?

Check your definitions with those provided on pages 37–38.

7. Further exploration of the transpersonal relationship

To the transpersonal belongs everything which is involved when we pray or are amazed by a miracle: those kinds of things that we can't find words for. In terms of the relationship with the client, the point of the transpersonal relationship is that the person of the counsellor is not present as a personality but rather as a vessel, a channel to enable the transpersonal relationship to work. The counsellor is emptiness; the ego is emptied out. When the transpersonal enters the therapy room, it comes as grace, it is mystery, and it is awe. It is that which we don't understand but which moves us. It is that which makes some people get well against all the odds. We may call it God's providence. It has to do with the therapeutic aspect of our work. It is present in any kind of caring work, in any kind of medical work, and in every relationship. Just because we don't mention it by name, that doesn't mean that it is not there. The five aspects of a relationship are more or less present wherever we meet other people; the transpersonal relationship exists in the space between people. It is where, in the German language, the Du (Thou) becomes manifest. It is where the I–You relationship melts into a shared intimacy, which is no longer primarily personal. It is a silent place. All the counsellor can do is to point a person in the right direction towards this experience.

The transpersonal relationship in counselling and formation is concerned with those aspects of the healing relationship, which cannot be put into words. It has nothing to do with ego or self. It is *trans*personal – beyond the personal. It deals with things at the edge of chaos, with the uncertainties of complexity, and with the unknowable frontiers of quantum physics. The transpersonal never wholly submits to explanation. Often it is wordless silence. It merely requires that we open our hearts and our souls in faith-full expectation – for who knows at what hour the bridegroom comes?

Of course, we need to learn as much as we can about being human through our own experiences, through books and through good teachers. There is no denying the importance of such learning, but such learning, if thoroughly pursued, always leads us ultimately to where we do *not* know. This unknowing is neither an insincere humility, nor a laziness about putting in the hard work to gain as much personal knowledge about healing relationships as we can. It is that which "passeth all understanding". If we create space for the transpersonal therapeutic relationship to become manifest in our work, healing can happen independently of our gifts of learning, our inevitable limitations or our greatest theoretical understandings. Ultimately, it is not we who are responsible for the new life experienced by our clients. In the preparation of the disciples for their work in healing the people, the greatest trainer taught: "It was no human agency that revealed this to you but my Father in heaven" (Mt 16, 17–18).
It is God, who makes all things possible, who speaks in us.

In the transpersonal relationship, then, we learn to cope with ambiguities, contradictions and paradoxes, which are at the heart of human experience: "Anyone who wants to save his life will lose it; but anyone who loses his life for my sake will find it. What, then, will anyone gain by winning the whole world and forfeiting his life? (Mt 16, 25) and "Do not suppose that I have come to bring peace to the earth: it is not peace I have come to bring, but a sword." (Mt 10:34)

The transpersonal relationship

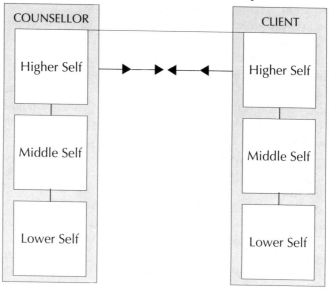

In Jungian psychology, the relationship between the unconscious of the analyst and the unconscious of the patient constitutes the transpersonal relationship. For the Christian counsellor, transpersonal relationship happens between the spiritual self of the client and the spiritual self of the therapist. Both definitions are accurate, because it is in the unconscious spiritual part of ourselves that we truly meet God, while our conscious awareness mediates the encounter through a sense of awe, sanctity or the numinous. Because the transpersonal relationship happens between the spiritual self of the client and the spiritual self of the therapist, it is marked by a sense of timelessness.

Any form of relationship which is not covered by the first four relationships as described in chapter one, is bound to be transpersonal. Because transpersonal relationship is essentially numinous and open to the supernatural, it is inevitably harder to define than Clarkson's four other Relationships. Faith is the way in which the numinous is made comprehensible, but

Faith cannot confine the numinous. By its very nature, the numinous belongs, in therapeutic terms, to transpersonal relationship.

The very difficulty that makes it hard to explain renders the transpersonal relationship appealing to extremism. It can become distorted, when not in conjunction with the other forms of relationship. There is a well-known anecdote concerning St Ignatius of Loyola, founder of the Jesuits. In the early days of his conversion, when zealous and chivalrous and vastly ignorant, he left it to his horse to decide whether or not to take the road which would lead to his killing an inoffensive Moor, who, when pressed in conversation by Ignatius, politely said he could not accept the Immaculate Conception of the Virgin. (*The Tablet*, 11 July 1998, 903). Throughout history, there have been far more serious occasions, when the numinous has been seen as the justification for violence. However, for the Christian counsellor to exclude the transpersonal relationship, either explicitly or implicitly, would be to diminish and falsify relationship itself. It refers to the spiritual dimension of relationships, but is not exclusive. It can be part of the working alliance, and of the person-to-person relationship. There is also a spiritual element in the transferential, countertransferential, reparative and developmentally needed relationship, because the spiritual is "all-pervasive" "If the analyst has been moved by his patient, then the patient is more aware of the analyst as a healing presence" (Samuels, 1985, 189).

The transpersonal relationship between a client and therapist is based upon an authentic, mutual high regard and acceptance. It transcends the other "definable" relationships. This relationship is "felt" implicitly as existing in the "between" of relationship. There are moments of being together, which are impossible to articulate in words. The relationship goes hand in hand with a shared belief in change, in healing, in transformation. It is the powerful and inexplicable healing force within counselling and therapy.

The flow of communication from the higher self

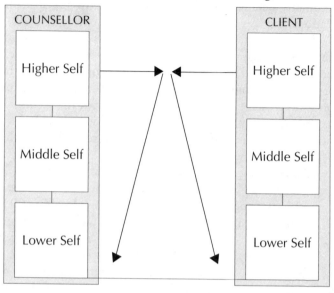

Archembeau (1979, 62) observes: "The psychotherapist and the client find themselves in a relationship built on mutual unconsciousness. The psychotherapist is led to a direct confrontation of the unreconciled part of himself. The activated unconsciousness of both the client and the therapist causes both to become involved in a transformation of the 'third'. Hence, the relationship itself becomes transformed in the process."

There is surprisingly little documented about the transpersonal relationship in psychotherapy, even though this relationship is at the centre of spiritual direction. Buber, as early as 1937 used the concept of "grace" to explore this relationship, but it was not until Peck (1978) followed his example in this, that the debate in the context of therapy really began. Thankfully, in recent years it has been gathering momentum. Transpersonal relationship is the ultimate factor that operates in the person-to-person encounter. This factor makes the difference between whether the patient gets better or not, and thus is not under human control. Berne (1966, 63) explicitly agreed with this, when he quoted Agnew as saying: "Je le pensay, et Dieu le guarit" (we treat them, but it is God who cures them).

The transpersonal relationship is characterised by a kind of intimacy and by an "emptying of the ego" at the same time. "The soul lives continually in the presence of God…In order to live thus, it carefully detaches itself from creatures, so as to be held by no outward affection. It is on this account that the soul seeks solitude and silence… it gradually builds in the heart, a sanctuary where it finds God and converses with Him heart by heart. Then there is established between the soul and God a sweet and loving intimacy" (Tanquerey, 602). The language is dated, but the concept has not yet been better expressed.

Witnessing the birth of a baby (Keen, 1992) is often an opening to awe and wonder. Crisis, illness or personal tragedy can bring people face to face with ultimate questions. At Christmas I met a bereaved young man. His wife had died from cancer after only three years of marriage. He said to me: "I am very angry with God. Why did He allow this to happen? I am not a criminal. Why do criminals get away? Why does He not punish them?" My reply was, "I can understand that you are angry with God and why you have many questions about what has occurred." There was a moment of silence – then he smiled; his smile indicated that he was thinking, "You understand me and God understands me." This was a transpersonal experience, for which no words would be adequate

The ego of the personal unconscious of the psycho-therapist is "emptied out" of the therapeutic space. This kenosis leaves space for something numinous to be created in the "between" of the relationship. This space can then become the "temenos" or "the vas bene clausum", inside which the transmutation takes place (Adler 1979, 21). This means that the counsellor must let go of any preoccupation with skills, knowledge, experience, preconceptions, even of the desire to heal. It means that s/he must just be present. Basically, we become "passivity" and receptiveness. We can encourage this to happen by preparing the conditions conducive to the spontaneous or spiritual act: the more the psychotherapist dissolves the individual ego that so often demands to be at the forefront, the more s/he allows wisdom, insight and transformation to occur as a self-manifesting process. Grof (1979, 155) speaks of "experiences involving an expansion or extension of consciousness beyond the usual ego boundaries and beyond the limitations of time and/or space".

The transpersonal relationship is found in the work of many authors such as Rogers, Rowan, Hillmann, Maslow, Assagioli. Maslow brings the term "peak experiences" into mainstream psychology. He uses the word re-sacralising: "Re-sacralising means being willing, once again, to see a person 'under the aspect of eternity' (as Spinoza puts it), or to see him/her in the medieval Christian unitive perception, that is, being able to see the sacred, the eternal and the symbolic within the individual personality. It is to see Woman with a capital 'W' and everything which that implies, even when one looks at a particular woman" (Maslow, 1968, 284).

Psychotherapists mention again and again the "mystery" of their work. Indeed, it is essential to it. As Grof says (1988, 238), "A therapist who is unwilling to recognise transpersonal experiences because of his or her philosophical bias is giving up a tool of remarkable power." It has been said that Freud interested himself in the "cellar" of human psychology, and Jung in the "attic". Following Kofler's Personality Model, this book attempts to integrate the height and the depth of human psychological and spiritual growth, including the spiritual, conscious, unconscious within embodiment. The transpersonal may be said to be in the attic, but the attic has a skylight to eternity.

8. How can we facilitate the healing process?

The healing is not in the healer neither does the healing power depend only on the seeker. It depends on both and is achieved through grace. Both need to provide the necessary conditions for healing. Certain factors will influence the birth or development of the transpersonal dimension in the therapeutic relationship.

Whether the therapist is open or closed to the therapeutic relationship in principle, if not in practice, may make all the difference. For instance, patients may not feel free to discuss their yearning for a closer union with the Church and with God, because they believe that their psychoanalyst, well known to be a committed Freudian, would only interpret their reaching towards God as a symptom of father fixation. Conversely, there are other clients who perceive the therapist as a healing priest, witch doctor or shaman. Much of the working alliance may be undermined by an excessive preoccupation with the healing power of the laying on of hands or prayer.

So, are we explicitly or implicitly oriented towards the spiritual dimension of the human being? Depending on where we have received it, our therapy training may legitimise spiritual disclosure. If one has been trained as a psychosynthesis or psycho-spiritual counsellor, for instance, it is to be expected that the soul or spirit will be part of the world to be explored. "What can the client talk about and hope will be understood?" and "What can the client not talk about, because of the fear of being misunderstood?" are important questions to be asked by any counsellor. Surely we shall fall short of therapeutic effectiveness, if we ignore spiritual intelligence. If the counsellor is unwilling to enter into the transpersonal relationship with his/her client, Jung's attic will be deprived of light.

9. Four stages of spiritual unfolding

As the transpersonal relationship has a great deal to do with spiritual unfolding, it is appropriate to show how this process takes place in human beings. In "The Essential Ken Wilber" (1998) we find that there are four major stages of spiritual unfolding discussed: belief, faith, direct experience, and permanent adaptation:

1. **Belief** is the earliest stage, and the most common factor in spiritual unfolding. Generally speaking, belief originates at the mental level. It requires images, symbols, and concepts. The mind itself goes through various transitional phases in its own development: magic, mythic, rational, and vision-logic. Each of these phases is the basis of a type and stage of spiritual and religious belief.

    a. Magic belief is egocentric. The subject and object are often fused. The individual believes that s/he can greatly affect the physical world and other people through mental wishes.

    b. Mythic belief is always sociocentric/ethnocentric. Different peoples have different myths. Mythic belief invests its spiritual intuitions in one or more physically disembodied god or goddess. They are endowed with ultimate power over human actions.

    c. Rational belief – to the extent that reason chooses to believe at all – tries to de-mythologise religion. It portrays God as an ultimate Ground of Being.

    d. Vision-logic belief is the climax of rationalisation. Sciences such as systems theory are often used to explain this Ground of Being as the Great Holistic System, Gaia, Goddess, Eco-Spirit, the Web of life, and so forth.

These are all mental beliefs. Usually they carry very strong emotional or sentimental connotations. They are not necessarily direct experiences of supra-mental spiritual realities. One can embrace them without changing one's present level of consciousness. Any mental belief sooner or later loses its forcefulness. The reason for this is that it is mental and not supra-mental or spiritual. Mere belief does not provide you with an actual transformation. This becomes slowly, but painfully obvious. For example, the mental belief in Spirit as the Web of Life will begin to fade in its power to persuade, because no matter how much you believe in the Web of Life, you still feel yourself to be a separate, isolated ego with personal hopes and fears. Magic or mythic belief can have even more detrimental effects than mental beliefs, because they do not lead to transformation, but rather act as a regressive force in one's awareness, moving the person not towards, but away from the transrational. In spite of these drawbacks, however, beliefs can mature as direct emergence of higher domains pushes against the self. Thus, mere belief can give way to faith.

2. **Faith** begins when mental belief loses its power to compel. Often between finding direct experience and letting go of mental belief, the individual is carried only by faith. The belief in God, in Oneness may no longer offer much consolation. However, the person may have faith that God, Oneness, is there calling out to him or her. Faith carries on when belief becomes unbelievable. Faith hears the faint but direct calling of the higher reality – of Spirit, of God, of Oneness. That higher reality is beyond the mind and therefore beyond belief. Faith stands on the threshold of direct supramental, transrational experience. Faith lacks dogmatic beliefs and therefore has no sense of security. It is not yet direct experience, and therefore offers no sense of certainty. Faith is thus a no-man's land. There are many questions and no answers. Faith possesses only a dogged determination to find its spiritual abode. It is propelled only by its own hidden intuition. It will eventually find direct experience.

3. **Direct experience** answers the nagging questions inherent in faith. There are usually two phases of direct experience: peak experiences and plateau experiences.

 a. Peak experiences are brief, intense and often life changing.
 b. Plateau experiences are more constant. These involve years of sustained spiritual practice.

Most people, it has to be said, remain at the first two stages of mental belief or faith. Some will have a genuine peak experience of a transpersonal realm. The mystics often use the terms "contemplative prayer", or "prayer of silence" to describe the preparative stages of a peak experience.

4. **Adaptation** means a constant, permanent access to a given level of consciousness. With practice, people can evolve spiritually into plateau experiences of these higher realms. These plateau experiences, with more practice, can become permanent adaptations.

There are some further important points to remember about spiritual unfolding:

a. People can be at a relatively high level of spiritual development and still be at a relatively low level of development in other areas. For example, some people are spiritually developed but still rather immature in sexual relations, emotional intimacy, physical health. Meditation, which is the usual route to peak and plateau experiences, is not about uncovering the repressed unconscious. Rather, meditation is concerned with allowing the emergence of higher domains. Spiritual unfolding needs to be complemented with good psychotherapeutic practice, if it is to expose the psychodynamic unconscious.

b. Many of these stages unfold in a specific sequence. However, one's overall development follows no set pattern. Each individual will follow his or her own unique unfolding.

c. A child can have very deep spiritual experiences. But as we grow older, we put obstacles in the way. However, we return to yearning for these same childhood experiences at mid-life. That is one of the meanings of Christ's, saying "Unless you become like little children, you will not enter the Kingdom of Heaven." Having these spiritual experiences is "entering" the Kingdom. Even though higher stages of spiritual development can only be achieved after years of practice, that shouldn't daunt a beginner.

d. Start with twenty minutes a day of centring prayer, as taught by Fr Thomas Keating (2002). Many people experience almost immediate effects – calming, opening, caring, listening.

e. Attending an intensive retreat for a few days each year often helps.

f. Those who are interested in transformative spirituality usually find an authentic spiritual teacher to be a helpful guide.

For the Christian counsellor, spirituality needs to be integrated into the therapeutic process at all stages. This cannot mean that the client is expected to be at the same stage of spiritual development as the counsellor. Assumptions about the client's spiritual awareness should not be made. The important thing is for the counsellor to be aware of the presence of God as the ultimate and "all-pervading" source of healing.

10. The use of the Bible in counselling

The Bible can be used constructively to assist the transpersonal relationship, but it can also can be abused or misused. The misuse and abuse of the Bible has contributed to many therapists and counsellors becoming atheists or agnostics. Carl Rogers' Christian family background was fundamentalist; in the environment in which he grew up, the Protestant work ethic was very important, and there was a culture of avoiding people because of their dubious morals or ways of living (Marquet, 1971). Certain condemnatory scriptural texts were overemphasised to the neglect of others, such as those teaching God's mercy and compassion. Karen Horney grew up in an atmosphere of inconsistency between belief and practice (Quinn, 1987). Her parents taught the family the Christian faith; however, they did not live it. Her father had the nickname "Bible-thrower".

Lots of questions with regard to the use of the Bible come to mind at this point: Should we use the Bible at all? Is it acceptable to quote the Bible to people in need? At what stage in the counselling process should we quote the Bible? Which parts of the Bible are most suitable for counselling? Roger Hurding's *The Bible and Counselling* (1992, 147-178), provides us with ways of answering these questions by observing distinctions between various counselling approaches to the use of Biblical material: between cognitive-behavioural approaches, analytic approaches, Christian personalism and Christian transpersonalism.

Cognitive-behavioural approaches tend to be prescriptive in their use of the Bible. They stress the importance of "right thinking" and "right behaviour". "Be transformed by the renewing of your mind" (Rom 12:2). Christian cognitive-behavioural approaches are mainly used within pastoral settings. Jay Adams' "nouthetic counselling" (1976) exemplifies this approach. The Bible is used for exhortation, admonition, confrontation and the call to repentance. Christian cognitive-behavioural approaches are, therefore, mainly used within pastoral settings. The word, *noutheteo,* means to warn, to admonish, to advise. We are reminded of the call to instruct one another (Rom 15:14), the need to learn from the sins of the past (1 Cor 10:11) and the links between warning and teaching in connection with achieving Christian maturity (Col 1:28; 3:16).

Learning, remembering and application of relevant biblical passages can be an important technique in counselling. It parallels the 'changing tapes' concept of cognitive-behavioural therapy. Cognitive-behavioural counselling tries to help a client to look at his maladaptive behaviour and so to find more realistic response to everyday events. For example, if we look at a client with a poor self-concept from a Christian perspective, the client may be encouraged to write out on a card and learn the following text: "There is nothing I cannot do in the One who strengthens me" (Phil 4:13). During the week between sessions, whenever the client finds he is about to say to himself, "I am worthless" he is to "change the tape" by referring to the statement from Philippians. Such inner changed communication will lead to different feelings and actions towards others and different responses from them.

A word of caution. People in need can be badly damaged by an insensitive or overzealous use of the word of God. We must not use or abuse it in order to perform open-heart surgery at every turn.

Analytic approaches look to the healer and the "wise". They tend to be reflective and "visionary". For example, an analyst might suggest to a client with a poor self-image that Psalm

139 might be helpful. S/he could reflect on verses 14-16, seeking the Holy Spirit's insight:

> I praise you because I am fearfully and wonderfully made;
> your works are wonderful, I know that full well.
> My frame was not hidden from you
> when I was made in the secret place.
> When I was woven together in the depths of the earth,
> your eyes saw my unformed body.
> All the days ordained for me were written in your book
> before one of them came to be.

Out of this reflective approach God may speak very powerfully to the client. S/he may experience God's love for her/him. The very roots of her/his existence within the womb and in early childhood may be touched. The counsellor must be patient and trust God's timing.

Christian personalist approaches are formative and pastoral. There are certain parallels with the humanistic and existential approaches, in that the focus is on relationship. Within Christian personalism, counselling respects the uniqueness of the person and utilises the relationship between client and counsellor, in order to deal with blocks to growth and maturity. Biblical principles shape the caring relationship. Howard Clinebell's *Growth Counselling* (1979) provides a seminal example of this kind of work.

Christian transpersonalist approaches are imaginative. In one sense, all Christian approaches to counselling are transpersonalist, because they all reach beyond the self to God as well as dealing with everyday human issues. In Christian transpersonalism the relationship with God receives the greatest attention. Emphasis is on God's reconciling and sanctifying work in the life of the believing client. The stress here is on the journey towards wholeness and holiness. The model of change is always Christlikeness. Paul puts it in the following way:

So for anyone who is in Christ, there is a new creation: the old order is gone and a new being is there to see. It is all God's work; he reconciled us to himself through Christ and he gave us the ministry of reconciliation.

(2 Cor 5:17-19)

By "imagination" we mean the forming of mental images (impressions, pictures, symbols) of ideas, events, actions or beings. These images represent a greater reality. This approach realises that creative reflection on the Scriptures can be of immense value in the context of counselling. It can either be used during the session or as an assignment. Such techniques either carry the client, in imagination, back to scenes described in the Bible or bring the text alive in contemporary settings. For example, the counsellor can ask the client what is his/her favourite or least favourite character in the Bible. If Joseph is the most liked, the question can be asked why? What is the attraction? Is it because he was the favourite of his father? Two main influences here are The Spiritual Exercises of Ignatius of Loyola and Carl Jung's idea of "active imagination". In the Spiritual Exercises there is a strong focus on discerning God's will through imaginative meditation. In Sheila Cassidy's translation, we meet the sentence, "Man is created to love, serve and praise God" (Ignatius Loyola, The Spiritual Exercises quoted in Sheila Cassidy's *Sharing the Darkness: the Spirituality of Caring*, London: Darton, Longman & Todd 1988, 149).

Morton Kelsey (1977, 188) takes Jung's practice of imaginative dialogue and applies this idea to Bible stories. He states that "Using the imagination we can step into the events recorded in the New Testament... we can participate in the eternal reality that broke through in history in the person of Jesus of Nazareth, and continues to break through whenever someone becomes truly open to the Holy Spirit. Basically, what we are asked to do is to let the images speak to us, and then to share in the victory and power, allowing them to show through in our outer lives in service to others."

How can we use this method? A simple way is to read or re-read a parable or incident described in the Gospels, prayerfully and in stillness. It helps us to use all the senses imaginatively to enter into the story or situation. For example, taking the story of the Prodigal Son, narrated in chapter fifteen in Luke, the client might visualise the young man setting out on the road to the far country, and famine striking the land. He might imagine the grim hunger the prodigal son felt, sense the apprehension of the return journey, feel the warmth of the father's embrace and hear the joyous sound of the celebration. It is important to allow oneself to be led by the Spirit. There are several ways of proceeding:

1. The client might simply be a witness of what happened to the young man on his journey. The counsellor might engage the client in imagined conversation: "How do you see the far country?" "What was it like for the young man at the end of his journey away from home?" "Was he at the end of his resources?" "How did he appear to feel about meeting his father again?"

2. The counsellor might invite the client to explore what it was like to be the prodigal son, the elder son or the father. He might ask the same kind of questions, but using the second person singular and the present tense, "What do you experience at the end of your journey?", etc. In this way the client can gain insight into the folly of self-will, the temptation to spiritual pride or the satisfaction and joy of forgiving others.

3. The Bible story can be brought into the present. Some people may find it difficult to enter into the story fully, historically, since they lack the basic historical knowledge about food, clothing or environment, or they do not comprehend the idiom in which the story is told. With such clients, the counsellor can read what has happened or has been done as though it were happening right now, within the client's own culture. This approach can pose a challenge to the imagination. It is not easy to enter into the mind of the prodigal son (or daughter) in terms of our life in modern times. It is not easy to translate the story of the tax collector into our times – not easy, but it can be very enlightening.

4. Kathy Galloway in *Imagining the Gospels* (1988, 5-7) shows ways in which the Bible can be brought into today's world and expressed more readily by: (a) keeping a diary, (b) writing a story, (c) composing a poem, (d) painting a picture.

She stresses the importance of action following the uses of imagination and the creative faculty: "I have found that imagining the Gospel is not just an aid to faith, it is also a call to action. In every story, I found the questions changing, as they moved from 'what would I do?' through 'what did I do?' to 'what must I do?' Jesus does not meet us to leave us where we are, but so that we can follow him into the future."

It is important to be aware of the strengths of the client in the various uses of the Bible, and to use it accordingly, and possibly to help him/her to develop the less familiar ways. Certain approaches attract certain types of personality. This holds good for both counsellor and client. However, the use of the Bible needs to fit into the overall process of counselling. It must not be artificially introduced, but must follow from the counselling process, just like any other technique which we use. We must make sure that it does not lead to spiritual abuse of the client.

11. Exercises

Write short notes in answer to the following:
a. What is the transpersonal relationship?
b. How, if at all, can we facilitate it in therapy?
c. What are the potential dangers in fostering the transpersonal relationship?
d. How far can meditation lead you to the transpersonal?
e. In what ways does emptying ourselves help us to establish the transpersonal relationship?
f. What are some of the ways of using the Bible in counselling?
g. Which way of using the Bible, if any, do you think would suit you best?
h. How do you see the transpersonal relationship in the overall counselling process?

And finally

i. Why do you think the author of this book put the
   transpersonal relationship at the beginning of his
   exploration of the five relationships?

12. Two case studies of the transpersonal relationship

1. MICHAEL is a forty-year-old missionary priest from
Europe, who had worked all his life in South America. He
had worked very hard to help the poor with many projects
which involved all his time and energy. When he came for
counselling he felt drained and his priestly life was meaningless
to him. He was not sure whether he could even carry on as a
missionary or priest. He did not see any sense in his ministry
any more.

During our first session, after we had dealt with the
contract and arranged to meet every Monday from 9.00 to
10.00 a.m. in my office, it became clear that Michael, my
client, was stuck in a deep mid-life crisis. He had badly
neglected himself through overworking. What once gave him
much meaning and satisfaction was now boring, a routine,
meaningless. He had also neglected his spiritual life. Prayer
was boring. Even celebrating the Eucharist was a routine, a
burden. He was fed up with all the projects for the poor. Our
dialogue went like this:

M: "I don't know why I am a priest and a missionary priest!
It does not make any sense. I used to enjoy it, but now I
don't find it fulfilling. It is very hard work and most of the
time very boring. I don't know why I have not given up my
priesthood.

C: "You seem to be stuck in something which is no longer
fulfilling?"

M: "Yes, I like the word 'stuck', because I don't know what
to do. I just carry on and find it less and less rewarding and
more and more of a burden. As a young priest I really

59

enjoyed working in South America, but now it is no longer so. It is boring, it is disgusting. I am disappointed with my missionary vocation. I don't know whether I am in the right place."

Together, we explored his strong feelings of disappointment, frustration and disgust. What was once so meaningful had become disappointing and boring. What once energised him was now draining him. Nothing seemed to make sense any more, not even his many projects for the poor. Moreover he was now forty years old! What has he achieved? Life seemed to be at an end.

As he explored his existential position, it became clear that something had to change. He was not clear what this something was. He thought that he might have made the wrong decision to become a priest and missionary. Would he now be happy if he could get married? Would he be happy if he had a family of his own? Would he be happy if he were a successful businessman?

After several sessions of exploration of his predicament it became clear that not one thing, but many things had to change. He had neglected himself very badly. With regard to his physical health – he was worn out; as for his spiritual life – he related to God only in a mechanical way; his relationships with people were very superficial; his relationship with himself was hardly noticeable, because he had no time for himself.

As he became aware of what had happened to him in his thirteen years of missionary ministry, and how he had neglected himself, he was prepared to change some of his habits and spend more time for his own sake, and for his relationship with God. He also felt that he wanted to spend more quality time with people.

This went on for several weeks. One day he shared an experience he had had during his meditation. He was sitting near the sea and reflecting on the calmness of the waters. All of a sudden he experienced the warmth of the sun. It was not just the warmth of the sun, it was the warmth of the creator who had brought this beautiful universe into existence. He felt the love, which was the motivation for creating it. As he shared this with me he stopped for a moment. There was a prolonged silence. Then he tried to articulate what had happened to him as he was sharing. "I have found new meaning for my life." His "stuckness" was gone.

I asked him: "How do you think you can maintain this?" He replied: "By having time for myself, others and God, and by not being so busy as I have been in my ministry over the last thirteen years. I need to have time for myself and experience myself as loveable; then I can share this love with others. I need more time to allow myself to experience God's love and warmth, and then to share it with others. This is the key to my future happiness."

We had a few more sessions to consolidate what he was going to change in his life. His energy level stayed high. So did his enthusiasm. We then terminated our counselling sessions. Ten years later, he wrote to me that he was so grateful for the sessions which we had had, because they changed his life and brought a second spring into his priestly and missionary life.

2. TONY, a middle-aged man came to me for counselling. It rapidly became very clear that he was heading for a depression. He was a counsellor himself, but did not want to carry on in this profession. He said to himself very often: "What is the purpose of all this? I can't find any meaning in this life. Why should I carry on dealing with difficult people? I would like to enjoy the rest of my life, but I don't know how". He had been a counsellor for twenty years. Before that, he had received counselling himself from a very warm female, atheistic counsellor. He was a lapsed Christian and believed that after death there was no further existence. Somehow, this had been reinforced in his counselling sessions. Consequently, the meaninglessness of living and the fear of death constantly pestered him. He came from an Anglican background. His father was a lapsed Catholic who was originally from Ireland.

Tony earned a great deal of money, had paid back his mortgage, has a lovely wife and three children, a happy home life. He plays sports, exercises regularly, eats prudently, and has everything he wants. When I asked him, "What do you plan to do now that you have achieved all these wonderful things? What do you want to do with your life? What is your life for?" He looked at me with surprise and said, "That is exactly my problem. I know how important this question is. I feel that somehow this question is welling up from within me; I do not know how to answer it, or what I should do".

I soon realised that I had to make the transpersonal relationship the centre of my treatment plan. I was in a dilemma. I did not want to impose my Christian values on Tony, but needed to rely on them in order to lead him; and I felt that this was really what he needed: for me to share spiritual values with him. Each time the question of an afterlife came up, I was so much aware from my counselling training that I should not impose my views on a client, that for a time I kept clear of the whole subject.; but then, one day he said himself that he wanted me to share my views on this matter. I told him of Christ and what Christ means for me. I told him about the resurrection and that we all are called to a risen state with Christ after our death. I shared how important Christ, the Mystic, was for my own personal spiritual journey and how I appreciate every day as a gift from God to come closer to Christ. He listened carefully and said at the end: "Thank you very much for your sharing. This will help me to reflect on the meaning of my life."

Next time he came to me, he said that he had thought much about what I had shared and that he wanted to become a Catholic, since his father had been a Catholic, although he had been brought up in an Anglican family. For twenty years, counselling and helping people had given meaning to his life. Now he wanted more than just doing, he wanted to become Christ like. He wanted to become a true follower of Christ. As the sessions went on, I noticed that his enthusiasm as a counsellor came back, although it was now very different from the way he had previously envisaged counselling. He wanted not just to help people sort out problems, but to help them to find meaning in what they were doing. I had to help him to find a delicate balance between counselling and an over-eagerness to share Christ with his clients that could lead to indoctrination. His profession as a counsellor became much more meaningful for him. He could become Christ-like by sharing his love with his clients as they struggled with their emotions and transferences on to him.

His road towards depression was reversed, because his positive emotions of love, trust, enthusiasm and joy gave him much life energy. We finished our counselling contract after ten sessions, because he felt that his problem of meaningless-ness in life had been turned round towards enthusiasm to live his life fully and to help others to do the same. In this way, the focus on the transpersonal relationship helped this particular client to deal with his problem. Other approaches and appropriate skills were there to some extent, but the transpersonal was where we were most profitably engaged. It is a question of discovering the central need of the client.

CHAPTER THREE

The working alliance

1. The nature of the working alliance 2. The place of the working alliance in Kofler's personality model 3. The skills necessary to establish a working alliance 4. Empathy 5. Exercise 6. The importance of the working alliance 7. Descriptions and conditions of the working alliance 8. A clear contract helps to avoid potential problems 9. Exercise 10. The historical development of the concept of the working alliance 11. Establishing the working alliance 12. Exercise 13. Management of the working alliance 14. The influence of expectations on the working alliance 15. Threats to the working alliance 16. Exercise 17. Two case studies of the working alliance

1. The nature of the working alliance

Counselling is first and foremost a relationship. This point needs to be stressed, because trainee counsellors often think they have to *do* something rather than *be* with the client; sometimes they think they have to solve their clients' problems. They may not fully understand and appreciate the importance of establishing a working alliance. Before engaging in any change intervention, the counsellor must try to gain the co-operation of the client. The client needs to overcome the resistance to working on himself/herself. The quality of the counselling relationship is the basis for the therapeutic process. The nature of the counselling relationship depends on the unique characteristics of the individuals involved. Therefore, no two counselling relationships will be the same. However, effective counselling relationships do share certain basic elements. All the different therapy disciplines stress the importance and centrality of the relationship for effective therapeutic work. They all ask the counsellor to try to accommodate the client's view of a particular problem, and to use the same language as the client. They agree that the counsellor or therapist needs to use joining techniques, so as to enter into the world and culture of the client, which is a prerequisite for establishing those conditions necessary to the therapeutic process. There is also firm agreement on all sides that the motivation of both counsellor and client is essential for the therapeutic relationship to succeed. Whatever form of counselling or therapy is taking place, each party is conscious of entering into a special kind of relationship. Now, this special relationship can only achieve mutually agreed goals through some form of *contract*, either explicitly or implicitly made. This contract we call the working alliance.

2. The place of the working alliance in Kofler's personality model

We shall now look at examples of the working alliance from various angles. First, we shall place it within Kofler's personality model.

Working alliance in Koffler's personality model

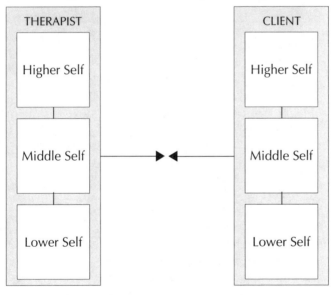

This relationship takes place between the Middle (or Conscious) "Selves" of the therapist and client. Both are supposed to be "in the adult", and aware of the nature of the contract. The contract, even if it is only implicit, has roughly the same properties, whether it is made between the Bishop and the ordinands; an executive director and his junior partners; the Superior General and the candidate who wants to join his congregation; the rector of the seminary and his students; the parish priest and his parishioners, or indeed between the bride and groom.

When difficulties arise between the two parties concerned, they are reminded of the contract which they made; they are aware of that overall relationship when it becomes difficult for them to function. They stick to each other, even though there may be moments where they are very angry with each other and hate each other. Because they feel safe enough to allow their feelings to surface, the relationship grows rather than gets blocked. Love and hate go hand in hand. All this, of course, presupposes a commitment which nowadays is frequently lacking.

The working alliance takes place between the
   conscious selves of client and therapist
The working alliance takes place between the adult
   of the client and the adult of the therapist
The working alliance must be established on the
   conscious level
The working alliance is a professional contract to
   engage in an existential encounter
The working alliance must not be in the child or
   parent ego state
I am in the child ego-state when I am behaving,
   thinking and feeling like a child
I am in the adult ego-state when I am behaving,
   thinking and feeling like an adult
I am in the parent ego-state when I am behaving,
   thinking and feeling like a parent.

(from *TA Today*,
by Ian Stewart and Vann Joines. 1987, 11)

It is worth remembering in this context that people coming for counselling are often already in the child mode: they can't cope just because they are not fundamentally in their "adult mode". This can present the counsellor with an obstacle that has to be recognised and partially worked through before the working alliance can be fully established.

3. The skills necessary to establish a working alliance

To establish a good working alliance, certain negotiating skills need to be possessed by both partners. They have to negotiate a contract between themselves: where they meet, for how long, how often, the cost, what the therapist's job means, what is expected of the client, and so on. Both of them need to be in the adult to negotiate this contract. They can't do it properly if the client is regressed and in the child state, or indeed if the therapist is in a demanding parent state. If the therapist finds him/herself trapped in this state, supervision will be necessary for the construction of the working alliance with the client.

It is essential that both are assertive enough to express their needs. This again pre-supposes a certain awareness of needs on both sides. Obviously, the client may not be as aware of his/her needs as the therapist is. Therefore, the working alliance does not finish being established in the first session. The two must work on the working alliance as long as the relationship lasts. Needs will become clearer, and therefore more negotiations are required. Sometimes the therapist or the client will ask open questions, at other times they will ask closed questions. The skill of "immediacy", of dealing with the present moment, is important. However, the client may not yet possess these skills or the state of mind required to communicate in this way; so, constant negotiation and re-negotiation will be needed, as the wok progresses. Often, client or counsellor will summarise what the other has said, or ask for further explanations. Sometimes each may mirror back what the other has said, to make sure they have understood correctly. It is particularly important that the therapist makes sure that the client feels understood, by using the skill of empathy, and possibly later on the skill of challenge or caring confrontation. Sometimes, the therapist or client may paraphrase what the other partner of the relationship expresses, to be sure that they understand clearly what is being said. The therapist will need to probe and prompt, to make sure the client will express what is necessary to fulfil the contract, and to establish a good working alliance.

The working alliance is a beginning and it sets boundaries. No amount of contracting can compensate for a therapist's inability to meet the client person-to-person. However, the paradox of the therapeutic relationship is that it is a far-reaching relationship, which is contracted for a certain time only, and paid for!

4. Empathy

We need to explain the term "empathy", since it is such an important skill in facilitating the working alliance, and indeed in all counselling situations. Basic empathy is the ability of a person to be in touch with the experience of another person by attending and listening, and communicating this understanding to that person. It means that we are able to put ourselves into the shoes of another person. Empathy is not the same as sympathy. In sympathy we lose ourselves in the other person's feelings. We get enmeshed and block growth and empowerment. Empathy, on the other hand, *is* empowerment. The Oxford Dictionary defines sympathy as "agreement with the other's feelings" while empathy is "an intellectual identification with a person's feelings, thoughts and attitudes" – an *intellectual* identification. Sympathy means that a person identifies *emotionally* with the feelings of another. There is a pitfall with sympathy. When clients express pain over a particular experience and counsellors identify with them emotionally, the counsellors will also feel pain. Like their clients, they may well become overwhelmed by such feelings. In such a situation, counsellors can become focused on their own feelings. They may no longer be able to be sensitive to the changing perception and feelings in their clients. Thus their ability to be empathic becomes severely depleted. With too much sympathy, you become hooked into the other person's feelings, so that you are no longer able to be objective. This very often reinforces negative feelings in the other person and leads to collusion. The empathic counsellor concentrates on *understanding* the client's frame of mind, trying to understand how s/he feels and why s/he feels that way. The client feels sad, because his/her father died. With empathy, the counsellor is free of the client's overwhelming experience of sadness. When we are empathic with a person, we put ourselves into his/her place, his/her shoes, as though we were that person, yet we retain a professional detachment from the other person's emotions. Empathy, particularly advanced empathy, is a form of challenge.

While we stress the importance of empathy in the working alliance, we do not intend to suggest that the counsellor should act in a cold manner. Obviously s/he must have warmth in order for counselling to be effective; but without empathy there is no basis for a meaningful relationship in the therapeutic context. Counsellors need to communicate empathy to their clients to maximise therapeutic effectiveness.

SUMMARY:

Skills involved in establishing the working alliance:
- Negotiation
- Assertiveness
- Open and closed questioning
- Immediacy
- The ability to summarise
- Initiative in asking for explanation
- Mirroring of statements
- Empathy
- Ability to challenge, paraphrase and prompt

———

5. Exercise

Consider as fully as possible the question below. Write down your answer, giving two or three examples, and then amend it over two or three days of counselling, until you are satisfied:

• How is empathy, as compared with sympathy, applied during therapy?

6. The importance of the working alliance

The working alliance is the basis of all therapeutic work. Without the working alliance it can't happen. A lecturer's needs may provide an apt comparison. A lecturer needs to know what time s/he is supposed to start and to finish; how many students are going to be present; how much s/he is being paid; to whom s/he is accountable; whether the students want to work with him/her; what s/he is supposed to do and who is going to help if there is trouble. Who is in charge, if all the lecturer's students want to do something completely different? Should the lecturer agree to that, or should s/he take direction from the organiser of the course? These are some of the things that need to be in place before any lecture takes place, and they are similar to those that ought to be in place before counselling sessions begin with a client. When everything goes well, we hardly think about the basic contract. However, when something goes wrong, it suddenly becomes important, since small problems could quickly develop into much larger ones. That is why we need the working alliance. A good and clear working alliance will help us to avoid many possible problems.

That said, it is important not to rush into creating the working alliance. Counsellors are very often dealing with very vulnerable people who just know they want help – and quickly. They want to *begin* by pouring out their story; so a contract at the *beginning* of the first session can sometimes block rather than facilitate.

The working alliance is what makes it possible for client and counsellor to work together. That is the crucial thing. In many cases it is very subtle, but it is essential nevertheless. In supervision, as I have already said, I have found from many years' experience that in 95% of cases, if there is a difficulty in counselling, it is due to a problem with the working alliance. It should never be taken for granted that difficulties have to do with anything else. If there is not a good working alliance, the result may be premature termination, or dependency of the client on the counsellor. A good working alliance is a fairly safe indicator of a successful prognosis.

Most difficulties are related to the working alliance. Expectations don't match, responsibilities are not defined, boundaries are not being kept or clarified. Most of the time, if there is a difficulty in counselling, in formation work, in a pastoral setting, in community living or in a couple's relationship, it is a difficulty produced by a faulty working alliance. Having said that, there is an interesting non-compliance in the medical field. A majority of patients don't follow their doctor's prescriptions. So there are doctors who are following their part of the working alliance, while their patients are not. Admittedly, lecturers and counsellors are dealing with a different kind of clientele, and on a different level; but what is true for medicine will be equally true for counselling. So even with a contract, there is no guarantee, but at least there is a safeguard.

SUMMARY:

The working alliance is:
- The basis of therapeutic work
- The tool for working together

Without a good working alliance difficulties arise.
Some difficulties may arise from:
- Unclear expectations, unclear responsibilities, boundaries not being kept.

7. Descriptions and conditions of the working alliance

The working alliance can fail to be properly established; it can also be destroyed, by either the client or the psycho-therapist, or occasionally by external circumstances, such as the intervention of a spouse, the demands of a government agency, hospital closure, war or natural disaster, or any combination of these.

The working alliance is clearly absent in some psychiatric cases, such as the force-feeding of a person with anorexia who is in danger of dying, or when Largectyl is forcibly administered to a homicidally psychotic patient under a section order.

An effective working alliance contains the necessary ground agreements between psychotherapist and client. Without such an agreement the psychotherapeutic work cannot take place; there can be no genuine assumption of responsibility for the client, and no genuine long-term engagement on the part of the therapist. The working alliance guarantees the contractual time and space for sessions, and it attempts to ensure mutuality of commitment. I am aware that I may be over-emphasising the need to "get things right" in the professional contract. This must, of course, be tempered by the counsellor's effort, from the start, to build a trusting relationship with the client. Where the working alliance is concerned, the I–You relationship (person-to-person) is should not be overlooked. The psychodynamic structure needs to be incorporated into the person-centred approach.

The supervisor often has to go back and re-examine a working alliance. The quality of the therapeutic alliance gives a good indication of the therapeutic outcome; there is a moderating relationship between a good working alliance and positive therapy outcome. The client may have to agree to forego certain customary props (e.g. wearing dark glasses) in order for the work of therapy to proceed under the best conditions. Neither therapist nor client can work effectively without adequate support (e.g. if there is a threat of psychotic breakdown, criminal behaviour, violence, self-damage). In order to be able to work competently, it is a necessary precondition that the psychotherapist does not feel personally threatened by fears of violence towards him or herself, or suspect that self-damage may be inflicted by the client.

There are limits to the responsibility of the therapist:

1. No one is under obligation to undergo therapy unless he chooses.

2. No therapist is compelled to take on very disturbed patients, or, indeed, any particular patient. If there were compulsion, what sort of relationship would develop?

3. The therapist has the right to refuse to continue, if the conditions are changed for any reason after therapy has begun (Little 1986, 55).

In certain situations the therapist may only just manage the relationship. One client may become very fearful, another may flirt with, or even fall in love with the therapist, another may fall into the penal system, or experience enormous internal or familial pressure. Under these circumstances, therapy is limited in what it can achieve, because all the energy is taken up in safeguarding the basic conditions of the working alliance.

The influence of third parties – a hostile employer or a possessive spouse – can greatly damage the working alliance. It can also exert pressure on the therapy, if the client's attitude toward the third party begins to change.

SUMMARY:
The working alliance can be destroyed by:
- the client
- the therapist
- external circumstances

The working alliance is absent in:
- the force-feeding of patients
- the forcible administering of medication

The limits of the responsibility of a therapist are:
- no obligation to do therapy unless s/he chooses
- no obligation to take on very disturbed clients
- the right to stop therapy if basic conditions change

In some circumstances therapy is limited, if, for example:
- the client is afraid of the therapist
- the client flirts or falls in love with the therapist
- the client experiences enormous internal or familial pressure

Unhelpful influence on therapy may come from a third party:
- an employer or a spouse, etc.

———

In chapter one we defined the initial working alliance as an agreement to work together even if later on neither party wants to do so. The client or therapist may think: "No, I don't want to be here, I don't really want to talk to you, and you don't particularly want to talk to me, but we agreed to do this job together, so here we are; we carry on, whether we feel like it at this moment or not." That's the crux of the working alliance for the counsellor – doing what needs to be done for one's clients, and persevering, whatever difficulties may arise. I think that this is often true of marriages. The working alliance keeps marriages going. This is certainly often true of religious life or priesthood. The working alliance is needed to keep religious life or the priesthood buoyant. Not everything in marriage, religious life or priesthood is going to be wonderful. Sometimes it is going to be very difficult. Couples in a marriage with a strong working alliance can say, "This is really hard, but our commitment is to stay together, to work through the hard bits." There is no working alliance if a couple says, "Oh well, we will have a good time while we are all happy and easy together, and later on, we'll see." A working alliance requires that two people remain committed to working on their relationship, no matter what happens. That is the kernel of the working alliance. Times of uncertainty or failure are inevitable. They are never a valid reason for giving up. Indeed, failure sometimes provides the maximum opportunity for growth.

In spite of always trying to create and maintain the ideal working alliance, the counsellor is bound to meet occasions when this proves impossible. Occasionally, a client will discover that counselling is not helping. S/he may just stop coming, because to continue would be a waste of money. Sometimes a referral proves necessary; and sometimes the working alliance is spoilt by the threat of violence or the danger of breakdown. Again, the metaphor of marriage is pertinent. An annulment registers the fact that the wedding ceremony did not initiate a true marriage; similarly, a working alliance can turn out to be radically faulty.

DEFINITION OF THE WORKING ALLIANCE:

The working alliance, as far as it is generally understood outside of counselling or therapy, is a co-operative relationship based on its purpose, and on the contractual way in which each partner intends to reach a specific goal in relation to the other.

In the counselling context the working alliance is the co-operative relationship between counsellor and client that underpins all effective therapeutic work. It is built on a mutual adult to adult contract that includes such areas as boundaries, expectations, confidentiality, space and time. The working alliance will develop as the process continues and needs to be checked out and renegotiated regularly.

---

8. A clear contract helps to avoid potential problems

A contract is a formal, explicit agreement between counsellor and client. It helps to ensure the professional nature of the relationship. The following items may be included in the contract: venue of the counselling sessions, time and frequency of sessions, boundaries of confidentiality, responsibilities of each party, goals of therapy, and the means by which they may be achieved, "homework", setting of other necessary boundaries and expectations, such as desirable or undesirable interventions by a third party, process of referral, supervision, fees, the terms of the therapeutic relationship.

The contract may be written and signed by both counsellor and client. However, most contracts are verbal. Part of the contract will include a discussion of the ground rules. The construction of a contract may seem formal and forbidding; however, in fact, it provides the client with safe boundaries and a clear focus. It may be a source of energy and confidence for the client because s/he experiences it as professionalism with its own value and discipline. Often it will establish trust, because counsellor and client know where they stand with each other. It also provides security for the client and the counsellor. Here are the usual components for a working alliance:

1. **Venue of the counselling session**: The venue needs to be a fairly quiet place, where there are no interruptions. The room should be simply furnished with two easy chairs, a box of tissues for the client, and the chair of the counsellor should be near the door for the sake of his/her safety, in case the client should appear to be growing violent.

2. **Time of the counselling session**: This is usually established on the phone, but sometimes face to face. The conversation is best kept as simple and to the point as possible:

Client: May I see you, please?
Counsellor: Certainly. Could you come tomorrow?
Client: That would suit me. What time?
Counsellor: About four o'clock?
Client: Would twenty-past four be OK?
Counsellor: That would be fine. Then we can talk about whether this would be a good time for us to meet each week.

This is a simple illustration of how the crucial aspect of time can be treated.

Counsellor and client should negotiate a time which is comfortable for both of them. It is important that both parties are happy with the arranged time and do not feel under pressure. The time needs to be constant, as far as possible. When the client knows the time for ending the session, s/he knows that any topic introduced at the end of the session cannot be explored immediately. The counsellor will help the client by reminding him/her of the short time left for the session, and therefore not allow him/her to get into deeper material at the end of the session. Time management is an important skill to learn. Inexperienced counsellors often notice that the client only "gets to the point" towards the end of the session. This is often due to the client's poor time management or fearfulness, but may also result from a lack of awareness on the part of the counsellor.

Another reason for the client's introducing new material at the end of the session may be his/her client's bid for extended attention from the counsellor. S/he may need to be reminded of the contract, and be reassured that the matter will be treated at the next session. This is good modelling for time management, which will help the client in everyday life. It can also help the client contain the seeming enormity of some feelings.

3. **Frequency of the session**: The frequency of the sessions must always be determined by the real need of the client, never by the financial need of the therapist. This would constitute financial abuse. It is unethical to suggest two appointments each week, if one is sufficient. However, it would be equally unethical to agree to take the client twice a week, just because the client's dependency leads him/her to ask for this. The therapist must not collude with the client's pathological need.

4. **Boundaries of confidentiality and socialising**: The counsellor explains the terms of confidentiality, and reassures the client that these terms will be strictly adhered to. What is said in a counselling session remains between the two people concerned. However, the counsellor will be free to bring

relevant material to his/her supervisor; this is normal practice in therapy. Anonymity will be preserved as far as possible. If some disclosure means that there is a danger to the client or to the public, the counsellor is free to do everything possible to deal with the situation in a discreet way, so as to protect the client and anyone else who might be affected. It is essential that the client is clear about his/her position with regard to confidentiality. In extreme cases, the counsellor needs to be free to pass on information to social workers or the police, so as to protect clients or members of the public. All this must be explained to the client as part of the initial contract. It will not then be such a shock or apparent betrayal for the client, if such a situation should arise.

Many counselling books forget to mention that the client is also bound by the ground rule of confidentiality with regard to material the counsellor may share in the counselling session. Confidentiality is a contract which binds both parties. The counsellor's material should, of course, be appropriate and discretionary, and normally will not be confidential.

The client should be asked to make clear at this early stage how s/he would like the counsellor to behave, if they should meet outside the session. Does the client prefer not to be known by the therapist in front of other people?

5. **Goals of therapy**: The goals of counselling must be clear. What does the client want to achieve? Is s/he here to deal with a specific problem such as a fear of spiders? Does the client want counselling for general personal growth? Is therapy a requirement for a training course? Are the parents of this child sending him to therapy, so as to teach him to be obedient? It is absolutely essential to clarify the goals of the client and, in some situations, to motivate the client and encourage him/her to make the best use of the opportunity.

The counsellor should help clients to articulate their needs. Sometimes, when clients arrive for counselling, they are not sure what they need. They have the feeling that something is wrong with them and that they need help; but it may take several sessions to perceive the real needs of the client, as compared with the problem as s/he presents it. A clear contract in this respect may take time to emerge. Moreover, the contract must not be so fixed that it cannot be renegotiated, as better insights will probably be gained during the counselling process.

6. **Means to achieve the goals:** Once the goals have become clear, counsellor and client will discuss how the client can achieve these goals, and what each of them will have to do. A treatment plan will be established.

7. **Responsibility of each party:** The counsellor agrees to be on time and available during the arranged time. S/he will use his/her skills and personality for the healing process of the client. The client, too, will be on time and will pay the arranged fees as agreed. They will both freely consent to abide by all the other clauses of the contract.

8. **Setting of other necessary boundaries:** For certain clients the normal agreements may not be enough. The counsellor may need to put in place certain specific agreements, which are determined according to the nature of the client's problems such as: "I will not stalk you", "I will not act violently", "I will not shout at you", "I will not come to a session after drinking alcohol or when drunk". Such agreements may be necessary to contain a specific client.

9. **Expectations:** It is very important that expectations are clearly expressed on both sides. For example, the counsellor may expect the client not to eat or drink in the room, but this must be clearly articulated by the counsellor to the client. Client expectation may be unreal, e.g. "The counsellor will heal me, I don't need to do anything." This could be transferential, an expectation raised by experiences with doctors or psychiatrists. Such unreal expectations would be counter-productive for the therapeutic process. The client needs to be fully aware that counselling is not a magical process, but that hard work on his/her part will be necessary. Another transferential issue could be that the client's problems would be sorted out after one or two sessions.. Many times

in my practice I have had to say to clients in the first session, "This problem will take much longer than you expect."

10. **Supervision**: The counsellor will explain to the client that it is a normal professional requirement for counsellors to have supervision and that s/he will take material from the session to the supervisor. The trainee counsellor will probably want to make arrangements with the client to be allowed to tape or videotape certain sessions, or all sessions, according to the counsellor's need. Obviously, the counsellor will respect the fears and feelings of the client, and will guarantee confidentiality and anonymity.

11. **Process of referral**: The counsellor will also explain the practice of referral in counselling. If material surfaces which needs the attention of another specialist, then the counsellor will initiate the process of referral.

12. **Terms of the therapeutic relationship**: The therapeutic relationship is for the benefit of the client, and therefore will last only as long as is necessary for the client. When the contract has been completed as far as possible, the counsellor will initiate the process of termination. Should the counsellor feel at some stage that s/he is no longer able to help the client, there should be a discussion leading to an agreed end to the counselling sessions, and perhaps to referral.

13. **Notes on counselling sessions**: The counsellor will keep some form of notes or records concerning all counselling sessions. The notes should be precise, brief and useful. There is no point in copying down everything the client says or does. Certain essential facts about the client must be recorded. For example, the counsellor needs to know the name and telephone number of the client's GP, and to have a brief record of the client's medical history. Notes should include details of any important matters that arise during each session. This can provide a useful record of the client's progress. The client must be aware that such records are being kept, and that according to present legislation, the client has the right

to see these records. These notes will then be available, when the counsellor prepares a report to be entered into the client's file.

Some practitioners argue for withholding such information, because files may contain information that might be harmful to the client. On the other hand, the knowledge that clients do have access to their files may encourage the counsellor to write more sensitively, and so avoid any distress on the part of the client if s/he were to read the file.

9. Exercise

In your own words, illustrate practical application of the following aspects of the counselling contract:

a. Venue of the counselling session
b. Time of the counselling session
c. Frequency of the sessions
d. Boundaries of confidentiality and socialising
e. Goals of therapy
f. Means of achieving these goals
g. Responsibility of each party
h. Setting up necessary boundaries
i. False expectations
j. Role of Supervision
k. Process of referral
l. Terms of the therapeutic relationship
m. Notes on the counselling sessions

10. The historical development of the concept of the working alliance

The effect of a good working alliance means that the client is willing to engage in the psychotherapeutic relationship, even when at some level he or she may no longer wish to do so. This relationship is considered to be a valuable element by many therapeutic approaches, although it is not always given sufficient weight. Opponents of behavioural therapy, for instance, have long argued against what they regard as the impersonal character of a working alliance; they regard it as indicative of a mechanistic approach to counselling (Wilson and Evans, 1970). In fact, the behaviourists whom they claim to oppose have never argued for an impersonal relationship between counsellor and client (Wolpe, 1973), and have even tried to identify central elements of the personal relationship that need to exist for therapy to be successful (Gurman and Rice, 1975). From the standpoint of behavioural therapy, a good and personal counselling relationship is a pre-condition to the therapeutic process.

Let us take a very basic example of a personal, rather than impersonal, way of behaving towards a client. How do you reply to the client who asks you: "How are you?" It will probably not help if you say, "Fine, thanks; so let's get started." As a therapist, you will want to answer in a way that will help to achieve the stated therapeutic task. You might say, "Fine, and how have you been?" or "As you can hear from my husky voice, I'm getting a bit of a cold, but I'm quite well enough to work with you today." The working alliance creates a sense that the client and therapist are joined together in a shared enterprise.

Psychodynamic and client-centred approaches go further. For practitioners of these disciplines, relationship is the "sine qua non" of therapy. For them, therapy is impossible without a good working relationship, based on a sound working alliance. Psychodynamic approaches stress the non-judgmental nature of the therapist. They stress the importance of neutrality in the relationship, but also the importance of warmth and empathy on the part of the counsellor, when establishing the working alliance.

The person-centred approaches tend to argue against the neutrality position, and stress that the interpersonal qualities of warmth, genuineness and empathy are sufficient for the therapeutic process (Rogers, 1951; Carkhuff and Berenson, 1977). However, the person-centred school also speaks of the necessary and sufficient conditions for the client's personality change: accurate empathy, positive regard, non-possessive warmth, and congruence or genuineness. These variables are fundamental to the formation of the working alliance, and they are important for any significant progress in therapy.

Early psychoanalytical literature. The concept of a working alliance is not found in work by earlier psychoanalysts. However, Freud is clear that the therapist must connect with the healthy part of a very disturbed patient. Freud also stressed that the therapist must develop friendliness and trust, and foster a positive transference. This should lead to an "analytic pact" between analyst and patient (Freud, 1937). Anna Freud (1927) mentions the need for creating a "treatment alliance", and stresses its importance for children. Greenson (1967) underlines the use of techniques to develop confidence in the patient, so that a therapeutic alliance can be built up. He lays particular emphasis on the importance of the real personality of the analyst. In psychoanalysis, the working alliance is conceptualised as "the relatively non-neurotic, rational and realistic attitudes of the patient towards the analyst's point of view; [the patient agrees] to work with the analyst despite the neurotic transference reactions" (Greenson, 1967, 24).

More recent psychoanalysts (Adler, 1980; Friedman, 1998) stress the importance of sensitivity in the development of the working alliance. The therapist needs to be aware of his/her own needs, without pushing those needs on to the client. For example, a counsellor who has perfectionist character traits, and who knows the importance of establishing a good working alliance, might be inclined to push for a clearly worked out contract before the client is ready. Under these circumstances, the client may refuse to agree to the contract, or may subsequently be unable to abide by it.

Bugental (1987, 49) states: "The therapeutic alliance is the powerful joining of forces which energises and supports the long, difficult and frequently painful work of life-changing psychotherapy."

Bordin (1979) distinguishes goals, bonds and tasks – three aspects of the working alliance. These seem to be required for any form of therapy to be successful. Most counsellors are familiar with goals and tasks, and are well equipped to work with them. However, when it comes to bonds, they often don't know what to do. Bonds are produced by those feelings and inter-connections that draw people – in this case client and counsellor – together. Bonds are not breakable merely because of physical separation. Where they exist, they need to be nurtured, though always in a professional manner, for the good of the client.

11. Establishing the working alliance

An effective working alliance between counsellor and client requires that the client feels that s/he is accepted and understood. According to Aronoff and Lesse (1976), successful counsellors show similar interpersonal traits. According to them, success requires that the counsellor: (a) provides a relaxed sanctuary, (b) engenders in the client a trust and confidence in the therapist's competence, and (c) demonstrates interest in, and understanding of, the client and his/her concerns.

Researchers have tried to identify those qualities and behaviours in a counsellor, which foster a facilitative relationship. As early as 1951, Fiedler stated that the most successful therapists show: (a) greater ability to understand the feelings of the client, (b) greater security in the therapeutic setting, and (c) greater capacity to show warmth, without being overly involved with the client.

Rogers expanded on this theme. He identified what he called the *necessary conditions* of a facilitative relationship. According to him, a counsellor must be congruent and genuine; experience an empathic understanding of the client; be capable of communicating this understanding to the client; possess unconditional positive regard, be non-judgmental towards the client, and experience a warm, positive, accepting attitude towards the client (Rogers, 1951).

Counsellors can be trained to develop the attitudes and behaviours needed to foster and maintain the working alliance. Some of these are:

1. **Acceptance**: There must be a climate of mutual acceptance, if counselling is going to be effective.

   a. It means that we do not control the client by expecting or pushing him/her to conform to our expectations. It may mean that we laugh genuinely as the client recounts an incident in his life. It may require us to accept the client's decision not to share a certain experience. It may also mean apologising for unintentionally hurting the client by word, act or gesture.

   b. We do not impose values, attitudes, roles or norms on the clients.

   c. We lay aside formal status, for example to be called Doctor, Mr., Mrs., etc. which interferes with an open relationship between counsellor and client.

   d. We sit silently with a client who is weeping, struggling, or experiencing a deep "aloneness".

   e. We provide privacy and adequate relaxing surroundings.

   f. We meet the client on time.

   g. We notify the client if we cannot make the scheduled appointment.

   h. During the session we don't allow interruptions, such as phone calls or messages delivered by secretaries.

   i. When we attend psychologically to the client, we indicate that we are willing to be "in tune" with the client.

Acceptance may show itself by facial expressions, nodding, friendly tone of voice, or appropriate close physical proximity; it may involve using different postures to convey that one is in tune with the client.

Acceptance does not imply wholesale approval. It is often an expression of non-involvement (Egan, 1998). If the therapist really cares for the client, s/he will make efforts to motivate and encourage the client to grow, while still allowing the client the freedom not to grow. Such acceptance is mediated through the awareness of God's presence in the counselling encounter. God accepts the client unconditionally, therefore I myself, the therapist, must also learn to accept the client unconditionally. We need to communicate this acceptance to the client. This facilitates the therapeutic alliance. Often, we simply assume that the client knows that we accept him/her. Such an assumption can interfere with the establishment of the working alliance. The counsellor can show his/her acceptance by (a) actively encouraging clients to share the ways in which they are unique or individual, and (b) by showing respect, care and concern for the client and whatever s/he shares.

2. **Non-possessive warmth and respect**: The client needs to feel valued and appreciated. The counsellor can express respect for the client non-verbally as well as verbally. Respect is shown by a counsellor whenever s/he is really interested in the well-being of the client; it is shown when the counsellor uses his/her professional training in the best way possible. Giving time to the client is an expression of respect. Not pushing the client into areas of discussion for which s/he is not ready is another expression of respect. The counsellor should show non-evaluative respect for the values, thoughts, feelings, wishes, behaviour and potential of the client as a free and responsible person. This is very much in line with Christian thinking and with Christ's way of dealing with people. According to Christian belief, the client is made in the image and likeness of God, endowed with intelligence and freedom. Unconditional positive regard for an individual does not imply unconditional approval of all of that person's behaviour. Christ could love the sinner while hating the sin. We need to learn to distinguish our evaluation of a person's behaviour from the existential love we have for that person. Keeping these two areas distinct is essential for effective counselling. We may find it hard to maintain unconditional, non-possessive warmth for particular clients, when they express their anger and hatred for us as counsellors. That is why we need the support and help of supervision. The counsellor should not accept any behaviour that is harmful, either to the client, the therapist or others, and this needs to be made

clear to the client as part of the working alliance. Occasionally, if anger or hatred becomes overwhelming, we may need to refer a client to another counsellor.

As counsellors, we can monitor our ability to communicate unconditional, non-possessive warmth for the clients by asking ourselves the following questions after a session:

a. Was I fully present to the client in this session?

b. Did I succeed in emptying myself of all my prejudices against this client?

c. Were my interventions respectful, and my challenges caring?

d. Did I use descriptive language rather than judgmental or evaluative?

e. Did I mirror back the love and forgiveness God holds for each of us?

f. Did I make every effort to understand the client and his/her problem?

g. Did I come to the session assuming the "good will" of the client?

h. Was I really listening to the client?

i. How did I communicate my acceptance for the client?

j. What messages did I send through my facial expressions, tone of voice and posture?

3. **Genuineness**: The counsellor needs to be authentic and genuine in the relationship. The authenticity of the counsellor cannot be superficial, but must be basic to the core of his/her being. The genuine counsellor does not hide behind his/her professional role. It is not easy to attain and maintain genuineness. We have learned over the years to hide our real self in our transactions with others. In this way we become depersonalised. Depersonalisation can become a way of life. Genuineness is role-free and means avoiding rigid formulae. It means responding authentically to the client in both a negative and positive manner. This is difficult, because the counsellor is trained to behave in a certain way, to use certain skills, to think according to the approach learned. A genuine counsellor is open, not defensive, real as opposed to putting on a front. The counsellor needs to be congruent in words,

tone, expression, actions and feelings. For example, if it will help the client, admitting discomfort when it is experienced may be more useful than attempting to present a relaxed image.

Genuineness implies "living" the core conditions of everyday life. The counsellor has to work on his/her own growth and integration.

The counsellor can look for evidence of his/her genuineness by reflecting on his/her interactive style. Genuineness shows itself in the following ways (Egan, 1985):

a. Role freeness: the counsellor does not hide behind titles, labels, degrees, or roles. S/he does not use labels as justification or disguises for manipulating the client.

b. Spontaneity: The counsellor is tactful and considerate. However, s/he does not constantly weigh what s/he says. The counsellor is responsive to the moment, rather than pre-planned. Spontaneity proceeds from natural feelings, disposition, or a particular mood, and it occurs without restraint. It is an act freely done or a thought freely uttered, in harmony with one's native impulses. The effective counsellor responds spontaneously in a way that seems to suit the present moment. As with all facets of relationship, spontaneity has to be appropriate to the client's growth. Reactions that come from the counsellor's own issues or from defensiveness need to be avoided.

c. Non-defensiveness: When questioned or criticised by a client, the counsellor shows empathic listening, together with a willingness to see things from the client's point of view. The counsellor does not retreat or counter-attack when challenged by the client.

d. Congruency: The counsellor is consistent in expressing his/her thoughts, feelings and behaviours. Are there discrepancies between what I think or feel on the one hand, and what I do or say on the other? Again, this congruency has to be employed so as to further the client's process.

e. Openness: The counsellor shows self-disclosure when appropriate. Self-disclosure and spontaneity are general indications that a counsellor is congruent, genuine and authentic.

f. Transparency: Therapist transparency encourages transparency in the client. It reduces ambiguity. Of course, we have to use disclosure appropriately and professionally.

g. Bonding: Therapeutic bonds are developed and maintained, and sometimes threatened in the course of counselling. There are many factors which influence bonding. Some are within awareness, others are out of awareness. Some are under the control of the counsellor, others are not. The client-therapist matching is important in establishing the working alliance. We can divide the factors for matching into two main categories:

• *Demographic characteristics*: age, race, gender, class and physical characteristics, which may present an obstacle to good bonding. If the counsellor senses that there may be such an obstacle, s/he needs to use the reflection process sensitively. In this way, through the use of advanced empathy, s/he may identify the existence of such an obstacle. Suppose there is such an obstacle, the counsellor can work through it. If this does not work, then the counsellor will need to initiate the process of referral.

• *Interpersonal response patterns*, and interpersonal differences such as beliefs/values, needs, demands, self-containment or lack of it. These may also affect the process of bonding. Some counsellors may be able to adjust to different clients as naturally as the chameleon adjusts to different environments. However, others may find this very difficult, and therefore it may be necessary to refer the client.

h. Counselling Credibility: The psychotherapist needs to possess face validity or "communicator credibility" (Dryden, 1984, 249) for the client. Each client will associate certain characteristics with an effective and reliable therapist, e.g. professional qualifications and academic background or an informal "human and warm" style. It has become customary to attribute to the term "counselling credibility" two distinct components: (a) ability variable = expertise, (b) motivational variable = trustworthiness.

Gelso and Carter (1985, 164-8) summarise five important aspects of the therapeutic working alliance:

1. The alliance needs to be established relatively early.
2. The strength of the working alliance which is required for a successful outcome, varies according to the difficulty of the demands of the treatment.
3. The bonding aspect develops more slowly than others: there must be personal agreement early in the work about the goals appropriate for treatment, and the tasks that are necessary to attain those goals.
4. The importance of the working alliance waxes and wanes during the various phases of the interventions.
5. Clients vary in the ability to form alliances. Therapists, too, vary in their ability to form, maintain and cultivate a working alliance.

Some clients may have previously suffered from a violation of a working alliance by a therapist, doctor or carer. These clients need particular consideration when encountering difficulties in forming or maintaining a working alliance. For example, one hears from time to time of someone who has had a limb unnecessarily amputated in a hospital because of an administrative error. Such a client will understandably find it difficult to establish a working alliance; most likely s/he will distrust members of a helping profession, counsellors included. Since this kind of distrust on the part of the client can drastically affect the working alliance, it needs to be invalidated:

1. by proving that that particular helper is an exception.
2. by enabling the client to build criteria for reliability, trustworthiness and the ability to respond to the counsellor.
3. by developing the intuitions of the client.
4. by resourcing them with appropriate assertive and self-defensive skills.

In this way, the afflicted client is being helped to deal with potentially dangerous situations in the future.

SUMMARY:

In establishing the working alliance, client/therapist matching is important. Problems may arise from:
a. Demographic characteristics: age, ethnicity, gender, socio-economic status
b. Interpersonal response patterns: attributions, values and aims

The therapist needs to possess face validity or communicator credibility:
a. Expertise
b. Trustworthiness

What are the needs of clients who have suffered a violation of the working alliance?
a. Understanding as to why s/he now finds it difficult to form a working alliance.
b. Invalidation of the mistrust:
- by proving that the helper who caused the injury is an exception
- by enabling the client to build criteria for trustworthiness
- by developing the intuition of the client
- by helping the client to acquire appropriate skills of assertiveness and self-defence.

———

12. Exercise

Consider this question:

Which aspects of the various approaches outlined above do you believe would be most conducive to developing a successful working alliance?

Give reasons for your choices and illustrations of how the approaches would work.

13. Management of the working alliance

Factors which facilitate the management of the working alliance include:

1. **Unconditional positive regard, empathy and congruence:** it was Rogers (1951) who first articulated these three as the necessary and sufficient conditions for growth and change. They are values and attitudes, but they are also skills, which can be taught, learnt, practised, supervised and "lived" as Gospel values. Unconditional positive regard, empathy and congruence are generally associated with an effective working alliance and successful outcome of counselling.

2. **Personal preparation of the counsellor** is perhaps the most important aspect of the working alliance. Self-exploration is important in training and supervision. Self-awareness and work on oneself will improve the quality of the working alliance. If I am aware of my own feelings, and of my scripts and thought patterns which influence my actions and reactions, I shall be in a better position to maintain the working alliance, than if I am completely unaware of what is going on in my relationship with my client.

3. **Personal happiness in everyday life** is an important factor for forming and maintaining a working alliance, particularly through difficult times. Therapists whose personal lives are not fulfilling can be liable to exploiting their clients sexually, emotionally or in other ways, which are not only less effective but totally unethical. They are less effective than they could otherwise be. Keeping fit is one of the central factors for being a good counsellor. As "wounded healers" we need to be aware of our woundedness and use it for the good of the client. We need to avoid "burnout".

4. **Third-party references** affect the working alliance. Who referred the client and why? Was it a dissatisfied spouse, a guilty employer, a friend whose life was miraculously transformed after seeing a counsellor for six sessions, a

colleague with some hidden rivalry, or perhaps a tired psychiatrist whose patience and resources had run out?

5. **The first interview**, and often just the first three minutes, can act as an overture for the whole therapeutic journey. It enunciates all the major themes. These will recur again over the following months or years. They indicate a substantial part of a person's existential reality.

The first interview is also the therapist's opportunity to give sufficient information, both practical and experiential, so that the client is able to give informed consent. The client has to make up his/her mind about whether to come to counselling. Therefore, the therapist needs to demonstrate the ability to accompany him/her on the rocky journey, using humour, warmth, care, challenge, empathy, listening, questioning, and interpretation where a psychodynamic approach is considered appropriate. Both parties need to have a reasonably sound sense of each other, and of what the journey together may involve.

6. **High levels of focus**: clear contracting; mutually agreed goals and procedures, appropriate levels of information; sharing the responsibility for getting the most from the treatment; clarity about fees and aspects of the client/counsellor relationship, including, where appropriate, reference to the extent of the counsellor's authority. – all these are important in setting the stage for a solid working alliance. It will then be a solid platform from which to deal with uncertainties, threats, interferences or ruptures in the working relationship. Given a sound working alliance, these apparent problems can often provide a touchstone for moments of breakthrough.

SUMMARY:

What helps to establish the working alliance?
- Unconditional positive regard, empathy and congruence.
- Personal preparation of the therapist.

- Personal satisfaction outside the therapy setting.
- Properly assessing third party references.
- The first interview, and often the first three minutes of it, can act as an overture for the whole therapeutic journey.
- In the first interview the therapist needs to use sufficient personal skills to relate warmly and empathetically with the client, so as to ensure that the client believes s/he is in good hands.
- Other factors for establishing the working alliance are: high focus, clear contracting, mutually agreed goals and procedures, appropriate levels of information, sharing the responsibility for getting the most from the treatment, clarity about fees and any aspects of the counsellor/client relationship that need to be addressed at this early stage.

---

14. The influence of expectations on the working alliance

One of the most important factors in establishing the working alliance seems to be expectation. "Response expectancy" is highly influential in therapy outcome. It is partly determined by the expectancy of the therapist and his/her specific helping techniques. Social learning theory also teaches how important expectancy effects can be in determining the outcome. We talk about placebo effects in medical research. Similarly, expectancy may be an essential ingredient of effective therapy. The influence of expectation, either from the therapist or from the client, certainly affects outcome to a considerable extent. Therefore, we need to optimise the effects of expectation. How can this be achieved?

Kirsch (1990, 200) answered the question in this way: "Treatment procedures and rationales should be adapted to clients' existing beliefs, and efforts should be made to provide experiential confirmation of therapeutic change." For example, a client believes deeply in the healing power of Christ. This belief needs to be built into the healing process of the client. This is one of the reasons why, for believing Christian clients, bringing Christ the Healer into the session is important.

The possible effects of expectation (whether it is conscious or not), and whether the expectation derives specifically from a person's history, or is culturally determined, should be discussed at the initial assessment session. For instance, the assimilation of media reports may have distorted a client's expectations with regard to therapy and therapists. For clients who use intellectualisation as a defence, a little knowledge on their part may prove "a dangerous thing".

Relationships with previous helping professionals (doctors, teachers, priests and therapists) will tend to colour the working alliance. The counsellor should enquire at the assessment interview about the nature of the client's prior working relationships. "I never see doctors". "I don't believe in doctors". Such a client may have a strong counter-dependant tendency. A history of good collegial collaborative relationships bodes well for subsequent psychotherapy. Defiance of, or over-compliance with, authority figures needs to be identified and monitored during therapy.

SUMMARY:

How do expectations influence the working alliance?
- Expectations are an important factor in establishing the working alliance and in the outcome of therapy.
- Matching client and counsellor properly will assist in creating beneficial expectations. It will assist the relationship if the client has found out a little about the counsellor.
- The nature of clients' prior working alliance will affect the expectations.
- If the client possesses a little psychological knowledge, this may be counter-effective!

———

15. Threats to the working alliance

There are many other, less disastrous factors which are a threat to the working alliance, such as lack of punctuality, non-payment of fees or failure to adhere to the agreement. But at the far extreme is some kind of action of violence, suicide, homicide or psychosis. These forms of action include the following:

1. **Suicide, psychosis and homicide destroy the working alliance**. These are the biggest threats to the working alliance in counselling. They are the ways in which people can destroy the working alliance. These issues need to be addressed and resolved, or revisited appropriately, as long as the therapy lasts.

2. **The working alliance can be affected by a client's emotional blackmail**. This may take the form of subtly threatening to jeopardise the therapist's professional reputation, or other guilt-involving manoeuvres. The client's medical or psychiatric record may be an obstacle; s/he may have a history of sadistic acting out, childhood or adolescent antisocial behaviour, prior suicide attempts, alcoholism, drug addiction or even the occasional use of mind-altering substances.

Examles of threats:
- The client takes a Valium before the session, to calm herself down.
- The sexually addictive person can only come to therapy after a casual sexual encounter on the way.
- The harassed executive frequently arrives late for the session, stressed out and exhausted by traffic conditions.

What response is needed?
a. We need to make "no suicide" contracts. This is a damage-limitation tool.
b. Yalom (1989) emphasises the importance of working with feelings and fantasies about death.

c. Hospitals and residential facilities are more suitable for patients than out-patient treatment, if there is serious suicidal, homicidal or psychotic risk.

d. There may be some unusual situations where it is deemed appropriate and beneficial for a client to be held responsible for monitoring his or her own intentionality in terms of, for example, suicide or psychosis.

3. **The issue of dual relationships**, for instance with spouses, fiancés or relatives, has to be sensitively and intelligently handled in order to maintain a healthy working alliance. We must not pretend that they do not exist. Rather, we had better learn how to cope with them constructively.

4. **Extra-therapy factors**: They can either facilitate or impede progress in therapy. Some therapies, in particular grief therapies, advocate "homework" for the client. What happens outside counselling may be as important as what happens during the therapeutic hour. Sometimes, an intervention when the client leaves a session may have an enormous effect on therapy.

5. There are many other, less disastrous factors which are a threat to the working alliance, such as lack of punctuality, non-payment of fees or failure to adhere to the agreement.

Fritz Perls used to refer to psychotherapy as a "safe emergency" (Perls et al., 1951). In systems theory, it is acknowledged that sometimes it is necessary to create a crisis. The purpose is to find the necessary turbulence or disruption or de-structuring, from which new growth and healing can arise (Menor, 1994).

Breaks, crises or ruptures in the therapeutic alliance are therefore not necessarily detrimental or catastrophic. It is a matter of holding the client within the area of rational good will, while allowing the maximum buffeting from unconscious, environmental or existential challenges.

We have now made a short exploration of the working

alliance. We have explained how in any relationship we use the working alliance. Some of it may be implicit and some of it may be explicit. However, you know when something has gone wrong. For example when somebody says "I am surprised, I never knew that I had to pay for this", and the therapist has that sudden uncomfortable feeling. Let's think of friendship. It might be that you suddenly realise that a certain friend sends you birthday cards, while you never send her one in return, or you think, "That's odd, we always invite those people out for dinner but they never invite us". Then you feel that there was a problem in the working alliance.

16. Exercise

Work out your own responses to the following:
1. What skills are involved in establishing a working alliance?
2. What skills are involved in contracting?
3. What kind of skills and attitudes do I need to acquire, in order to create better working alliances and contracting?
4. Make what you would consider to be a reasonable contract with regard to your job or situation in life.
5. Give some illustrations of why you might feel obliged to stop the counselling process with a client.
6. Visualise yourself in detail establishing a good working alliance with your client.
7. What can you learn from the first minutes of a first interview, if you listen carefully?
8. Describe some factors which facilitate the establishment of the working alliance.
9. Enumerate some factors which interfere with the establishment of the working alliance.

17. Two case studies for the working alliance

1. ANNA, an African girl, aged eighteen, who was studying to become a nurse, came for counselling. She came because she had a great fear of blood. Her goal was to get rid of this

fear, so that she would feel normal, and would not be disturbed whenever she saw blood, especially in the operating theatre where she was supposed to assist the surgeons.

I listened carefully and attentively to her and mirrored back some of her statements to let her know that I understood her, so as to establish a working alliance with her. Anna was of the opinion that this problem could be sorted out quickly in one or two sessions. I made it clear that from my experience such problems take some time; we decided that we would meet ten times, and then reconsider our contract. Our sessions would take place in my counselling room, every week on Tuesday from 10.00 to 11.00 a.m. She would pay twenty pounds for my services for each session and if, for one reason or another, she was unable to come, she would phone me at least twenty hours beforehand, so that I could make alternative arrangements. If she neglected to inform me, she would be bound to pay the fees. I agreed that during this time I would be fully available to her, using all my skills to look at her problem, and if for some reason I was not able to keep to my agreement, I would let her know twenty hours ahead, so that we could make alternative arrangements. Even if I were suddenly taken ill or suffered a bereavement, although the notice would have to be shorter, I would still let her know that I could not be with her for the session. All this was done in a person-to-person relationship and not too seriously, but clearly.

We then went on to talk about confidentiality. We agreed that whatever was shared in the session remained between the two of us, and would not go beyond the room. This was to enable her to share freely and without reservation. We also mentioned the exceptions to confidentiality, for example danger to herself or to others. I made it clear that in such cases I would have to inform the relevant authority. I further pointed out that I was under supervision, and asked for her permission to tape the sessions, so that I might take some material to my supervisor. We agreed that some material might be used for research purposes; however, strict anonymity would be preserved. She had no problem with that whatsoever, and just laughed. I was not sure what the laugh meant, so I mirrored back what I saw. It turned out that she was not sure what the fuss was all about with regard to confidentiality, since everybody knew her problem in any case. Nevertheless, I mentioned the importance of confidentiality on both sides in the counselling relationship.

I stressed my professional relationship with her: I would not socialise with her, or discuss any business with her outside the session, should we happen to meet. We also discussed greeting each other, if we should happen to meet somewhere. She felt that we should try to be normal and therefore greet each other as people do who know each other. She realised that clear boundaries were important for our relationship. These would include time boundaries; we would start on time and finish on time.

The treatment plan was fairly clear, since the ailment was a phobia about blood. Therefore, we would use the techniques of desensitization. I checked out how she felt. She said that she was happy to start the process. The initial working alliance had been established.

2. PETER, twenty-two years of age, of African origin, came to me for counselling, because he was in danger of loosing his job in a bank. He loved working in the bank, but had been warned by his bank manger that he had to be on time and not be rude with the customers. Peter was very surprised that the bank manager was so strict with him. He had been late coming to work only three times in a month and only for half an hour. He did not consider that he was rude with people. He was just himself. Peter could not understand why the bank manager would make such a "fuss" over such a small matter.

As I listened to him telling other stories about his private life like having intercourse with girls when he was only fifteen years old, I became aware that "boundaries" were the main presenting problem. We needed to establish a good working alliance. Thus, I asked some very concrete questions to make sure that my hunch about boundary issues was verified. I asked him directly whether he had any friends. His reply was yes, but they usually lasted just a short time. Most of those friends were girls. I then put the question to him: "Have you many girl friends at the same time?" His reply was, "No, only three usually." "What kind of relationship is it?" "We go out for a meal and then sleep together, once a week." "Do you do that with all three?" "Yes, but not the same day."

As he talked to me, I became aware that his language was not very polite and that he would need to improve that to be able to work in the bank. Very gently and deeply lovingly I pointed this out to him with a soft smile on my face. He took it very positively and was ready to work on himself. In his former job as a street sweeper, this was not a problem. He was dissatisfied with sweeping streets, but he had wanted to earn money when he left school at an early age. Now he wanted a better job, a job where he would meet people. That was the reason why he applied for this job in the bank. For one reason or other he got the job. Basically he was an intelligent, hardworking young man with great aspirations who had never had a chance to show his real talents.

We were near the end of the first session. I stressed that we need a very clear working alliance in order to be effective in our counselling. I had found out from my exploration of his family background that he had never learned healthy boundaries. So I stressed that it was very important that he would be on time for his sessions and at work, that he needed to observe how he spoke to the customers; I asked him to give me feedback on these points at our next meeting. When the time was up, he still wanted to talk to me. I was strict with him and said that he could bring all he wanted to talk about next time. I pointed out that we had to finish on time. I wanted to model boundaries for him.

The next session was important for the success of the therapy. I spent quite some time, after he had shared how he related to people and customers, in explaining what had happened in the family. He needed to learn time boundaries, emotional boundaries and sex boundaries. He understood that he had developed certain behaviour patterns and use of language that now caused him problems, because nobody had told him what was right or wrong. He had a fine way of manipulating teachers as he had manipulated his mother in allowing him to do what he wanted without realising what he was doing to himself. Now he was aware. He was very intelligent and started using his intelligence to grow rather than to manipulate people,; I had managed to show him how he was manipulating others. I intentionally instilled hope in him, described what his future could be like and that he could become a bank manager with his talents, if only he learned to change some of his behaviour patterns, particularly his language.

It was a great pleasure for me to work with Peter. He was always on time. When he became emotionally abusive, he apologised. He decided on his own initiative to have only one girl friend and to learn to treat her with respect as a person, and not just as an object of sexual pleasure. Having clear boundaries and knowing why this was important helped him motivated himself to put every effort into changing his behaviour patterns and language. After eight sessions I felt he could manage himself and we terminated our counselling contract. I told him that he could always come back if he needed it, but that I felt confident that he would do well by having developed a more reflective mental approach to his behaviour and language, and to the consequences of both.

CHAPTER FOUR

The transference relationship: the client's perspective

1. A description of transference 2. Freud's position with regard to transference 3. Exercise 4. Freud's development of the concept of transference 5. Carl Rogers and transference 6. The re-experiencing therapy of Merton Gill and transference 7. Past experience and present reality 8. The counsellor and transference 9. The all-pervasive nature of transference 10. Transferential relationship 11. Resistance to transference 12. Some transference-inviting questions 13. The importance of transference for learning 14. Some common transference patterns in therapy 15. Transference and idolatry 16. Exercise 17. Managing the transference relationship 18. God-representation 19. Exercises 20. Two case studies of transference.

1. A description of transference

Transference means "carrying over". In order to learn anything, we carry things over from a past situation into a present or future situation. This process is basic to learning; so, if we couldn't transfer, we would never remember anything. However, we frequently "carry over" factors – often problematic ones – from a past relationship into the present. In the language of counselling, transference refers to the past experience of a relationship being "carried over" and applied to the therapeutic relationship.

The transference/countertransference relationship is sometimes referred to as the unfinished, or the biased relationship. Clarkson calls it the distorted relationship. This definition comes closest to the mark. This kind of relationship distorts the working alliance, because something is being "carried over" that is out of place in the therapeutic situation. Indeed, invasive transference/countertransference in the relationship threatens, and can even destroy the working alliance.

SUMMARY:

Transference means "carrying over". This process is basic to any learning.

Transference can be thought of as follows:
- Unfinished material from the client's past.

- Biased attitudes derived from the past.
- Distorted perceptions derived from the past.
- It distorts the working alliance.
- It threatens the working alliance.
- It can destroy the working alliance.

———

Transference refers to the situation, in which the client, often unconsciously, notices in the therapist feelings, attitudes, attributes and behaviour patterns which recall those of another person, particularly a parent, in his/her earlier life; then the client responds to aspects of the counsellor's personality, as if the counsellor were the person of whom the client is reminded. Transferences can be detected by the following characteristics: they are inappropriate, intense, ambivalent and inconsistent. When you feel inappropriate anger towards someone, and the anger is quite out of proportion in the here-and-now situation, then very likely the source of the emotion is transference. A client may have very strong emotions towards his/her counsellor, both positive and negative, and these emotions may stem from unresolved conflicts of childhood. The client transfers the anger, hatred, love or ambivalence, which s/he experienced as a child, on to the counsellor.

Transferences are described as *positive*, when they manifest positive feelings towards the counsellor, as for example when a male client likes his female therapist very much, or even loves her and feels very attracted to her. He may tell other people how wonderful his therapist is. In this way, a client may develop an unhealthy and clinging attachment to the counsellor. Transferences are described as *negative*, when they manifest negative feelings towards the counsellor, for example when the client reveals a palpable dislike for the therapist; this may have been transferred from the dislike the client once felt for his/her father, or for a schoolteacher. Feelings of insecurity, nervousness, anger, rage or resentment often belong to a negative transference. *Negative* transferences will often interfere with counselling. They can lead to direct verbal attacks on the counsellor. They can also mean that negative feelings are acted out, rather than explored. A common factor of negative transferences is an unwillingness to work through resistances. Even intensive positive transferences can interfere with the therapeutic process, because they make excessive emotional demands on the counsellor and therefore prevent the genuine exploration of feelings. However, the trained counsellor can use these strong feelings to uncover the unresolved conflicts of the past; then s/he can help the client to resolve the conflicts.

Generally speaking, we could describe transference as the tendency of one human being to project on to another, feelings, attitudes or behaviour patterns that originally related to someone else. Transferences very often give the counsellor the opportunity to work through old conflicts that have surfaced. The counsellor needs to be especially careful how s/he responds to the behaviour patterns and attitudes that transference provokes, because s/he is dealing with the client's subconscious.

Liechty (1995, 92) summarises Becker's meaning of transference in the following way: "the dynamic of drawing personal symbolic power from external sources". He goes on to state: "Transference is the psychological mechanism by which an individual feels grounded in the object world and at the same time feels powerful, important, and unique standing as it were, above nature." According to Becker, since we have this need to feel powerful, important and unique, we choose several transference objects which symbolise strength, power and beauty. Such transference objects include cars, money, the flag, famous people, specialised collections, technical gadgets, romantic or intellectual interests, a club, association, a social movement.

Becker's presentation of transference links even a perversion like fetishism to the same inner motives of strength, power and beauty. He writes:

> Transference is a form of fetishism, a form of narrow control that anchors our own problems. We take our helplessness, our guilt, our conflicts, and we fix them to a spot in the environment. We can create any locus at all

for projecting our cares onto the world, even the locus of our own arms and legs. (Becker 1973, 144)

According to Becker, people use transference as a way of dealing with the pain and terror of feeling powerless, ungrounded, weak, alone. The earliest transference objects are parents and caretakers, a blanket or a teddy bear. We invest a specific transference object with power to protect us and to help us not to feel alone.

There is ambivalence in both positive and negative transference objects. This ambivalence is based on the investment of power. The child invests power in the parents "to control terror, to mediate wonder, and to defeat death by that person's strength". But then, as a consequence, the child experiences "transference terror". According to Becker (146), this terror exists in losing the object, in displeasing it, or not being able to live without it. The terror is still with him, but now it is in the form of the transference object.

Life without some form of transference would be unbearable, if not impossible. Becker goes on to affirm that transference is the very basis of our drive towards truth, beauty and goodness. The problem is that transference objects are mediated unconsciously, without a person's control. The harmful side effects can be reduced when the transference patterns enter our consciousness, so that we can develop some control over them.

SUMMARY:

Transferences
Some of the characteristics of transference:
- they are inappropriate
- they are intense
- they are ambivalent
- they are inconsistent.

How can we detect a transference?
Transferences may be positive or negative.
- Positive transferences: liking the therapist very much, loving the therapist inappropriately, being attracted to the therapist excessively, idealising the therapist.

- Negative transferences: great dislike for the therapist, feelings of nervousness, fear, insecurity, anger, rage, resentment towards the therapist.

What is transference in a wider sense?
- Negative transferences may interfere with counselling, such as direct verbal attacks on the counsellor.
- Even intensive positive transferences can interfere with therapy, for example rescuing.

Becker's interpretation of transference:
- We invest power in external objects and then draw power from them.
- There is ambivalence in both positive and negative transference objects.

What is transference terror?
- It occurs as the result of losing or displeasing the transference object.

———

2. Freud's position with regard to transference

Freud was a nineteenth-century physician, and as such had a very mechanical view of the therapeutic relationship. This changed, however, as he observed what happened between Breuer and his patient Bertha. Breuer visited Bertha twice each day, often in her bedroom. One day, she was very distressed, and said that she was pregnant with his child. Breuer was certain that she was a virgin. The pregnancy turned out to be hysterical. From studying this and other relationships, Freud made two important discoveries: the theory of templates and the repetition compulsion.

Freud's theory of templates (1962, 97–108) suggests that in early relationships we establish patterns into which we try to fit all our important subsequent relationships If I had a cold and negative relationship with my father, for instance, I would very likely see male authority figures in a negative light. Similarly, if I had had to fight with my brothers and sisters to get my parents' attention, I would probably fight with my peers to get the attention of the boss.

The repetition compulsion means that people have a need to create and recreate for themselves replays of relationships and situations, which they found particularly difficult in their early childhood. We have all met people who keep on recreating situations that had bad effects upon them. Some people, who were persecuted or ill-treated in early years, e.g. by their mother, constantly push us to punish them. Freud states: "We have come across people all of whose human relationships have the same outcome: such as the benefactor who is abandoned in anger after a time..." (1920, 22).

Why do people go to such trouble to create a situation which will cause them pain and suffering? It looks as if the person is trying to put a happy ending on childhood's negative outcomes. However, this may be a misguided interpretation. The situation with a happy ending would no longer resemble the original situation, which was essentially one of conflict, anger, frustration and guilt.

When people come to therapy, according to Freud, their reactions will be influenced by two tendencies: they will see the therapeutic relationship in the light of their earliest relationships, and they will engender replays of earlier difficult situations. Freud used the term *Uebertragung* (transference) for these perceptions, responses and provocations. This means, as we said at the start of the chapter, that the client transfers on to the counsellor the old patterns and repetitions of behaviour. Freud's followers realised that transference could represent a replay of a childhood relationship. If the patient's father had been cold and disapproving, s/he might see the counsellor that way too; alternatively, s/he might see the counsellor as loving and warm, because subconsciously s/he was compensating and making the counsellor into the father s/he had always wanted; in this way, I could try to give myself the father I always wanted. During the course of therapy, the patient might switch from one kind of transference to the other.

A male therapist may draw a mother transference, and a female therapist a father transference. The transference phenomenon is strong enough to express itself, regardless of the gender of the counsellor. One of my clients, a teacher, had an authority problem that originated from his domineering mother. It showed itself in his relationship with the principal of the school, and in his relationship with God. Another, female client was very angry with her male therapist; whatever he did was not good enough. After some time, she was able to share that she had been abandoned by her father when she was very young. Although she had adored and completely trusted him, he had abruptly left her mother and herself without providing for them. Once the situation had been explained, the therapist understood the client's rage.

The theory of transference applies not only to clients in a therapeutic setting, but also to other relationships in daily life. Wherever we are, we are constantly replaying some aspect of relationship from our early childhood. It can be seen in authority relationships, in love affairs, in friendships, in business dealings. Becoming more sensitive to transference phenomena will not only help the counsellor, but clients who need help with their relationships. Michael Kahn (1997, 29) says that the first relationships are the themes of one's interpersonal life, while subsequent relationships are the development and recapitulation of those themes.

SUMMARY:

Freud and transference

At first Freud's views on relationships was mechanical. Studying Breuer's experience with one of his patients, and reflecting on relationships, he discovered the theory of templates and the repetition compulsion.

According to Freud, in therapy the client's reactions will be influenced by two tendencies:

- seeing the therapeutic relationship in the light of earlier relationships;
- experiencing the therapeutic relationship as replicas of earlier difficult situations.

———

3. Exercise

Briefly explain in your own words, and with your own illustrations:
1. The theory of templates.
2. Repetition compulsion.
3. Why people create a situation, which causes them pain and suffering.

4. Freud's development of the concept of transference

Initially, transference was considered by Freud (1905) as interfering with the method of treatment he was developing. Only later on, did it become a tool or vehicle for performing psychoanalytic therapy. Freud considered transference as helpful if it consisted of positive feelings. Liking the therapist was seen as necessary for the therapeutic journey. The only time positive transference was not considered helpful by Freud was if it had too strong an erotic dimension. This could interrupt the therapy. An example of this was Bertha's erotic transference to Breuer.

Freud saw the client's negative feelings towards the therapist as obstacles. The therapist's task was to interpret the transference, in order to help the client understand the true childhood origins of those feelings. This would free the therapy from the burden of anger, resentment or suspicion. Freud's patient Dora abruptly terminated therapy. On reflection, Freud realised that he had missed the signs that a very negative transference was in process (1905, 7-122).

Later on, Freud realised that the best place to work through things was often from within the transference, inside the relationship formed by client and counsellor. (1973, 454). This was an enormous change for Freud, as far as the therapeutic relationship is concerned. He had taken two important steps away from the mechanical relationship between doctor and patient. He recognised that the nature of the relationship could facilitate or block the therapeutic work and that, in some way, the therapist was in charge of this effect. He also realised that there was important work to be done on the subject of the relationship itself. Transference enables the therapist to show convincingly to the client how early fantasies, expectations, impulses distort present reality. In the transference, everything that interferes with the client's life in the here-and-now shows up clearly. Therefore, the therapist would do well to use the transference to show the client the distortions of present reality.

The therapeutic relationship contains within it the whole story of the client's life, so to speak. Freud thought that successful therapy was achieved by remembering, recalling the early experiences, and by realising how they affected one's present life. Freud saw transference mainly as distortion, and as resistance to true remembering. Transference means wanting to change the therapeutic relationship into something that it is not designed to be. Here is a not uncommon example of a client reporting negatively on how he distorted his relationship with his analyst: "I thought she was angry at me. I thought she did not like me. I thought she was disgusted by my fantasies". Even in positive transferences, the therapeutic relationship is distorted: the counsellor becomes all-important to the client. He/she is the constant topic of conversation, of idealisation and praise. He/she enters as an important person, even into the client's dream or fantasy world. Freud believed that, by pointing out to clients these distortions through transference, they could be helped to see the distortions that had occurred throughout their lives. However, he knew that these steps were not enough to sort out all the problems that the analyst would inevitably encounter when treating a patient.

SUMMARY:

Freud's development of the concept of transference

- Initially, Freud considered transference as interfering with treatment.
- Later on, he saw transference as a vehicle for therapy.
- Transference was helpful, if it consisted in normal positive feelings towards the therapist.

- According to Freud, strong erotic feelings interfere with therapy.
- At first, Freud saw negative feelings towards the therapist as obstacles for therapy. Therefore, the therapist interprets the transference feelings.
- Later, Freud saw that transference was the tool to work through things.
- For Freud, transference was distortion and resistance to true remembering.

---

5. Carl Rogers and transference

For Carl Rogers, genuineness, empathy and unconditional positive regard are the three attributes necessary to a successful therapeutic relationship. He saw each of these as a continuum. For him, the art of becoming a therapist consisted in moving further and further along each of these continua. In person-centred therapy, where there is genuineness, empathy and positive regard, strong transference is rarely the case (although some degree of transference is present in most cases.) When the projected feelings encounter empathy and unconditional regard, transference phenomena disappear; they lose their source. According to Rogers, the client-centred psycho-therapist "attempts to understand and accept such attitudes, which then tend to become accepted by the client as being his own perception of the situation inappropriately held" (1991, 218).

Rogers clearly acknowledged the existence of transference attitudes in analytic and non-directive psychotherapy. He understood that the analytical approach to theory tends to transform transference attitudes into the full development of a long-term dependent relationship. Transference is most likely to develop where the counsellor is seen and experienced as authority, as in psychoanalysis. The client builds up an experience of the psychotherapist as knowing more about the client than the client does about him/herself. Thus, the client will hand over the reins of his life into the hands of the more competent psychotherapist. The client may as a result enjoy comfortable feelings of relief and liking. At times, however, there will probably be feelings of hatred for the person who has become so all-important.

The more the therapist evaluates, questions, interprets, controls, directs and criticises, the more dependency is created and the more intensive transference becomes. Rogers asserts that this is not the case in person-centred therapy, where the problems of dependency are less likely to interfere with the counselling relationship, because the idea of the counsellor's authority is not stressed.

SUMMARY:
Carl Rogers and transference
- In person-centred therapy the emphasis is on genuineness, empathy and unconditional positive regard. Therefore, strong transference feelings are rarely the case.
- Some transference feelings may be there in most situations.
- Transferences are stronger where the therapist acts as an authority figure and fosters dependency.

———

6. The re-experiencing therapy of Merton Gill and transference

Merton Gill (1982) has written a great deal about the therapeutic relationship. Gill believes that because the patient's difficulties were acquired through experience, they must be changed, transformed and healed through experience. We cannot reason them away. Understanding the roots of a problem is necessary; but understanding cannot be achieved through mere explanation. It emerges gradually, as clients re-experience relevant aspects of their past lives. This re-experiencing must occur within the therapeutic relationship.

113

According to Gill, re-experiencing will be therapeutic if the impulses, feelings and expectations are experienced under the following conditions:

1. They must be experienced in the presence of the person towards whom they are now directed.
2. The re-experienced feelings must be expressed towards the person towards whom they are now directed. It is not enough for the patient to experience the feelings silently, or without divulging them.
3. The person towards whom the feelings and expectations are now directed, must be determined to discuss the patient's feelings and impulses without defensiveness, with interest and objectivity.
4. The client must be helped to learn the original source of the re-experienced impulses. In this way, remembering and re-experiencing become organically blended.

This emphasis on re-experiencing changes the concept of transference. Material re-experienced in the transference is then directed towards the therapist, who will respond accordingly. This material includes the feelings, thoughts and opinions, the observations, questions and wishes that the client has about the therapist. It also includes the feelings, thoughts, opinions, observations, questions and wishes that the client believes the therapist has about him or her.

It is natural for the client to be frightened of re-experiencing and expressing these emotions, and learning their roots in front of the therapist; s/he will most likely be resistant. Therefore, the therapist has to create a safe environment which will encourage the client to reveal his/her feelings. The therapist has to help the client through the resistance.

The therapist needs to be aware that allusions to the therapeutic situation are often encoded as references to other situations. The therapist must also be sensitive from moment to moment as to what is going on in the therapeutic situation. This will help him/her to detect the stimuli to which the client is responding. For example, say a female client talks apprehensively about being criticised in her place of work.

The therapist needs to reflect on what happened in recent therapy sessions. Was there anything which the client may have experienced as criticism? If so, the therapist will address it as tactfully as possible.

According to Gill, the client will use elements of the therapeutic situation to elaborate or extend the transference phenomena. Gill developed two kinds of transference interpretation. The first aims at helping clients to become aware of their feelings about the therapist. The second aims at helping clients to appreciate how their long-standing attitudes influence their understanding of the therapeutic events.

7. Past experience and present reality

Part of the problem is that sometimes we carry things over from the past, and fail to update them with here-and-now reality. We don't check them. Let's take the topic of trust. You might meet hundreds of priests whom you can trust. Then you transfer that trust on to a priest, whom you shouldn't trust, for all kinds of reasons. That shows you how positive transference can be a problem. You have learned to trust, but have now made yourself vulnerable by "carrying over" your trust to the wrong person.

This is sometimes the case with medical doctors, although people are more careful now. Many people have had good experiences with doctors and surgeons. However, you may meet a surgeon, who implies, "Don't worry about it; we will just cut you open and see what is in there. Just leave it all to me. I know what I am doing." Then you hear about the terrible mistakes the surgeon has made. That is another example of where we transfer positive experiences inappropriately, not checking whether this person knows their business, or whether this person can be trusted in this respect. We don't inform ourselves properly about what our problem is, what the operation will involve, and what the likelihood is of something going wrong. The lesson to be drawn from all this is: be wary of transferring positively from one experience on to another. Positive transfer poses the danger of being disappointed. Think for yourself, check things out. This is not being distrustful, it is common sense.

Education provides us with plenty of examples. In secondary school, maybe our experience of teachers has been largely good. We transfer positive experiences on to the next teacher; but if this teacher turns out to be humiliating, shaming or not to have a good grasp of his/her subject, then you must adjust your thinking. Maybe s/he is different from the others. This is the difficulty with positive transference.

Negative transference poses a similar danger, but in the opposite direction. Suppose you have had negative experiences with people who have been in positions of authority. In a new situation, you meet another person in authority, and what happens? You expect the same kind of negative experience. And, lo and behold, if you treat them as if you expect negative experiences from them, they will reproduce your negative experiences. That is what is known as a repetition compulsion. We take things from the past, we transfer them on to current or future situations, and we generalise. We say, "I have met one Serbian soldier, all Serbian soldiers are the same." This is the basis of prejudice, of course.

SUMMARY:

Not correcting past experiences in the here and now
- Problems arise when we do not update carried-over experience with the here-and-now reality.
- Positive transferences can be a problem, because, having learned to trust, you trust the wrong person.
- Negative transferences can also be a problem, because you don't trust a person whom you could trust, and, because of your non-trusting attitude, that person rejects you.

The lesson to learn is
- Think for yourself in the here-and-now. Check whether you can trust or not trust in the present situation.

———

8. The counsellor and transference

The counsellor is not the "saviour" or the "liberator" of the people who come to him/her for help. They may idealise him. The counsellor can only point the way, facilitate the journey, but in the end cannot take the journey for the client. The client has to do it for him/herself. But at the end of it all, there is still a lot of work to be done and none of it is complete before death. The effective counsellor is realistic enough to see that his role is not to provide an anaesthetic against the difficulties in life. The effective and realistic counsellor is not there to provide a permanent inoculation against all the difficulties of life. He is there to help clients discover in themselves their own resources to meet these difficulties.

SUMMARY:
The counsellor and transference
- The counsellor is not the "saviour" or "liberator" of the client.
- The counsellor facilitates the process of healing and becoming resourceful.

———

9. The all-pervasive nature of transference

Transference/countertransference relationships will happen in any community, and even between husband and wife. Someone transfers past material on to members of their community or family, who then countertransfers material back! This material may consist of fears, other emotions such as anger, wishes or behaviour patterns. In some specific situations this may foster growth, but in many other situations this interferes with relationships and the wellbeing of communities and families. Similar events take place in the seminary situation, between students and staff, or between the priests of a diocese and their bishop, or between members of a congregation and their provincial, or between the parish priest and his parishioners. It is important for members of any community to become aware when and how they transfer and countertransfer, and how this affects their relationships with others. A better understanding of this relationship, and more awareness of it when it occurs, would help us considerably in improving community life.

How aware am I of the way I relate to others in my family or community? Do I project the face of my father, mother, brother, sister, uncle or teacher on to others in the community, family, diocese, parish? How can I detect when I am doing it? Often it is linked with strong pain and emotion, which are completely out of proportion with regard to the present situation. When I experience such strong reactions, I can stop and reflect: "What is going on in me at the moment? What exactly is upsetting me so much? Where do these strong feelings come from? If I am willing to listen to them, and to ask them how they experience me, other members of my family, community, seminary or diocese can help me to detect my transferences or countertransferences. Growth counselling itself is one way of helping both the leaders, and those who are led by them, to come to terms with the problems induced by transference.

SUMMARY:

The all-pervasiveness of transference
Transference happens:
- in community between members of the community and leader,
- in families between husband and wife and children,
- in seminaries between rector and staff, and staff and students,
- in dioceses between bishops and priests,
- in provinces between provincial and members of the province,
- in parishes between parish priest and parishioners.

———

10. Transferential relationship

This relationship may initially be formed between the lower (or subconscious) self of the client and the middle (or conscious) self of the therapist. Once the therapist becomes aware of transference, s/he endeavours to make the client aware of it as well, so that the relationship can be renewed, with both partners working at the level of the middle self (diagram 1).

Diagram 1

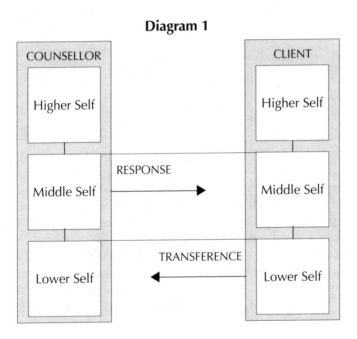

Sometimes, neither therapist nor client is aware of the transference and countertransference; for example the client transfers the father on to the therapist, and s/he unconsciously countertransfers a punishing father (diagram 2 overleaf).

Diagram 2

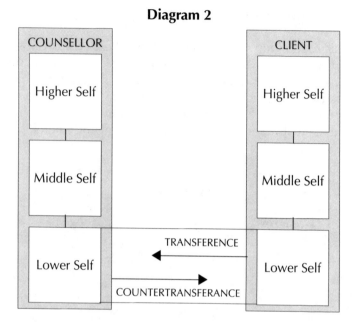

There is a solution to this knotty problem. The therapist needs to ask him/herself what is impeding the therapy. Once the client's transference of his/her punishing father becomes apparent, the therapist must refuse to fall into the role the client has subconsciously chosen for him/her. Instead, the therapist should respond, in an understanding way, to the middle self of the client. After this interaction has been going on for some time, the client will stop seeing the therapist as a punishing father, and will relate to him/her as a caring therapist.

11. Resistance to transference

Some clients seem unwilling or unable to enter transference, so as to disentangle it. They often avoid engaging with any possible transference, by using the defence mechanism of intellectualising or rationalising. For example, a client may say, "Of course I should feel sad because you are going on vacation, and I shan't see you for some weeks. I am supposed to miss you, but I don't think I shall!" This could stem, paradoxically, from a powerful resistance to the development of an abandonment transference, which is being denied, or repressed beyond reach of the conscious self. The counsellor may respond in a variety of ways. S/he may choose to confront such a rationalisation of denial. S/he may invite the client to slow down, and allow sensation and feelings to play their part. S/he might decide on a physical response, encouraging the client to breathe and re-own the emotion. Whichever route is taken, the aim should be to allow the client to relive the earlier trauma of desertion. This can happen through regression, hypnosis, or spontaneous reactivation of an earlier ego-status. Thus the client can re-experience the physical, emotional, cognitive and symbolic reality of the transference through the supportive relationship with the counsellor.

A special kind of resistance is shown by schizoid or autistic clients. These are in the main psychiatric disorders with psychiatric causes, and it takes considerable experience for a counsellor to be able to decide when symptoms identified as psychiatric might respond to counselling therapy. It can be deduced in some of these cases that there is a transference at work, which consists of not having any genuine interpersonal relationship. This probably began in childhood. People did not relate to them in ways, which would have been beneficial to their growth. Parents may have been over-invasive, neglectful, or abusive of them or their siblings. If they come for counselling, they will very likely transfer a fear that the counsellor may be as invasive or abusive as the parent was. Their withdrawal is part of the transferential relationship. In such a situation, it may be deemed necessary and humane to enter somehow into a relationship. The counsellor may need to risk fear in order to make the beginnings of a human, person-to-person relationship, so that the client can then learn when and how to trust, and how to find self-protection in an appropriate way, without cutting him/herself off from nourishing human contact. It is very important for a counsellor, who has decided to try to help a schizoid or autistic client, to obtain as clear a history as possible of the person's psychiatric history and treatment, so that a careful diagnosis can be made. This will avoid false expectations.

12. Some transference-inviting questions

"How do you feel, as you say that to me?" "How do you feel about me?" "What do you think when I say that?" "What happens in you when I say that?" "How am I like your mother?" "How am I like your father?" "How am I like your sister?" "How am I like your brother?" "What do you imagine I might do next? I imagine you think I will reject you. Tell me". "Do you imagine I might punish you?" "Do you imagine I might leave you?" "Do you imagine I might not be available to you?" "Do you imagine I might have no time for you?"

We can facilitate the transference passively by being a mirror. Or we can facilitate the transference actively by displaying emotion or behaviour similar to that which the client is projecting. For example, a counsellor is late for a session with a client who fears abandonment; perhaps the counsellor would decide to say, "This is what you were afraid would happen, and now it has happened".

Sometimes, the client is not able to do any reality testing; because s/he is so locked into past experiences, that s/he is unable to experience present reality. Therefore, whatever the counsellor does or says, is used by the client to confirm her/his projections. These projections may be, "You are not saying anything, because you think I am useless and worthless" or "You are just saying that, so that you don't have to admit that you think I am useless or worthless".

13. The importance of transference for learning

Information available to us from past experiences influences our present experience. People who cannot use past experiences for present or future events are severely handicapped. They cannot learn from past experiences. Transference, as we have said, is necessary for learning, although one may not be conscious of this process. It is common to speak of anticipation in this context. Anticipation allows us to rehearse a situation, to plan for it and then to prepare for it. It inevitably involves transference or "carrying over" from the past.

With healthy people, transference and anticipation are usually updated with regard to here-and-now situations. They revise their assessment of past experience, as soon as new experiences begin to corroborate or contradict it. For example, a parishioner may have come to the conclusion that all priests are bossy. A new, and very tolerant parish priest arrives. The parishioner anticipates a new bossy parish priest, and feels resentment towards him, as he preaches or leads a meeting. Eventually, however, it dawns on the biased parishioner, that this priest is not bossy, but very caring and collaborative.

A healthy personality processes information from the past, by comparing it with information from the present situation. When experiences from the past become cemented, there is no adaptation to new circumstances. Here transference becomes a different kind of problem, because it is impeded.

Transferences can be about people, places, situations, values, sounds and smells. Often the most damaging transference refers to the repetition of past behaviour patterns in the very counselling setting where they are meant to be being resolved. The counsellor may allow transferences, even invite them, or else minimise them, depending on the patient's needs. Transferences and countertransferences may disrupt, inspire or destroy the working alliance. Working with transference means focusing directly on the intrusive feelings, in order to make them explicit.

SUMMARY:
The importance of transference for learning:
- We learn from past experiences.
- Transference is necessary for learning.
- Anticipation is transference.
- Anticipations are often corrected through new here-and-now experiences.
- Transference is a problem, when it is cemented in past experiences, and consequently there is no possibility of adaptation to new situations.

———

14. Some common transference patterns in therapy

Some clients idealise their counsellor by profuse compliments or by bragging about the counsellor to others. They may imitate the counsellor's behaviour and wear similar clothes. They may dream about the therapist and want to be with him or her to a disproportionate extent.

Others attribute supernatural powers to the counsellor. They see him/her as all knowing and divine-like. The client may experience the counsellor as all knowing, all wise, and even as all-powerful. Clients can magnify the personal qualities of the counsellor out of all proportion. They consider them as the experts, who know what is going on inside them; they may be afraid of what they consider to be the counsellor's supernatural power; their admiration may be tinged with fear. These positive transferences can place a heavy burden on the counsellor, who may think s/he has to live up to these expectations. Human beings want to depend on others as children do. So the counsellor can sometimes be attributed with omnipotence, which is the attribute that the child once experienced in his parents or parent substitutes.

We can see this tendency, particularly in groups or political parties. Members of a group are sometimes too ready to submit to the leader, and to the structures established by him/her. At the behest of the leader, they may do things in the group, about which they later feel ashamed. They succumb to the illusion of the leader's greatness, and accept this illusion over reality. They may become enraged, when their illusions are threatened. This unhealthy bond between leader and followers is rooted in the regressive transference. Mass media can promote the demagogue because, under their influence, adults can become like children, seeking protection from the symbolic icon of strength and power that is constantly being suggested to them. Strong demands are placed on the leader, who has to fulfil the role placed upon him or her by the members of the group; the leader needs to be vigilant, to ensure mutual control between leader and group.

The counsellor's training and experience enable him or

her to provide insight, together with emotional and physical warmth, as the individual needs them. Clients will often hope for advice, but that is not the counsellor's role. If the client's relationship needs are met, it can happen that s/he will increasingly display helplessness and dependence; s/he can become vacillating, when the counsellor is not there to offer support. Other forms of transference lead the client to see the counsellor as self-protective, watchful, reticent, resentful, angry or hostile; as one who always talks but never listens; as one who always changes the subject or is unwilling to explore; as someone who is dismissive of ideas.

SUMMARY:

Some common *positive* transference patterns:
- Idealising the therapist.
- The therapist is a provider of advice.
- The therapist is not really a professional, just a very close friend.
- Attributing superhuman powers to the counsellor.

———

15. Transference and idolatry

According to Becker's definition of transference, idol worship is a clear example of transference dynamics. The idol is a transference object. Idols are made by human hands, to represent external forces in the environment. Through transference dynamics, these idols become psychologically invested with power, to the point of being given dominion over human existence, while in reality they remain merely objects of wood, stone, or metal.

The important question between the ancient Israelites and their neighbours was not whether there was a God, but rather what kind of God he was. It was not easy for the Israelites to sustain a worship of a God, who could not be made into a transference object. In fact, the Israelites did set up transference objects, witness the golden calf. They built special altars. They set up the political institution of kinship, which would act as human focus for the power of God. The prophets periodically tried to cleanse idolatrous practices, which we can now classify as transference objects. Yahweh, the prophets insisted, could not be controlled by the people; He would demand social justice rather than cultic sacrifice.

What are the transference objects of our own time? What is the price we pay for the transference objects which we make for ourselves? These transference objects can order our lives, so that counselling becomes necessary. Counselling can help us to gain insights into the shadow side of these domineering transference objects. These transference objects may be a car, a house, a dress, a job, social voices, or parental voices, which tell us what to do and how to behave. We pay a high price for these transferential objects in the form of stress, phobias, and broken relationships. By becoming aware of these transference objects and their influence upon our lives, we can bring about change. This process is not purely intellectual, and the change is not easy, because we have learned to find security, safety and groundedness in our transferences. To recognise that these solutions are illusionary throws us into chaos. Therefore, the client will resist revealing these sources of power. It is not an easy job to free ourselves from our attachment to idols.

SUMMARY:

Transference and idolatry
- According to Becker's definition of transference, idol worship is an example of transference dynamics.
- The idol is an example of a transference object.
- The Israelites struggled not to get involved in creating transference objects.

———

16. Exercise

Answer these questions as directly as possible:
1. What are my transference objects?
2. Car, dress, house, a job, social voices, parental voices, a party?
3. What is the price to be paid for them?
4. How can counselling help us to discover our transference objects and their influence upon our lives?
5. What are some of the transference objects in my faith and religion?

17. Managing the transference relationship

One of the strongest ways of changing human relationship patterns is that of working through transference and countertransference, in the following ways:

Transference Interpretation: This is the main tool for working through transference. For example, the therapist might say: "You are angry with me, because I did not greet you. Your anger seems, however, exaggerated to me." The therapist allows transferential material to accumulate, to support an interpretation when the time is right. At that point, denial by the client is less likely to occur. Exploring and experiencing transferential patterns should include physical, emotional, behavioural and cognitive elements. All these form the basis of interpretation.

If the client over a long period of time insists on seeing the counsellor in an unrealistically negative or positive way, it is important that the counsellor refuses to identify with the projection. For example, in the situation where this problem has become apparent, the counsellor needs to convey that the client is not trapped, and is free to stop coming, if that would be beneficial. The client can gently be led to understand that this is a different proposition from when s/he was a small child, who could not leave the parental home. The counsellor should beware of "telling" the client this; it is better to "draw out" the new understanding of relationship.

There are several possible ways of dealing with transference, depending on the approach taken. The following is an integrative approach. What does the counsellor actually do where transference is concerned?

a. S/he uses the experience of the client as presented through narrative, emotion, body language.
b. Collects evidence.
c. Analyses.
d. Confronts.
e. Recognises where the transference originates and why.
f. Uses cognitve understanding.
g. Supports emotional catharsis.
h. Moves from reliving to remembering, with the affective charge ameliorated by helping the client to reflect on what produced the emotions.
i. Helps the client to develop skills, so as to spot transference in future relationships.
j. Guides the client to avoid situations that echo the original unmet need, or else to become adept at dealing with such situations. The client must be led to understand the difference between these two processes.
k. Helps the client to develop reality testing. For example, the counsellor may help the client to identify the kind of people to whom the client has repeatedly been attracted, and to change his/her attractiveness patterns.

Interpretation, empathy, confrontation and interruptions by means of countertransference are the main ways to work with transference relationships. Manifestations of transference can be minimised by choosing to ignore indications, analysing the interaction, re-establishing or confirming adult reality testing, establishing a clearer contract or a more appropriate working alliance. The counsellor may humorously exaggerate a client's transferential moan: "Oh, no one loves you, not even your psychotherapist!" (However humour needs to be used with care, usually where a firm relationship is already established, and the counsellor has some evidence that the client is able to enjoy the humour.) Another expedient is to refuse to adopt the parental role. For example, if a client asks the counsellor's permission in a childlike way, the counsellor can respond: "What is stopping you?" In this way, the counsellor refuses to be the granter of permission, and the working alliance is re-established.

What do you do if a client, who is confronted by the source of a transference, is gripped by fear or rage, and threatens to leave? The counsellor can remind him/her: "This is your opportunity to work through your fear or rage with me. If you don't, the chances are, you will find yourself in similar situations in the future." Once again, the appeal is to the working alliance.

What do you do when a client gives vent to rage or grief towards the end of the session? The counsellor may remind the client that there are only five minutes left. S/he may ask what the client needs before leaving. The counsellor may make some suggestion about what the client might need to do in order to come to some closure before leaving. This is done so as to avoid the experience of abandonment, which might be understood as punishment for fully experiencing the emotions. When counsellors attempt to provide some form of closure under these circumstances, they show that they believe the client has sufficient ego to strengthen the working alliance.

Intentional interruption: Often the counsellor may wish intentionally to interrupt the transference, particularly if working in the transference has become temporarily or permanently dysfunctional.

To resolve transference, the counsellor may allow the transference to develop, to become fully alive, and yet be experienced as something alien in the here-and-now reality. Then the counsellor may invite the client to test reality through the use of his/her senses. One expression of intervention might be: "When you were little, it is true that no one listened to you. Is that still true now? Do your friends not listen to you? Have I not been listening to you during this session?"

Confrontation: Nowadays, it seems that confrontation, particularly in working with clients who do not accept that they have a particular problem, has become the main therapeutic technique of the whole process. Confrontation is a strong technique. As with so many counselling skills, it is capable of constructive and destructive use. The counsellor must be able to be fully with the client. S/he needs to be empathic and tuned into the feelings of the client. Confrontation must be faithfully balanced with the client's state of mind, associations and feelings. It must be done in a "caring" fashion, not through "hammering" home what is perceived as the truth. Only in this way will confrontation work.

Empathy: We need to reiterate the importance of this central tool for the counsellor. The Shorter Oxford dictionary defines empathy as: "The power of projecting one's personality into, and so fully understanding, the object of contemplation." Other synonyms are "empathic attunement", "resonance", "communicative matching".

The question arises: "Is empathy not mainly a reparative operation, rather than a tool for the resolution of transference? Or is it usually a characteristic of the person-to-person interaction? Sometimes, the counsellor uses empathic interventions to replenish or to re-activate the natural developmental tendency. In this situation, the purpose is not to understand the transference but to supply the experiential content of previously deficient relationships. Most people were not listened to as children, and therefore, if in the therapeutic setting they experience the counsellor as attending and listening to them, they are provided with an aspect of relationship which they did not receive as children. In this sense, empathy *is* reparative.

However, there is another function of empathy. The counsellor shares experiences, images or metaphors similar to those of the client. This can act as a bridge to the person-to-person relationship. In dealing with transference, empathy is often used to pair rational understanding (interpretation) with empathic understanding (emotional resonance). It is supposed to support the client and build the working alliance. This, it is hoped, will shore up the psyche and help the client to work through the transference. For example, "I can see and feel how painful it is for you not to know more about my personal life. Still, it wouldn't be appropriate or helpful for me to discuss this with you, because it is important for you to experience fully your reaction to this exclusion, which appears to be similar to the way in which your parents excluded you from their personal lives."

There is another way in which empathy is used. This use is in terms of countertransference. When empathy occurs, there is always projective identification. Empathy is the outcome of an interactive process between client and counsellor. The counsellor receives and processes projective identifications from the client; this in turn allows the counsellor to show that s/he understands. One of the main sources of healing is understanding: understanding oneself, being understood by others and by God.

18. God-representation

What is the God-representation? It is the totality of all experiential levels which we acquire in the course of our life, and which we link with the name of God. The God-representation includes perceptual and conceptual elements. We use our senses to acquire information about our surrounding environment. When parents talk about God, the child may imagine God as a tall man. A very tall bishop once went to visit a school in London. When he had left, the little children asked the teacher afterwards whether this was God who had visited them. Many elements of the God-representation that we acquire in our life are concepts and ideas. Our education is very much based on this way of learning. Our theology deals with this aspect of human thinking.

The God-representation also includes proprioceptive, visceral, sensorimotor and eidetic elements. These terms need defining. What is a proprioceptor? It is a sensory nerve ending in muscles, tendons, and joints. It provides a sense of the body's position by responding to the stimuli from within the body. Certain body feelings may become linked with the God-representation, such as a feeling of being grounded and a sense of wellbeing. Possibly the feeling of falling may be linked with this. There is also the visceral element. The viscera are the bodily organs that occupy the great cavities, especially the stomach and intestines. God's presence may be felt in these areas. It may be a feeling of being fulfilled, content, or peaceful. Then there is the sensorimotor component of the God representation. A sister I knew was finding it difficult to pray while kneeling or sitting. As a girl, she had learned to dance and was very fond of dancing. For her, the normal positions of prayer – sitting, kneeling or standing – were difficult. Dancing would link her with God. She felt very relieved when I explained to her how we acquire the God-representation and of what it consists. Finally, there is the eidetic element. Some people have visual images coming from their imagination but projected with extreme sharpness and accuracy. Their God-representation may consist very much of such images.

There are people who have a strong experience of God linked with certain parts of the body. A priest told me how important the hand of God is for him. He studied all the passages of the Bible referring to the hand of God. He even dreamt that the hand of God was holding him as he was hanging on a rock high up in the mountains. He felt nothing "bad" could happen to him. He trusted God. He felt strong in God's hand and secure.

These representational levels are not equally distributed; in most people, one level prevails over the others. Some people have more of an intellectual concept of God. Others use many images to describe Him, while for others, like this priest, parts of the body are important, like the hand of God or the heart. The Sacred Heart is depicted as Christ's physical heart. Indeed, how could it be otherwise?

How do we explain these differences? We can trace back God's representational characteristics to experiences, either in reality or fantasy, that we had with those who cared for us as children, and other people who influenced us in the course of our development. Freud gave us the clue. He said that the God of the adult was in fact his childhood father now disguised as Godhead. Freud mentioned only the father as providing a source for the God-representation. He did not reflect about the role of the mother or other people. Anna-Maria Rizzuto (1976; 1980) has done much work in this field. We are still talking here about transferences. A priest at the age of seventy told me that he had been "struggling" all his life with his God-representation. He knew that God is love from his studies, but he did not experience God as love. In fact, he was frightened of God. He also knew where this came from. He shared with me that he had had a strict father, who would punish him if he did not do what he wanted him to do. He may also have absorbed some of the Old Testament attitudes to God, which sometimes end up stressing the wrath and anger of a punishing God. Even at the age of seventy, this priest had not been able to update his God-representation emotionally.

These characteristics of the God of childhood remain as the fundamental components of the God representation for the rest of a person's life. We have to update this representation again and again as we receive new information. It seems that many people hardly ever re-elaborate their God-representation as they grow up, and some of them therefore become agnostics or atheists. They find it difficult to hang on to the God-representation of their childhood. Much valuable work can be done to help people update their God-representation, not only conceptually, but also holistically. Using the arts may help in this process, by re-presenting God's presence through imaginative material. Contemplation of Jesus in the Gospels, and approaching the Father through him, can be a great help in dispelling false images. We need to remember that God is not "He", but the Trinity. The three persons form a "Community". With this in mind, a client might be invited to contemplate Rublev's icon of the Trinity.

How does the God-representation originate? This process starts early in a person's life. Some elements may even go back to the pre-natal stage of development. Whether a baby is wanted or not will influence the relationship of that baby with the mother, even in her womb. It is very likely that an unwanted child may have feelings of rejection going back to the pre-natal stage. These feelings of rejection may become components of the God-representation. After birth, a wanted baby will experience an intensely affirmative relationship with his mother and father. There are profound experiences of eye contact, bodily care, feeding, playfulness, laughter, crying, and also experiences of neglect and rejection. The mother or primary carer provides the child with many such experiences. These become the very essence of his/her way of relating to himself/herself and others. The face of the mother may become an important factor. It is the first mirror in which the baby can find and recognize him/herself. The maternal face is then likely to become the principal component of the God-representation. The child learns from his/her exchanges with the mother, and also from other exchanges, with the father or childminder. These are the only meaningful adults that are round the baby, and therefore available to form his/her God-representation. We must not forget that God is that particular being that the child can neither see nor hear, but can experience deeply, because of the "indwelling" of God. Therefore, the child has to make every effort to give concrete shape to this being, in a creative way.

The child may also hear about the devil, God's enemy. Thus the child begins to include both God and the devil in her/his way of thinking. The child begins to learn to attribute goodness to God and badness to the devil, dividing the universe into these two areas – the goodness of God and the badness of the devil. However, many children do not manage to make this clear distinction. Although they attribute badness to the devil, they cannot completely purify God of all rejecting, frightful or unresponsive traits. These elements creep into the God-representation as a result of the child's exchanges with his parents.

The growing child or teenager may not include a concept

of God in the process of updating his personal reality. If this happens, the person may forsake belief altogether, or go through a religious crisis. To update the God-representation, the person needs to go through times of soul-searching. There will be much questioning. There may be much pain involved, because change is needed. Many avoid change and renewal because of the fear of the unknown. Yet change is needed because the childhood God no longer fits into the newly acquired universe of the adolescent and adult. Some people find it difficult to believe in a loving God. They may even think that God could never love them. Some cannot believe in a God who would punish them. We need to remember that not all non-believers have a conflict with their God-representation. Some people may be so busy with everyday affairs that they have no time for God.

What are some of the conclusions and educational implications of the God-representation as described above? Belief and faith are not only grace; they are parts of a psychic process that we can study, understand and build upon. The process of learning, rather than the concepts themselves, binds a person to his private God-representation. It is the result of conscious and unconscious ways of wrestling with relatedness to oneself, others, and the world. There is a private logic of conviction involved in trusting oneself, others, the world and God. The person will experience it as something happening to him or her. It is not rational logic that gives faith to a person. How it arrives and is sustained is difficult to describe.

Faith is always a developmental process. The fact that we believe today does not guarantee that we believe tomorrow. Therefore we need to pray for the grace of perseverance. Faith is never a final state. Are we able to face and integrate whatever happens to us? Are we creative enough to make this personal synthesis of the various events in our life? We have our expectations about what the world and the Church should be. What happens when our expectations are not met? The Pope, the Church, the world, may fail us beyond endurance or beyond our capacity to rearrange ourselves. We may not feel able to adapt to the change, and then we may let go of our faith.

Belief and faith are the result of a very complex developmental process. It takes the whole personality into account, not just the intellect. Therefore, we must take this into consideration in our Christian formation programmes, which are often geared mainly towards the intellect. In fact, the formation of the God-representation precedes the child's formal religious education at school, as we have pointed out above. Children come to school, with their own God-representation to some extent already formed.

Faith and belief are psychologically based on the logic of conviction of interpersonal relatedness. Can I trust or can I not trust my parents and other people? If I cannot trust people, can I trust God? Education provides us with a conceptual frame of reference. Does it also update our feelings of trust? Or are the feelings denoted by "I cannot trust people" reinforced through our educational systems? Our faith does not primarily depend on our intellectual capacity to synthesize and organise events in our lives. It depends more on the psychic ability to convince ourselves of the meaning of our relatedness to ourselves, to others, the world and God.

We have seen how the child's creation of the God-representation emerges out of exchanges with parents or other carers. Older siblings, grandparents, uncles, teachers, priests and many others will gradually contribute to shape the God-representation. This God-representation requires continuous re-elaborating so as to be updated to the needs of the growing child. This process is subtle and delicate. Adults need to be sensitive, and to respect the subjective experience of the child.

Religious educators, formators, counsellors, pastoral workers, and parents must take into consideration this process whereby the God-representation is formed. It takes place at the core of the child's capacity to relate to himself, to others, to the environment and to the world. The child's or candidate's religious development can seem to be unusual. It is important that we understand the child's or candidate's confusions and situation. We need to understand their wishes and sufferings. This will help them to resolve their "difficulties" with God, because they are mainly relational difficulties.

Here we see again the importance of our relationship with people entrusted with our care.

The best preparation for formators, counsellors, parents, educators, and parish priests for dealing with the God-representation of those entrusted to their care is to retrace the creation and history of their own God-representation. This will give them firsthand understanding of their own God-representation; it will help them to understand the experiences of those entrusted to them, with regard to the evolution of the God-representation.

We need to be able to distinguish between the objective reality of God and our subjective comprehension of God and His ways. God as an objective reality is infinite: all-loving, all-powerful, all-merciful, etc. We know about God as objective reality from theology and philosophy. God as subjective reality is our personal experience of God, our God-representation as described above. We may experience God as a policeman, as a dictator, as a person who punishes, even where there is no fault. Yet we know, from all we have been taught, that God is not like that: we find the God-representation par excellence in Jesus. One of the functions of integrative spiritual counselling or psycho-spiritual counselling is to harmonise our subjective experience of God with the more objective reality of God. This is a lifelong process. We have to pursue continually the process of updating our God-representation, otherwise unhelpful transference/countertransference will occur. The Christian counsellor needs to contemplate, perhaps to pray the Gospels, through using "lectio divina". Only through prayer and spiritual growth can the counsellor ensure that spirituality is integrated into his/her work.

SUMMARY:

The God-representation
- is the totality of all experiential levels which we acquire in the course of our life, and which we link with the name of the Triune God.

- There are perceptual, conceptual, proprioceptive, visceral, sensorimotor and eidetic components of the God-representation.
- Not all the representational levels are equally part of every person's experience.
- The process of building our God-representation begins early in life and needs to continue throughout the whole of life.
- The devil personifies evil. God personifies goodness. However, there is not always this clear distinction in our God-representation.

Educational implications of the God-representation

- Belief and faith are not only grace, but also a psychic process.
- Faith is a very complex developmental process.
- Faith and belief are psychologically based on the logic of conviction, and on interpersonal relatedness.
- Formators, parents, counsellors, educators, and pastoral workers need to retrace the creation of their own God-representation.

---

19. Exercises

Consider the following questions. Then look back over this chapter, to make sure that you have fully understood the points that are being made:

1. What is transference? What is unfinished relationship? What is anticipated relationship?
2. Are you aware of some of your transferences?
3. What do you do when clients transfer on to you? What choices do you have to make?
4. What do you do as a leader when members transfer on to you?
5. What do you expect from your boss, or superior? Might this be transferred material?

6. How can we detect transference?
7. What are the choices in therapy when clients transfer on the counsellor?
8. What were Freud's views with regard to transference?
9. What were Carl Rogers' views on transference?
10. What is the re-experiencing therapy, according to Merton Gill?
11. Can you say something about the all-pervasiveness of transference?
12. At what part of Kofler's personality model does transference occur?
13. Can you think of some transference-inviting questions?
14. How far is transference important for learning?
15. What are some common transference patterns?
16. Comment on transference and idolatry.
17. Give some ways of managing the transference relationship.
18. How do you see yourself using the transference relationship?
19. What is the God-representation?
20. Why do we talk about the God-representation in connection with transference?
21. What are some of the components of the God-representation?
22. What do we need to do with our God-representation?
23. What are some of the educational and counselling consequences of the God-representation?

20. Two case studies of transference

1. AMABEL. The subject of this short case study is a 46-year-old Asian female religious, whose stated goal for counselling was to look at her over-developed sense of responsibility, which had earned her a number of nicknames among friends.

Amabel was the first-born child in a family of five children, two boys and three girls. Her culture required of her that as the first-born girl, she should look after her young brothers and sisters. This responsibility, when it was not properly fulfilled, earned her much anger and punishment from her father. She recalled many incidents when she was actually almost frozen in a corner because of her fear of the father. Her refuge during this time was her mother, who also went through the same kind of ill-treatment from her husband, Amabel's father. Amabel and her mother, therefore, formed a strong bond between them. Amabel's mother supported her, and Amabel went to her mother whenever she felt anxious and lost.

From the very first time Amabel met her female counsellor, she showed a certain warmth and attachment towards her. The counsellor took note of this, but allowed it to continue, believing that it might be helpful. As time went on, however, and Amabel was in process, the counsellor noticed that Amabel was becoming more and more dependent on her, and decided to challenge Amabel about it. Amabel was starting to bring issues to the session which she hoped the counsellor would solve for her. The counsellor was herself a member of a religious order.

During one of the sessions at this time, the following dialogue occurred:

Counsellor: Amabel, I notice that even though we have had six sessions together and you seem quite free to talk to me, you still address me as Sister. I wonder what that means.

Amabel: It is because I respect you.

Counsellor: I see. How many people do you address by their title?

Amabel: (scratching her head) None really. I address them all by their first names, except my Provincial.

Counsellor: That is interesting. Do I take it, then, that you do not respect those other people?

Amabel: No. I do respect them.

Counsellor: You do respect them and yet you address them by their first names. What is the difference between me, to whom you show respect by addressing me as Sister, and those whom you address by their first names only?

Amabel: There is no difference really, but with you – I

140

just feel more comfortable to address you as Sister.

Counsellor: Could it be that I remind you of somebody else in your life whom you could not address by their first name?

Amabel: Oh, yes. You remind me of my Provincial. The way you talk to me – even your height – it is exactly like her.

Counsellor: Amabel, *am* I your Provincial?

The session was then given over to breaking the transference, and for some time Amabel worked very well.

However, as time went on, the counsellor noticed that Amabel found it very difficult to share certain issues, and would start blushing whenever she wanted to talk about such issues. This was the case when she discussed relationships with the opposite sex. Referring to a number of sessions during which Amabel avoided answering certain questions, which had to do with relationships with men, the counsellor said to Amabel:

Counsellor: Amabel, I notice that every time we touch the issue of relationships with men, you seem to avoid answering the question directly. I am just wondering whether I am leading you into some painful area when I do that?

Amabel: I am shy to speak about such issues with you.

Counsellor: Tell me more about your shyness.

Amabel: I cannot talk about my intimate relationships with men with my mother. I never did in the past.

Counsellor: Amabel, it seems that I was once your Provincial and now I am your mother. Who am I really for you?

Amabel: My Provincial is like a mother to me. So the two are almost the same.

The counsellor now realised the double transference, and had to deal with breaking the pattern. It took several sessions for Amabel to realise that the counsellor was neither her mother nor her Provincial, and that she was not dealing here with either her mother or her Provincial, but with her counsellor, who may have looked like her Provincial or listened like her mother, but was quite different from both in other respects! After that, Amabel was able to stop calling her counsellor Sister, and was able to speak freely about her relationship with a particular man whom she loved dearly.

2. MARY, who was twenty-eight years old, came to me for counselling because she suffered from depression. In the very first session she shared that she had two degrees, and was a teacher of Christian doctrine. "It is a contradiction that I teach this subject since I can't believe in a God whom I experience as domineering." She also mentioned that she had problems with her principal. We explored the family background and I found out that her mother was very domineering. This gave me a good insight into what might be the essential problem. My hypotheses were that I needed to deal with repressed anger and transference problems. She also mentioned that she would like to talk to her father on the phone, but her mother would always answer the phone. I encouraged her to ask to speak to her father before she came back for the next session. I helped her to see how life could be very different in the future if only some obstacles were removed, such as repression of anger and negative mother transferences. I encouraged her to observe her belief system and give me feedback next time. With this, we finished a very fruitful first session.

When she came for the second session, she was a little disturbed. She shared how she woke up and said to her husband, "What are you doing here? Who am I?" They had been married for two years. Then she showed me a paper on which she had written down thirty-three assumptions in her value system that she refuted as wrong. She had worked on herself so much that she went through an identity crisis. I encouraged her to slow down a bit. She had not managed to talk to her father on the phone. Mary knew now that she had a right to do so. Mary realised how possessive and domineering her mother was. She was ready to work on herself to be more assertive. We looked at her assumptions and worked on being more assertive by doing a chair exercise and using the ego states. Two of her essential assumptions were: "A girl should never be angry" and " a good girl should always do what her mother tells her, because mother knows better than she." I helped her to stay in her adult ego state and express what she felt about her mother and what she wanted to say to her on the phone. I also wanted to help her to become aware of what she was feeling about her mother. This was a great struggle, because she was totally unaware of her anger that showed itself in her clenched fists while talking to her mother on the chair. She had learned to smile rather than to show her anger. By the end of the session she was very tired. I suspected that things were happening in her unconscious.

Mary arrived at the third session very bright, all smiles, and said that she had experienced anger for the first time. She was very excited about that. There was a definite change in her. The heaviness had disappeared and she was much more assertive in sharing how she had talked to her father and how different her relationship with her mother was. She no longer felt that she was the little girl. She experienced herself as an equal, and therefore she could say to her mother what she had not been able to say before. Her mother, too, seemed to have changed. Her mother seemed to listen to her for the first time. She was no longer so domineering, because Mary was more assertive and stayed in the adult ego state whilst she was talking to her mother. In fact, she now enjoyed talking to her mother, whilst before she had been afraid of her. I was not so sure how permanent this would be and we kept on working on her relationship with her mother. So far we had not talked much about the Principal at school and her relationship with God. I had been aware that these were transference relationships and wanted to work first on her relationship with her mother. I hoped that the other two relationships would improve automatically once we had worked through her relationship with her mother.

The next four sessions were spent looking at her relationships with her Principal and with God. We worked to break down these transferences. She reported that she had a better relationship now with the Principal. She could talk to him without fear and he would listen to her. Prayer became much more meaningful for her. She started talking to God, could express her anger towards Him without being afraid of Him. Her love for God increased. After some time she shared how she experienced God as loving and protecting her. She was happy to teach Christian doctrine now. It was much more meaningful for her. She no longer had to say that God was a loving father whilst actually experiencing him as a hard taskmaster. In fact, her love for Him grew daily. She was a deeply spiritual person and very intelligent.

In these seven sessions she had made so much progress that I felt that there was no need to carry on the therapeutic process. I knew she woud be able to do it on her own. I don't believe in long term counselling, if you can achieve the same result in fewer sessions. The model of the five therapeutic relationships helps me to focus on essential therapeutic aspects. This speeds up the process considerably. I consider the relationship with my clients as very important for the healing process and therfore, make every effort to foster this relation-ship in my sessions. I am aware of my relationship with them and pick up negative countertransferences very quickly during the session, and I want to make sure that they do not interfere with my relationship with the client; I want to use them in a facilitative way. With Mary, then, I had managed to resist her mother transference, and so helped her towards more mature attitudes and behaviour

CHAPTER FIVE

The countertransference relationship: the counsellor's perspective

1. Working on oneself 2. Freud, post-Freudians and countertransference
3. A potential countertransference 4. Exercise 5. What is countertransference?
6. Patterns from the past disturbing the here-and-now reality
7. Unfinished relationship 8. What are some of the effects of countertransference?
9. How can we manage and use countertransference? 10. Failures in the transference
and countertransference relationship 11. Exercise 12. How can we assess the
effectiveness of transference and countertransference? 13. Summary of transference
and countertransference 14. Exercise 15. A case study of countertransference

1. Working on oneself

Michael Kahn (1991, 125) wrote about a client he particularly liked. This client said to him one day: "On Rogers' eight-point empathy scale I'd give you about a three." Kahn describes how he felt a rush of indignant hurt flash through his body. This lasted only a moment. Then he set to work suppressing it, by saying to himself, "This is wonderful. I have been waiting for the negative transference for months, and here it is." But obviously, the hurt was not gone. Deep down, it was still making itself felt. The pain would not be eased by the counsellor trying to ignore it. It would eventually cause trouble in some form or other. Unconsciously, the hurt might lead the counsellor to retaliate, or he might try, at almost any cost, to demonstrate what an empathetic therapist he really was. He would probably not be aware that he was doing either of these things.

This story demonstrates how important it is for therapists to undergo their own psychotherapy and supervision. Depth psychologists tell us that much of what happens in the therapist's mind, as well as in the mind of the client, is unconscious. Even when counselling, our deepest wishes, fears and impulses are hidden away from our awareness. However, they powerfully influence our conscious attitudes and our behaviour. With this knowledge to guide us, when we come to examine our pastoral settings and formation work, we may be able to discern what is going on in our unconscious, and what kind of negative impact this involuntary process might be having on our parishioners or students. This is one of several ways in which we have to prepare ourselves carefully for pastoral or formation work: part of the preparation needs to be working on ourselves.

2. Freud, post-Freudians and countertransference

A few years after Freud discovered transference, he noticed that something similar occurred in the counsellor with regard to the client. To this phenomenon Freud gave the name Gegenuebertragung – countertransference. As we would expect, he saw it as an obstacle to therapy (1910, 141-51). Freud's ideal picture of a therapist was of an absolutely objective observer who keeps his or her personal concerns and problems away from the consulting room.

Later, some of Freud's followers started to question this view. While it was true that countertransference often had negative effects upon the therapeutic process, it could help the counsellor to obtain insights into the client's problems, which could not be extracted in any other way (Heimann, 1950, 81-84). Interest in the study on countertransference grew. After Jung broke away from Freud, he developed the concept of countertransference and, far from regarding it as an obstacle, saw in it a potential for transformation (Wandlung).

No matter how much therapy the counsellor receives, there are always two hidden dramas, which are played out in the consulting room – the drama of the counsellor and the drama of the client. Obviously, the more aware the counsellor is of this fact, the safer the client will be.

SUMMARY:
Freud, post-Freudians and countertransference:
- Freud saw countertransference as an obstacle to therapy.

- Later therapists discovered the positive aspects of countertransference when used appropriately.
- For Jung, countertransference had potential for transformation.

_____

3. A potential countertransference

Petruska Clarkson gave us an illustration of a potential countertransference from her life. She was invited to teach in Scandinavia. Very vividly, and with full awareness, she thought, "I am going to teach people in Scandinavia. What do I know about the Scandinavians? They are very good at tennis, make pornographic movies, they get very depressed and commit suicide."

You can see how we grab for knowledge when we need it, and then generalise and compartmentalise. We come up with certain names, and then we build a whole experience from hearsay, readings and other information. Petruska was conscious of that happening. Most of the time, people are not conscious of the process. But you can imagine that Petruska could have got on the train or the plane to do a workshop with these people, convinced that they would all turn out to be depressed, tennis-playing perverts!

4. Exercise

I am sure that we have all had experiences like that. I would like you to consider, and reflect on, an experience of this kind that you have had. If it is possible, in the company of a friend, look at a pattern of difficulty that you have in your life. Look at where it comes from, how it is derived from past experience. A very simple example is that of authoritarian figures. Most of us have difficulty with them. This is usually because there has been some authoritarian person in the past of whom we were fearful. We transfer the past experience on to the present. Or take betrayal. If you have been betrayed a lot, the expectation is that the next person who comes along will also betray you. Or you could explore a prejudice you have towards someone else. These are all ways in which you can discover transference patterns in your own relationships. You can perform this exercise as profoundly as you wish. Be responsible for yourself. Maybe, just explore a little bit the existence and nature of countertransference relationships in your present everyday life.

5. What is countertransference?

The history of the study of countertransference reveals great controversy about how the word should be defined. Today, countertransference is usually defined as the therapist's feelings and attitudes towards the client. We divide counter-transference into two different types:

1. **Proactive countertransference:** This refers to the process whereby the counsellor brings his own material – feelings, values, behaviour patterns – into the therapeutic relationship. The material really consists of the therapist's pathology. Winnicott (1975, 195) called this the "abnormal counter-transference". He stresses its potential pitfalls, because counsellors' unresolved conflicts intrude into the therapeutic relationship. This is another reason why counsellors need to have their own therapy, so that they can deal with this material without its interfering with the therapeutic relationship. The counsellor needs to learn what is his/her material, as distinct from the material of the client. The better s/he is able to differentiate between the two, the more effective s/he will be as a counsellor.

We also need to look at any countertransferential conditioning which will predispose us to act in certain ways. We may be different from the client as far as culture, gender or age is concerned. This difference may, if its repercussions take place in our unconscious, interfere with the therapeutic relationship. For example, we may have acquired certain stereotypical ways of looking at different people. "Old people are out of touch with present day reality", "Young people are inexperienced", "Black people are inferior", "Women should work in the kitchen", "White people are dangerous", "Priests can't listen properly", "Priests will indoctrinate clients", and so on.

In the proactive countertransference, the stimulus for the transference comes from the counsellor. It may be unfinished business from childhood. It may stem from the counsellor's values or expectations; it may be emotion that is getting in the way. The counsellor pro-acts. We carry countertransferential phenomena across, not only verbally, but also non-verbally, through body language, and the atmosphere that we create.

Material for the proactive countertransference can include issues, dreams, feelings, atmospheres, fantasies, projections, fears, anger, jealousy, desires, any of which may be brought into the therapeutic setting by the counsellor. In the strict sense of the words, proactive countertransference contains solely archaic material. In the wider sense, the material of a proactive countertransference consists of anything the counsellor brings into the therapeutic setting, not just residual, archaic material.

Proactive countertransferences can be destructive or facilitative. An example for a destructive proactive countertransference is when a young counsellor expects the older client to find fault with him, in the same way as the counsellor's father did. As a result, he rejects the client at the first sign of negativity. An example for a facilitative proactive countertransference occurs, when a counsellor enjoys working with people who have low self-esteem, rather than with bereavement issues. This countertransference is based on the counsellor's individual style and personal preference.

2. **Reactive countertransference**: This refers to the process, in which the counsellor reacts to the material in the client. The stimulus comes from the client. Winnicott (1975) called this the "objective countertransference". He stressed that the counsellor is reacting objectively or accurately to the client's behaviour in the therapeutic relationship. The counsellor may react to the client's projections, to his/her personality or behaviour patterns. This is a non-pathological process. It

marks the capacity of the counsellor to comprehend the wider reality, particularly the unconscious reality of the client.

Reactive countertransference refers to those reactions and responses, which are induced by the client in the counsellor. These responses and reactions resemble the intra-psychic patterns of the client's past. When we say past, it may mean either the historical or the fantasised past. The counsellor may experience feelings or behavioural modes, which are elicited through the process of projective identification. The counsellor then responds in a way which does not correspond to his/her own personal issues, but which is induced in the therapist, in answer to the client's expressed or unconscious needs. For example, a counsellor may experience idealisation by the client.

Little (1986, 71) used the reactive countertransference interpretation to describe such a situation. A female client accidentally met Little after a concert in the musicians' room. The client was greatly surprised and said excitedly: "I didn't know you knew X". Her excitement seemed somehow exaggerated. Next day, after reflection, he discovered what the client had really meant – "What right have you to be here?" After this, it became possible to show her (as Little had often tried to do) how she had been trying magically to control the therapist. She wanted the therapist to be with her everywhere, in her imagination. Much of her concert going had been to do with the therapist. Finding little of reality there, her fantasy had been disturbed.

The reactive countertransference may be destructive or facilitative. An example of a destructive reactive counter-transference is when the counsellor accepts the projected identification and acts on it in an unhealthy way. The client sees the counsellor as her neglectful mother, and the counsellor responds by forgetting appointments; or the counsellor goes on holiday without giving the client due notice. The client hypnotically induces this behaviour in the counsellor. The counsellor acts outside his awareness, and contrary to his/her personality.

A facilitative reactive countertransference is exemplified by a counsellor's affection for a loveable client. A counsellor is permitted to be appreciative of a creative client. This kind of countertransference can be considered the heart of the person-to-person therapeutic relationship.

SUMMARY:

What is countertransference?

Countertransference is the therapist's feelings and attitudes towards the client. There are two main types of counter-transference:

1. The proactive countertransference
   - The counsellor brings his own material into the relationship.
   - Countertransferential conditioning: We may be different from the client as far as culture, age, gender is concerned.
   - We carry transferential material across not only verbally but also non-verbally.
   - Proactive countertransference can be destructive or facilitative.
2. Reactive countertransference
   - The counsellor reacts to the material of the client.
   - The reactive countertransference can be destructive or facilitative.

———

6. Patterns from the past disturbing the here-and-now reality

The notion of patterns from the past coming in to disturb and limit our current state of mind is familiar to us all. This enables us to relate to other people's experiences of this kind. The notion plays its part in every culture. Common trans-ference patterns include thoughts like these: "authority figures will shame or hurt or blame"; "tall people will hit you"; "small people are harmless". There are many other prejudices that we suffer from, particularly fear in testing situations, like interviews, tests, examinations, and public speaking. These may all be transferences, although other factors can clearly help to determine these prejudices or attitudes.

Another way of thinking about transference is to think of it as an anticipated relationship. We anticipate positive or negative experiences from people or situations, when they resemble others encountered by us in our past. We anticipate that what happened in the past is going to happen again. An important element of the anticipation is that we behave or feel as though it is completely accurate. These experiences are not updated to here-and-now reality; they are exaggerated, because of their accumulated apprehension. Imagine going on the stage before an audience. This is always a rather nervous experience, because there is a rush of adrenaline. However, when you start anticipating the moment negatively, and find yourself thinking, "I can't do this", you deny yourself the opportunity for growth. You don't carry over the confidence you gained in rehearsal; instead, you carry over some fear from the past, and place yourself in a position from which you cannot learn. You are limiting your life. The outcome is that your experience is not updated to here-and-now reality, and this limits the extent to which you can function responsibly. From this example of what can happen on the stage, we see that we can anticipate something as if it were real, when in fact it is not grounded in reality. Sometimes a client may feel, "Nobody will ever be there for me when I am in trouble!" This is anticipated relationship, transferred from the past.

SUMMARY:

Patterns from the past disturbing the here and now reality:

- Prejudices of any kind: race, culture, gender, situations, etc.
- We anticipate the transference situation positively or negatively, and then experience it as such in advance.
- Often, experiences are not updated to here-and-now reality.

Transference is what the client feels towards the counsellor, and countertransference is exactly the same in reverse: it is what the counsellor feels toward the client. For example, a very common form of countertransference occurs when a counsellor begins to think that s/he is the only one who can help. "It all depends on me", or: "I must ignore myself and my own needs in order to help my client." As a result, no matter how tired or exhausted I am, I drive myself to keep giving and giving, although my giving gets worse and worse. There are many ways in which we act out the counter-transference. I am referring to a kind of patronising transference experienced by carers: "People can't do it for themselves, I've got to help them, I've got to do it for them," instead of letting people find their own way. Empowering people so that they can discover things for themselves is the sign of a good teacher. There are many ways in which we can bring our own problems into the helping relationship.

But the story gets a lot more complicated because sometimes there exists the client's countertransference to the therapist's transference and the therapist's countertransference to the client's transference and so on and so on! The central point here is that, while you are travelling through this rocky landscape of transference and countertransference relation-ships, certain feelings get in the way. Somehow they distort the relationship, they bias it, they prevent it from fully developing. That's what we mean when we talk about transference and countertransference getting in the way of relationships.

7. Unfinished relationship

The reason why we like the word "unfinished" is that often a relationship is like a piece of unfinished business; suppose, for instance, you really wanted to tell that rejecting mother of yours, while she was dying, how painful her rejection had been, yet you could not tell her so. You carry that unexpressed feeling with you. The next time you meet a mother figure, you suspect that she is probably also going to reject you, so you find that you can't confide in her. The original experience poisons the new relationship. The piece of unfinished business goes with you from relationship to relationship. That is what is meant by "unfinished" in this context.

Or suppose you have had a fight with someone, and you didn't get the last words out. You think "I would have liked to say to them..." You know that feeling? I'm sure you do. Mean things like that stay in our mind. There are unfinished conversations. When I next see that person, it is right there on the tip of my tongue. If I get too stressed or tired or tempted, it might just pop up. Have you noticed that? And then you think, how could I have done that? That is the unfinished business that we want to complete through therapy. This is another way of understanding transference: we have carried over something incomplete or unfinished. We want to finish off that business; we want to really tell that person, "Don't treat me like that!".

SUMMARY:

Unfinished relationship can be the result of:
- unexpressed feelings
- unfinished conversations
- unfinished business, which needs to be completed.

———

8. What are some of the effects of countertransference?

Countertransference describes the feelings or attitudes that arise in the counsellor or formator during the therapeutic or formation relationship. In many cases, if the counsellor or formator has not worked on him/herself sufficiently, and is not growing in his/her own journey, proactive transference may distort and limit the counselling work or the work of formation. In other cases, the feelings and attitudes of the counsellor or formator, if they are aware of them, can be used effectively to strengthen and sustain the working alliance. Michael Kahn deals with this topic in his book *Between Therapist and Client* (1991, 132-142).

The destructive uses of countertransference

1. Countertransference can make us blind. We fail to explore important areas because of countertransference. For example, the client hints at sexual matters. The counsellor does not feel at ease, and becomes anxious and recoils from the presenting material.

2. Countertransference can motivate us to focus more heavily on material that belongs to our own issue rather than the client's. For example, if a male counsellor has a serious unresolved conflict with his father, he may overemphasise the relationship that exists between the client and his father.

3. Countertransference can induce in us changes of mood or feeling, which express themselves physically, in ways which, however subtle, may strongly influence our clients; sometimes we don't realise how important our expressions are to them. Consciously or unconsciously they pick up messages from our faces, tone of voice, posture or shifts in posture, muscle tension, verbal and non-verbal communication. For example, if unconsciously I have a need for clients to admire me, then my clients will probably pick this up, either consciously or unconsciously, and this may shape their behaviour; they may learn that it is acceptable to have friendly feelings towards me, but not aggressive feelings or negative feelings. This would limit the therapeutic process. Of course, no counsellor can or should attempt to control physical reactions completely, but we need to be aware when they become intrusive.

4. Countertransference can motivate us to use our clients for vicarious satisfaction. For example, say a counsellor has dependency needs. This need may drive the counsellor to encourage his/her client to act too independently, because in this way the counsellor hopes to overcome his own dependency. The result may be that the client will hide a conflict by means of superficial independent actions. Another example is the counsellor who lacks sexual freedom, and who

encourages the client to become sexually more free. This is one reason why counsellors should abstain from giving advice.

5. Countertransference can motivate us to play the roles which the client's transference encourages us to play. For example, the client considers the counsellor to be absolutely wonderful. This is an idealising transference. The counsellor starts playing the role of Saviour. Another example is the client who is very learned and also sees the counsellor as a learned man. He sees the two of them as having intelligent talks with each other. Unconsciously, the counsellor may fall into the trap, and play the role of the wise man, by showing how knowledgeable he is, rather than getting on with the work of counselling.

6. Countertransference can motivate the counsellor to make certain interventions, which are not in the interest of the client. For example, a client talks about his mother in such a way that it stirs angry feelings in the counsellor. The counsellor may then react by saying negative things about the client's mother. Another illustration is a client who talks about seemingly unimportant things. The client's talk stirs counter-transference feelings of impatience and irritation. However, the likelihood is that the client is afraid of going deeper. The counsellor may be preoccupied by his/her own feelings of irritation and impatience, and overlook the client's fear. The counsellor may give vent to his impatience by saying, "You seem to be avoiding things that really matter to you." The client may feel criticised, which in turn intensifies his fear of sharing.

The facilitative uses of countertransference

Countertransference is closely linked with empathy. How do we reach empathy?

1. It must be a countertransference which is triggered by the client and not by the counsellor's own issues.

2. Once the countertransference feeling or attitude is created, it becomes empathy only if the counsellor can keep an optimal distance from the feeling or attitude.

> What needs to happen with the feeling? It must not be repressed, neither must it be allowed to swamp the counsellor. The counsellor should not fight the client emotionally, or over-identify with the client's feelings. Preserving a safe distance from the feeling allows a felt understanding of the client.

A male client speaks of women in a way that his female counsellor hears as derogatory. After several such remarks, she grows increasingly angry. She finds it difficult to be objective. The thought comes into her mind that the client may not be aware of the impact of such remarks on a female counsellor, or on women in general. She asks herself, "Why would this client want to hurt me?" Her anger subsides. She has begun to form a new attitude, which she can use for therapeutic purposes.

Another example is a client who is very boring. The impression of the counsellor is that it is all the client wants of him – a person whom he can bore. At first the counsellor feels a lot of irritation. Then he realises that he is feeling lonely and useless. When the counsellor questions him, the client says that he is quite satisfied; he needs somebody to listen to him. The counsellor's feeling of loneliness becomes more intense. One day he is surprised by a strong hunch. Is it possible that the client is showing him what it was like for him as a small child? Possibly both parents were very boring, showing no affection, merely a-matter-of-fact approach. The child was lonely and felt useless. A new understanding and exploration of the client's possible pain has opened up, and the countertransference has been channelled into empathy.

SUMMARY:

What are some of the effects of countertransference?
1. Countertransference can distort and limit the counselling work and the work of formation.
2. Countertransference feelings can be destructive of, or strengthen, the working alliance.

Destructive uses of countertransference:

1. Countertransference can make us blind to the client's true situation.
2. Countertransference can motivate us to focus more on our own issue rather than the client's.
3. Countertransference can induce in us subtle physical reactions, which may strongly influence our clients.
4. Countertransference can motivate us to use our clients for vicarious satisfaction.
5. Countertransference can lead us to play the roles which clients' transferences encourage us to play.
6. Countertransference can motivate us to make certain interventions, which are not in the interest of the client.

Facilitative uses of countertransference:

Countertransference is closely linked with empathy.

How do we reach empathy through countertransference?

1. The countertransference must be triggered by the client, not by the counsellor's own issues.
2. Once these countertransference feelings have been experienced by the counsellor, empathy begins. It proves fruitful when the counsellor keeps an optimal distance from the feeling.

———

It is important to understand where Transference and Counteretransference occur in the therapeutic relationship. If we try to work too consciously on material that remains in the unconscious of the client, we may aggravate a problem. Conversely, if we allow the lower self to impinge too far on matters that should be negotiated by client and counsellor at a conscious level, disruption of the relationship may occur. In other words, we have to approach these delicate matters at the right level. The diagrams that follow are intended to locate the relationship according to the situation being considered.

The transferential and countertransferential relationship, according to Kofler's personality model

Transference

This diagram demonstrates the client/counsellor positions when the relationship initially takes place between the lower self of the client and that of the therapist. The therapist becomes aware of the transference and works from his middle self to the middle self of the client; as a result both become aware of the transference.

Transference

CLIENT		COUNSELLOR
Higher Self		Higher Self
Middle Self	Counsellor RESPONDS ← with awareness	Middle Self
Lower Self	Client's TRANSFERENCE →	Lower Self

Transference/Countertransference (diagram overleaf)

This diagram demonstrates a relationship where neither the client nor the counsellor is aware of the transference and countertransference process, for example when the client unconsciously transfers his father on to the counsellor and the counsellor in turn unconsciously countertransfers a caring or punitive father on to the client. Both the "higher selves" and the "middle selves" are dominated here by the "lower selves", and therefore cannot function properly .

Transference/countertransference

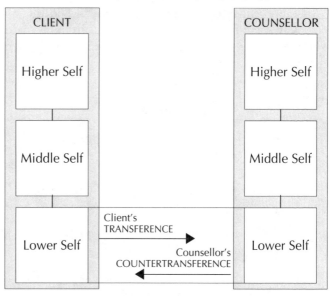

Immediately detected transference (diagram opposite)

This diagram represents the relationship when the therapist, immediately aware of the client's transference of a punishing father, refuses to fall into that role, and instead responds in an understanding way to the middle self of the client. After this interaction has taken place for some time, the client no longer sees in the therapist his punishing father. Most of the interaction takes place between the "lower" and "middle" selves, but the "higher" selves can guide the process. Integration, which includes the spiritual, remains the overall intention.

Immediately detected transference

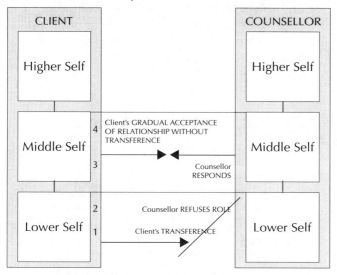

9. How can we manage and use countertransference?

The counsellor must learn to distinguish between proactive and reactive countertransference. Then s/he can use the reactive countertransference as data to help predict or anticipate the client's patterns of thought, emotion or behaviour. It is assumed that counsellors will have resolved most of their own pathology, at least in those areas which might interfere with their work with clients. As counsellors we must be able to identify and counteract our own pathological patterns. We need to know when and from whom to seek help, if the patterns become dominant.

When we are engaged in therapy, it is worthwhile reflecting that client transference and counsellor reactive countertransference are likely to provide the richest and most accurate options for intervention. In supervision, it is often found to be the other way round: here, most phenomena are caused by the counsellor's proactive transference and the client's reactive countertransference. It cannot, of course, be proved that either of these positions is more than speculative.

Anyway, frequent alterations between the proactive and the reactive are beneficial for both client and counsellor. The counsellor should be intent on locating the point at which the smallest intervention will lead to the largest degree of shift in the problem. One reactive word from the counsellor is sometimes sufficient.

10. Failures in the transference and counter-transference relationship

Failures in this area can destroy the working alliance. Sometimes, insufficient transference material comes to the surface. This can be because the relationship being carried over is either too personal, or too devoid of evocative meaning for the client. However, insufficient energy behind transference and/or countertransference is rarely to blame. Where failure occurs, the transference or countertransference is often strong to the point of being overwhelming; but, owing to the powerful force behind it, or to the counsellor's lack of experience, the transference/countertransference cannot be appropriately controlled. This leads, in the most extreme cases, to psychotic transferences, which disrupt the working alliance through threats, or even through attempts to injure the counsellor, or to damage something or someone close to the counsellor.

Paradoxically, the nature of psychotic transferences may render them potentially therapeutic; the power behind them can sometimes be channelled in alternative and positive ways. The real problem arises when a psychotic transference badly undermines or destroys the working alliance. The client may be under the illusion, for instance, that you are putting sexual fantasies into his/her head. The client may experience this as a fact, and may not be able to distinguish the feeling, fear or fantasy from the reality of the therapeutic relationship. In that case, the transference has become counter-productive, and the working alliance has broken down. If a transference is to be workable, the client needs to be able to distinguish between imaginative and objective reality.

SUMMARY:

Failures in transference and countertransference relationship, which can destroy the working alliance, occur when:

- There is insufficient transferential material.
- There is too much transferential material.
- There is psychotic transference: attempts or threats to injure the counsellor, etc. The psychotic transference ruins the working alliance.

———

11. Exercise

A client tells you that she is hurt because you were two minutes late. She seems disproportionately disturbed by this. The client has a childhood history of trying to please her parents and being rebuffed. What would be your reply? What would be your intervention?

Would you say:

    a.   "Your responses are unrealistic."

    b.   "Your perception of reality is distorted."

    c.   "You are confusing me with your father or mother."

On the other hand, perhaps it would be better to draw out of the client her own conclusions about how she might have suffered from her relationship with her parents, when she was young, and how this is being transferred to the counselling situation. It is often better to take this course, rather than making suggestions which the client may well refute in a defensive manner, especially if she feels annoyed by your probing. However you approach the subject of transference, avoid sermonising.

Write your own response to this or a similar situation.

12. How can we assess the effectiveness of transference and countertransference?

1. Work in the transference and countertransference relationship is effective to the extent that sufficient replication of the fantasised patterns penetrate the therapeutic relationship. This replication of the fantasised patterns will provide here-and-now material to explore, justify, and work through the archaic patterns.

2. There must be sufficient investment in the working alliance and curiosity about transference phenomena. This will sustain interest, and will maintain the investment in exploring the meaning of repetitive transference patterns.

3. Has the client the ability to be conscious of the transferential patterns, the ability to use this to increase his/her self-understanding, the ability to let go of these patterns and to develop others, the ability to generalise a novel, future-oriented relationship?

4. The most important criterion for effectiveness of countertransference is the ability to:
   a. learn how to separate out proactive from reactive countertransference;
   b. increase skills and opportunities, so as to minimise the distorting effects of proactive countertransference;
   c. develop skills and awareness, so as to utilise reactive countertransferences for the benefit of the client.

5. For the above to succeed, the counsellor needs personal therapy and good supervision.

6. In supervision we can experience and explore the parallel process. By doing so, we can improve vision, action and reaction. Parallel process is the reproduction during supervision of those interventions, feelings, and behaviours, which occurred during a counselling session. Parallel process is a way of describing the pattern of the client-counsellor transference/countertransference relationship. Both client and counsellor act, often unconsciously, in ways which may

influence the other "hypnotically". The "hypnosis" may be exerted in one direction, or it may be mutual. All these processes are very complex.

The phenomena of transference and countertransference are interconnected in ways which we do not yet understand. The concept of mutual hypnotic induction may help us to answer some of the questions. Hypnotic induction is similar to projective identification from either the client or the counsellor; it may also be mutual. It happens unconsciously, in the form of ulterior transactions, the meaning of which lies in the communicative space between the dialoguing partners. Now, the concept of parallel process assumes that the interpersonal field of client and counsellor is replicated in the supervision process, and the mechanism for this replication is itself assumed to be projective identification – or mutually interacting hypnotic induction. Therefore, it is postulated that a circular interaction serves as the dynamic field for what is called parallel process.

We know that counsellors often behave in supervision in the same way as the client behaves in counselling. Thus, if the client experiences a sense of helplessness and leans on the counsellor, the counsellor may feel the same helplessness as s/he leans on the supervisor. The counsellor is acting out in supervision a transient identification with the client.

Parallel process works in both directions. The supervisor stirs the counsellor, who then behaves accordingly with his/her client.

In a client's reactive countertransference, s/he may respond to counsellor-induced material. Similarly, a supervisee may be part of a projective identification process initiated by a supervisor. This process would be outside the conscious awareness of either of them. Hypnotic induction is a common phenomenon, which occurs in everyday life. From chaos theory we learn that large results can be achieved from small causes. Let us apply this to supervision. The parallel processes are explicable by nature's mechanism for preserving wholeness.

SUMMARY:

How can we assess the effectiveness of transference and countertransference?

1. Is there sufficient replication of the fantasised patterns?

2. Is there sufficient investment in the working alliance, and sufficient curiosity about transference phenomena?

3. Has the client the ability to be conscious of the transferential patterns, use them and let them go?

4. For countertransference to be effective, one must learn:
   a. to distinguish between proactive and reactive countertransference;
   b. to minimise the distorted effects of proactive counter-transference;
   c. to utilise reactive countertransference.
   d. to make the best possible use of personal therapy and supervision;
   e. to explore the parallel process during supervision.

---

13. Summary of transference and countertransference

1. We have outlined four categories of transferential phenomena, which must be conceived of as interacting. They form an inseparable systemic whole.

2. In the last two chapters we have discussed these categories, as follows:
   a. What the client brings to the relationship (proactive transference)
   b. What the counsellor brings to the relationship (proactive countertransference or counsellor transference)
   c. What the counsellor reacts to in the client (reactive countertransference)
   d. What the client reacts to as a result of what the counsellor brings (client countertransference or reactive transference of the client)

3. We have demonstrated that any of these four categories may form the basis for a facilitative or destructive therapeutic outcome.

14. Exercise

Make sure you can answer the following questions:
1. What is a countertransference?
2. Are you aware of your own countertransferences? What are they?
3. How do you deal with them?
4. Do you use them for individual therapy? If so, how?
5. How can you use countertransference in a formation setting?
6. What is a reactive countertransference?
7. What is a proactive countertransference?
8. When does a reactive countertransference become facilitative?
9. When does a proactive countertransference become destructive?
10. How can you use the concept of countertransference in a pastoral setting?
11. How can you use this concept of countertransference in a community setting?
12. How would you handle psychotic transferences?
13. How do you prepare yourself as a counsellor, using the concept of countertransference?
14. In the context of transference/countertransference, what blocks our learning about ourselves and our clients?
15. How can we use anticipation constructively?
16. When does anticipation become destructive?

15. A case study of countertransference

PETER, a European missionary, who worked for ten years in Africa, shared the story of the death of his mother. He was not there when she died. As the counsellor was listening to his story, she became aware of distinct and disquieting feelings. The story had triggered in her mind the memory of her own mother's death. She felt very sad, and was moved by her own sadness, to the extent that she felt she could no longer listen, or be fully present to the client. At this stage, she could no longer be empathic, because she had become emotionally involved in the loss of her own mother.

During supervision, the counsellor duly shared this experience, and spoke of how she had instinctively wanted to shorten the session: it was very difficult for her to continue with the client. Her supervisor helped her to understand that her countertransference in this instance was proactive; she was the source of it; the supervisor encouraged her to address the problem during her own therapy session. In time, the counsellor was able to observe, "After considerable reflection, and by working with my own therapist, I realised that it was my own unfinished business that was interfering with my client's progress. While I remained unaware of unfinished business in my own psyche, it was bound to disturb the therapeutic relationship with my client."

CHAPTER SIX

The developmentally needed *or* reparative relationship

1. Christianity and the cross 2. What is the developmentally needed *or* reparative relationship? 3. Regression and reparative work 4. How is this relationship beneficial? 5. Diagnosis 6. Establishment of the relationship 7. Discipline and the developmentally needed relationship 8. Reparative relationship linked with the developmentally needed relationship *or* trauma 9. Be careful what you do as a counsellor! 10. The heart of the developmentally needed or reparative relationship 11. Management and maintenance of the reparative relationship 12. Jesus' death and God's forgiveness – a reparative experience 13. Practical measures 14. Exercises 15. Anger and reparative experience 16. Exercise 17. God's reparative relationship 18. The reparative effect of laughter 19. Criteria for evaluating the effectiveness of the reparative relationship 20. Exercises 21. Two case studies of the reparative and developmentally needed relationship

1. Christianity and the Cross

First, we shall look at the meaning of suffering and the Cross from a Christian and Jungian perspective.

The Cross has become for us the symbol of suffering and redemption. The relationship between Christianity and the Cross reveals the reality beneath layers and layers of suffering and pain, endured by the human race. Our Christian faith tells us that Jesus redeemed us through His suffering and death on the Cross; He was innocent, yet He had to suffer.

Our therapeutic journey is similar to the journey of Jesus: we too have to suffer, face our pain, before we can be healed. This similarity can encourage Christians to face their pain and suffering, so that they may also experience the resurrection and new life, which follow the often painful therapeutic journey.

What Jung said about the Symbol of the Cross

In various different contexts, Jung alluded to the Cross as the perfect symbol of human suffering, and in particular psychic suffering. Here is a selection of his statements:

> "The moment of the eclipse and mystic marriage is death on the Cross. In the Middle Ages the Cross was therefore logically understood as the mother" (1963, 26).

"The Cross is by implication the Christian totality symbol: as an instrument of torture it expresses the sufferings on earth of the incarnate God, and as a quantity it expresses the universe, which also includes the material world" (1963, 122).

"Complete redemption from the sufferings of this world is and must remain an illusion. Christ's earthly life likewise ended, not in complacent bliss, but on the Cross" (1954, 400).

"Whichever course one takes, nature will be mortified and must suffer, even to the death; for the merely natural man must die in part during his own lifetime. The Christian symbol of the crucifix is therefore a prototype and an 'eternal' truth" (1954, 470).

"The Cross as a form of suffering expresses psychic reality, and carrying the Cross is therefore an apt symbol for the wholeness and also for the passion which the alchemist saw in his work. Hence the Rosarium ends, not unfittingly, with the picture of the risen Christ and the verses: 'After my many sufferings and great martyry, I rise again transfigured, of all blemish free'" (1954, 523).

Bearing these quotations in mind, we shall gradually explore the connection between the Cross and "developmentally needed" or "reparative relationship".

2. What is the developmentally needed *or* reparative relationship?

Petruska Clarkson (1995, 108) describes the developmentally needed or reparative relationship, as "the intentional provision by the counsellor of correction or replenishment, where a previous relationship has suffered from abuse, deficiency or overprotection." The counsellor provides corrective and replenishing actions, ways of behaving, attitudes, or feelings, in order to *repair* the damage caused by the earlier harmful relationship. Reparative relationship is made possible by the phenomenon of regression, which is the psychological ability to cathect parts of the psyche at earlier stages of its development. Although the provision is said to be "intentional", this does not mean that the counsellor is always fully conscious of the reparative relationship. Sometimes, an accidental word before or after the session can do the trick. For example, a client may have a plaster on his hand; it is natural for the counsellor to ask, "Are you all right? I hope you haven't hurt yourself." Some form of reparation is necessary in all effective counselling.

3. Regression and reparative work

Regression is a very common phenomenon. It is capable of great creative, as well as great destructive power. Many theories consider regression as essential to effective counselling, while not to be able to regress can be seen as unhealthy. The trauma must be retrieved, so that renewal and transformation can occur. In this way, regression becomes part of the healing process, within the developmentally needed or reparative relationship. However, there is, as usual, a negative side; regression is frequently found to be a defence mechanism. There are two types of regression: one malignant, the other benign.

Regression and fixation: We can distinguish between various forms of regression: (a) some regressive states are acute, disturbing and disintegrating; (b) some forms of regression are temporarily hindering; (c) Some regressive states are chronologically fixated. So regression needs to be distinguished from fixation.

Regression and the role of time: Regression is a recognition of our existence in time. We can move backwards and forwards in time (linear) or synchronistically (acausal). Healing is rendered possible by the plasticity of time in the body and in the psyche.

Regression and creativity: Regressive phenomena are often considered to be related to creativity. We can voluntarily regress into our depths, where we reach a passivity and receptivity of inspiration or of peak-experience. This is frequently followed by activity, control and hard work in one's chosen sphere. Maslow (1968, 143) acknowledges the role in creativity played by child-like states, or regression to earlier selves. Central to any creative action are the relaxation of "ego functions", such as the will to control completely or acquisitiveness, and the employment of the imagination. The process of inspiration often begins in fantasy and dream, in the regressive "play" of the mind.

The difference between transference relationship and reparative relationship: In transference relationship, an act, feeling or word will be replayed within the archaic drama. For example: "My father never had any time for me." Through transference, interpretations and empathic reflection, the client can begin to feel the real pain and disappointment beneath the statement, so that the statement does not remain a crude assertion of fact. In the reparative relationship, on the other hand, the counsellor's word or gesture provides the client with the experience of understanding and internalising a loving object for the first time. However, gifts from counsellor to client are strongly to be discouraged, as frequently something intended to be reparative will be misjudged, and can in fact reinforce the client's transference. For example: "I knew the Easter card you gave me was only meant to trick me – just like my father!"

The new reality: The actual relationship between counsellor and client, resulting from reparative techniques, should constitute a new reality – the indispensable therapeutic factor. This new relationship can correct distorted internal relationships, and so open the client's emotional life to a healthier development. The process will not always be easy. The counsellor will have to decide when to be supportive and when to confront caringly or to challenge, when to calm the anxious client, and when to reassure the "frightened child".

What kind of new relationship will the counsellor provide?
This will depend on several factors:

1. The developmental theory the counsellor follows, including theories concerning appropriate parenting and caretaking

2. The upbringing of the counsellor

3. The basic training of the counsellor

4. The countertransferential implications of the counsellor's class, economic status, skin colour and culture.

Often the new relationship will require "reparenting". Reparenting exists in both *optimal frustration* as well as in *the empathic resonance*. The counsellor helps the client to reshape his/her parenting experience by means of optimal frustration of factors causing harm, while employing empathic resonance, which runs contrary to the client's unhelpful experiences in childhood, to form a new vision of parenting.

If you read about psychoanalysis or psychoanalytic work, most of the time you will find yourself reading about transference and the countertransference relationship. However, the ever-increasing discourse concerning reparative or developmentally needed relationship is just as integral to many of the therapies that you will encounter. A word of warning, though. Because reparative work is so potent, it is very easy to misuse it. In many countries, most evidently in the United States, there are numerous legal cases, where people are taking action against therapists, because of the injurious reparative work they have done. Reparative work is highly problematic in practice, because the therapist may unconsciously manipulate, according to his/her own experiences as a child or parent. Countertransference needs to be carefully monitored, and supervision sought when there is any doubt as to the necessary approach.

SUMMARY:

What is the developmentally needed or reparative relationship?

- It is the intentional provision of the corrective, replenishing or reparative relationship. This is needed in cases where childhood relationships were abusive, deficient or overprotective.
- Regression enables the reparative relationship.
- Regression is capable of great creative as well as great destructive power.
- Regression needs to be distinguished from fixation.
- Regression is recognition of our existence in time.
- Regressive phenomena are often considered as related to creativity.

---

4. How is this relationship beneficial?

In its simplest form, we can say that this relationship means just being there for someone, every week, in a reliable way, respecting them, listening to them, treating them like decent human beings: this is both reparative and corrective. How many of you were adequately listened to when you were children? How many of you felt understood and respected when you were children? For many people this has not been their experience. For most human beings, our experience is that we have not been listened to, we have been hurt, we have been betrayed, we have been neglected; or else we were given too much freedom, and were never subject to tight enough control. Perhaps there were no rules: nobody cared if we stayed out all night or never did our homework; this parody of freedom is another kind of abandonment, leading us to believe that nobody cares about us. You often see this battle with adolescent girls. Often, a daughter really wants her parents to say, "But I expect you in by 11", so that she can say to her friends, "My Mum always wants me to be back by 11" – it gives her protection and a sense of security.

It also gives her something to kick against because it makes her different from her peers. Either way, it is not always the nice understanding bits that we want from our parents; a lot of the time it is structure or control.

For young people, aspiration can be set free by certain kinds of discipline. Sometimes, what they want is for people to believe in them, and for somebody to make the hurdle a little bit higher. Have you ever had that experience? Have you ever had children respond to this kind of challenge by saying, "Yes, I want to. I can do that." Because someone believes in you, you raise your capacity. You work a little bit harder, and you put more energy into it, and you achieve things of which nobody would have thought you capable.

Some young people, when they look forwards towards a career, conceive professional aspirations that their families had never considered, and they may be discouraged. They may hesitate to enrol to become doctors of psychology, for instance, because in the families that they come from there is no history of higher education. So there is no in-built capacity to envisage such an ambition. So, when someone with authority says, "I want that Ph.D. proposal in at the end of the week", that offers a kind of alternative vision. Rather than, "Well, that is fine, darling, anything you do, as long as you try, that's OK", what a young person may really want is for someone to believe in them, and to raise the height of the hurdle. This is reparative work. A word of caution is necessary here. It is possible to exert undue pressure on a young person by giving him/her expectations which are unattainable. Goals have to be relevant to the capacity of the individual. The counsellor needs to remember that talents are God-given. Aiming at things that are "too high" can create feelings of inferiority, when failure inevitably occurs.

The developmentally needed aspect of such encouragement is linked to the whole field of developmental theory. The reparative aspect involves factors which will be discussed later.

The main thing to remember is that the counsellor, when working in this way, is conscious of providing a relationship that repairs something of a prior relationship.

175

SUMMARY:

The need for developmentally needed or reparative relationship

In its simplest form it means being there for somebody.

- Most people were not listened to when they were children.
- Parents did not have enough time for them.
- Many people were hurt in childhood.
- Some were betrayed in childhood.
- Some were neglected.
- Some had too much freedom.
- Some were never given any controls.
- The counsellor provides a relationship that repairs something of a prior relationship.

———

5. Diagnosis

First, the counsellor has to identify the injuries or deficits of the client's childhood experience. This process will depend on the counsellor's own understanding of human growth and development. What theory of human development does the counsellor follow? From what cultural background does s/he come? Given these boundaries, the counsellor has to assess the nature, intensity, duration and variety of reparative or developmentally needed relationship required by the client.

Diagnosis for the developmentally needed relationship

Sometimes, a client's difficulties refer back to a particular developmental period of the client's life, rather than to a traumatic childhood event. There is a difference between the behaviour of an eleven-year-old exploring the nature of satisfaction to be had from his achievements, and that of the fifteen-year-old who is trying to break loose from his parents through hostile attacks on them. There is a difference between the two-year-old look of a client, who is testing the counsellor's limits of tolerance by coming late to a session, and the thirteen-year-old expression that the same client's features wear, when s/he is fantasising about the counsellor's private life! How we respond to these differences is a very important factor in the therapeutic process. Counsellors need to experience the different facets of their own history of development, as well as that of others. This experience, combined with intuition and acute awareness, will enable counsellors to respond in the most appropriate manner, taking into account the age at which the need of the client started to develop; this age is a dominant factor in his/her condition.

Diagnosis of the reparative relationship

The counsellor needs to identify the nature, severity and duration of the injury or deficit of the client. There are three main categories of such injuries:

1. **Trauma**: Some think that a trauma can be purely imaginary. This is a debatable issue. The subjective reality of the client is the important aspect in the healing process.

2. **Strain**: This is the long-term experience (not necessarily traumatic in the immediate sense), of pain, rejection, deprivation, neglect, pressure, exertion or seduction – of one or more of the many ways in which a child can be subjected to undue difficulties in growing up healthily. We could call this accumulated trauma.

3. **Extra-familial limitations and catastrophes**: Some examples are: a Hutu child, who spends most of his or her formative years in starvation and flight from one refugee camp to another; a ten-year-old boy, who is forced to join a rebel army, and is then captured by government soldiers and imprisoned; a woman who loses a child in stillbirth. We can include here the long-term effects of pollution and radiation, and of the lasting scars of "the underclass of society" through illness, social isolation and educational deprivation. And of course, there are the stripping, continual humiliation, even rape, that take place in a prison camp, where the victim has almost no control over his or her daily life.

SUMMARY:

Diagnosis and identification of the nature of the injury or the kind of developmental deficit
- First, the counsellor has to identify the injuries or deficits of childhood.

The developmentally needed relationship:
- Sometimes the difficulties arise from, and refer to, a particular developmental period of the client's life.
- The important question is: what was the age of the client when the need was created?
- The counsellor needs to identify the nature, severity and duration of the injury or deficit of the client.

The reparative relationship
There are three main categories of injury:
1. Trauma: Sudden disaster, with immediate impact.
2. Strain: Prolonged experience of pain, rejection, deprivation, neglect, pressure, coercion, seduction.
3. Extra-familial limitations and catastrophes.

———

Skills needed for the reparative relationship

Most of the skills mentioned in former chapters are relevant to the developmentally needed or reparative relationship. However, I would like to mention some specifically. One of these is the skill of immediacy. Gerard Egan (1998) distinguishes three types of immediacy: 1. General relationship immediacy; 2. Here-and-now immediacy; 3. Self-involving statements. Although all three types of immediacy are important for the developmentally needed or reparative relationship, I see the self-involving statements as being particularly suited to the reparative relationship.

1. **General relationship immediacy** is a skill through which we explore our relationship with people. General relationship

immediacy is the exploration of a relationship over a period of time. This can be very useful at certain intervals of the counselling process. It can also be of great value for the exploration of relationship within a community, a parish council, a team, or in enhancing the relationship between two friends.

2. **Here-and-now immediacy** is the exploration of the relationship in the present moment. This exploration can take place at a particular event in the counselling session, at a precise juncture during a community meeting, or at a moment shared between two friends or spouses. It is not the whole relationship that is being explored, but a particular intervention, interaction or event.

3. **Self-involving statements** are present tense, personal responses to the client. They can be positive or negative. Some examples of positive self-involving statements are: "I like the way you dress." "I like what you have just said." "From what you have just said, I see how intelligent you are." "You seem to be very creative in what you have done." These statements affirm the client, and are useful in building up low self-esteem. In that sense, self-involving statements are reparative.

Even negative self-involving statements can be reparative. They can be effective with clients who have never learnt to develop respect for healthy boundaries. "Your interrupting me constantly isn't helpful", " Please stop shouting at me, I get very angry with you when you shout", "It upsets me when you touch me, because it threatens our professional relationship", "Please don't phone me after midnight" are examples of this kind of constructive negative response. They are intended to reinforce particular boundaries.

How do you make an immediacy statement?

1. Indicate that you want to talk about the relationship between the two of you.

2. Make sure that your relationship with the client is solid

enough for him/her to accept whatever statements you are going to make, especially if they are negative.

3. Use I-statements, and own what you want to communicate (I feel, I think, I see it like this, I wonder etc.).

4. Don't blame anyone, but rather describe the relationship that exists between the two of you.

5. Ask the client for his/her view about the relationship.

6. For the here-and-now immediacy use the present tense (e.g. "As I listen to your story, I feel sad").

Expectations and the reparative relationship

There is a natural desire to reach for and repair the original neglect, injury or developmental deficit. We can call it a self-actualising tendency. Clients may be confused as to what is ethical, malpractice, or reasonable expectation. The expectation of the counsellor may permit, rule out, or encourage regression and developmentally needed or reparative experiences. The influence and expectations of the family or other institutions can also affect the outcome of regressive or reparative experiences. Some families allow a seven-year-old child to make a temporary regressive event for himself, for example, having a bottle again when a young sibling is born. Some institutions may support, control, encourage or limit regression. In the therapy room, the very presence of materials like toys or paint can make clear to both counsellor and client the nature of one dimension of what can be expected: creative play is to be involved.

6. Establishment of the relationship

Often there is no need for the reparative relationship to be formally established, because clients naturally regress again and again. Many people come for help because they want to learn to avoid regression in daily life.

180

Regression: As we have seen, regression occurs in many life situations, and often during counselling or psychotherapy. Regression can occur spontaneously. It can be initiated and facilitated by the counsellor. It can be recognised as the state of the client's presentation in a particular session. In some cases, it can be a specific feature of a contract or working alliance.

Spontaneous regression: Sometimes, clients come into the session already in a state of regression, sometimes they regress during the session. The latter eventuality may be in response to something the counsellor has said or done. S/he may not have intended it. The counsellor has to deal with it. Any helpful intervention for a person in an extreme state of distress is likely to be reparative.

Facilitated regression: Facilitation may mean, first and foremost, providing a safe and calm space for exploration. Beyond that, it may mean something more creative: providing a noisy instrument like a drum, or messy material such as paint. These can enable the client to meet certain archaic needs. Sometimes facilitation requires simply a touch on the shoulder; sometimes it may be a metaphor or singing a song. The task of the counsellor, having established that there is enough ego strength to sustain the client through the re-experiencing, has to find out the actual deficit. Once this is perceived, the counsellor can attend to the real need, facilitating regression in any number of ways, but always trying to avoid over-indulgent smothering.

Induced regression: Milton Erickson (1987) was a past master at the spontaneous and speedy induction of regressive states. This enabled him to achieve dramatic and permanent cures.

Recognised regression: It is important to recognise the point at which a client becomes regressed – whether before or during the session. This is not always easy, because some people live their lives in an extended period of age regression.

Contracted regression: This is one of the most beneficial forms of working with regression. The client intentionally and specifically contracts with the counsellor to regress for a particular period of time, to monitor his/her own responsibility and experience. Counsellor and client agree to cathect into here-and-now reality on an agreed signal or at an agreed time. The client is fully in charge of his/her own processes. This assists with the client's self-management, not only in the therapy setting but also in daily life. For example: "In this session I want to regress to the time when I lost my mother, re-experience that pain, let it out of my body and choose to live again."

SUMMARY:

Establishing the developmentally needed or reparative relationship

- There is often spontaneous regression.
- Some clients need to learn not to regress.
- Some clients come into a session already in a state of regression.
- Sometimes clients regress during the session.

———

7. Discipline and the developmentally needed relationship

There was a very bright and very attractive baby girl. People would stop her mother in the street to tell her what a wonderful little girl she was, and how beautiful she was. The mother did not have much of a relationship with her husband, because he was always off somewhere. The child was always adored and worshipped. When she was only four, her headmaster, a personage of great significance in the village, was writing poems to this little girl about how beautiful she was. Her mother allowed this. Now, this child grew up to rule the roost wherever she went. Nobody ever told her what she couldn't do.

When she grew into a woman she had more than half a dozen abortions. This shows us what can happen to a person who grows up, without anyone being able to contain her. Nobody knew how to put any limits on her. So she eventually found a very perverted way of putting terrible limits on herself. And that is why when working with her it was a question of providing control. Quite a lot of the time, the first thing she would say to me was, "Tell me to go home and not to shout at my children", and I would say to her, "I will only tell you that, if you promise that you will listen to me. Good. Now listen. I can't control you. You are not two years old. I can't sit on you. All I can do is work with you according to our working alliance. So will you promise that if I tell you what you ask, you will do as you are told?" She said, "Yes, I promise." Finally, I said "You are not to go home and shout at your children." We are talking about someone in her thirties or forties.

This was quite a tricky case. Only in a very disturbed situation, where a client clearly requires such treatment, should a counsellor intervene in a way that is controlling or seriously restricting. I was focusing on a developmentally needed relationship, because what went wrong for that child happened around the age of eighteen months or two years of age, where issues about potty training, control, and fundamental discipline are usually dealt with. However, she had never had that chance. She was deprived of basic human discipline, because she was treated as a beautiful doll.

SUMMARY:
Discipline and the developmentally needed relationship

- Discipline is important for a child when s/he grows up. A lack of discipline in childhood often manifests itself in disruptive adult behaviour.
- Sometimes restrictions are needed for the developmentally needed relationship.

———

8. Reparative relationship linked with the developmentally needed relationship *or* trauma

The reparative relationship can be linked with the developmentally needed relationship, or it might simply be linked to strain, or perhaps to some trauma experienced during the person's childhood or adulthood. I don't think that all our traumas have to do with childhood. Rape, torture, abuse, fear, living in war situations or being burgled, all constitute traumas or strains in adult life, for which sometimes we need to go through reparative experiences in order to be able to trust people again. Even a car accident can traumatise a person. A certain trust in the world may need to be regained. When you have been terribly ill, you may feel as though some kind of trust with the world has been broken. For quite a long while you can't quite believe that things are not going to fall apart. After some time, we heal up, and then we start trusting again.

SUMMARY:

The reparative relationship linked with the developmentally needed relationship
- Not all traumas have to do with childhood.
- Traumas or strains of adult life: rape, torture, physical or emotional abuse, war, car accident, burglary, serious illness, prolonged illness.
- We may need reparative experiences to repair the injury incurred in such situations.

———

I particularly remember a woman who was born and grew up in post-war Germany, where there was much deprivation and poverty. She eventually became very successful in her own right, but even more so since she was married to an international banker; they had vast amounts of money. But psychologically she was always poor. That went with her like a ghost. Wherever she went, no matter what circumstances she was in, she was poor. And interestingly, you find the opposite sometimes: some children growing up in what objectively would be a poor environment, are always rich. They always have a sense of abundance about them, and it is not related to how much money there was or how much food there was in the pot. It has something to do with them, it goes with them. Poverty is not necessarily financial. One can be deficient in material goods, or one can be deficient in ideals, aspirations, literature, music, spirituality, religion, relationships and many other things. All these deficiencies can contribute to the developmentally needed relationship.

9. Be careful what you do as a counsellor!

All the things that fledgling counsellors instinctively want to do, such as give presents, give advice, hug a client, or hold or client's hand, require a warning. Why do we say, "Don't do these things"? Because – unless they are done with great care by an experienced counsellor – they spell danger for the client. Why do we say that these acts of good will and generosity are dangerous?

Let us take an example. A woman has been sexually abused as a child. There she sits, and she is weeping, and there you sit as a counsellor, and she suddenly says, "Will you please hold my hand?" Can you feel your reaction? Part of you says, "I want to be the trustworthy man who is there for her." However, you hesitate. You don't know whether the person who was the abused little child is going to experience your gesture as yet another kind of abuse, or if it is going to be the grown-up woman who is ready for a reparative experience. Then maybe you do reach out and touch her, but she cannot cope with this, so she re-experiences the abuse and makes a formal complaint against her counsellor, saying he has assaulted her! This does happen, and not only to men, but to women as well, although men are particularly vulnerable in this way. The reason we say "Don't" is, that if you are going to behave in a way that leaves your behaviour open to false construction, you must really know what you are doing. My general advice to the trainee counsellor is, do not give presents, hold hands, hug, or give advice! If the definite need should arise for any of these things, be extremely careful.

SUMMARY:

Be careful what you do as a counsellor

- Generally speaking, don't give advice, hug or hold hands.
- It is very dangerous, and open to misinterpretation

The appropriateness of special interventions

There are exceptions to most rules. Although we have just discouraged such things, there are rare occasions in counselling and therapy where it *may* be appropriate or necessary to hold somebody's hand, to reach out to them, to give them a piece of your clothing, to give them a gift or accept a gift. There may be times when any one or all of them may be right. As we have already said, in order to intervene in this way you must have a lot of self-awareness, and have analysed why you might want to act in the particular manner you have chosen; you also need to have a good deal of awareness of the other person, and of all the many ways in which such an action may lead to things going wrong. That is the reason why it is so important that we receive our own therapy and supervision: so that we know who we are, and what our tendencies are, and what we are likely to get confused about. Incidentally, we must not assume that women are not subject to false accusations or to falling into eroticism. But of course it is true that men are particularly vulnerable. Special interventions can so easily go wrong because they are easily misinterpreted, but that doesn't mean that, given the right circumstances, they are not some of the most powerful means that we have at our disposal. Be careful!

Intervention of empathy

One major exception is the Rogerian intervention of empathy. When we are empathetic with people, when we respond to them with care, with attention and reflection, with respect, honesty and congruence, we are actually providing a reparative development. This is because most of us haven't had the experience of such a relationship, either as children or as adults. Having the experience as an adult is partly a reparative experience. That is why the Rogerian method has such enormous penetration. It could not achieve such a profound effect on someone who had really felt well listened to as a child; for such an individual, while reflecting on their childhood and being offered a counsellor's empathy, the reaction would probably be, "What's all the fuss about?". For most of us, on the other hand, it is an experience of "somebody understands". That is the way I react.

Petruska Clarkson used to tell the following story: "I was on a flight to San Francisco. It was the end of the summer, and I had been teaching all year and was exhausted. I was tired; it was hot. I had been flying for something like eighteen hours. I was feeling hot and tired, sticky and grumpy. Somebody was squashing me so I squashed them back and we had a sort of very gentle little fight, very polite, of course. Then the air hostess came over and said, 'Dr Clarkson, I know that it is very hot and you are probably very tired, aren't you? It's not so long to fly now, and I can really see this is very difficult for you.' I was like putty in her hands. I felt so understood. She saw how irritable and tired I and everybody else was, and it was fine. I have read some of the books that are used as trainers from British Airways, and the staff are encouraged to intervene in this way. It works. So what I am saying is that an empathic response is the main tool that we can freely use most of the time with good effect."

10. The heart of the developmentally needed *or* reparative relationship

Most of us were gifted at some particular moment in our life, because at some point we were quite lost and somebody reached out to us. Perhaps they saw us and believed in us, or they listened and they cared, or perhaps they intervened, phoned the police. Somebody was there for us, and I think that that is the heart of the developmentally needed or reparative relationship. The important words are that "somebody is there for you".

SUMMARY:

The heart of the developmentally needed or reparative relationship
Somebody was there for you in a meaningful way:
- Listening
- Phoning
- Understanding
- Caring

When using special interventions, be aware!
- Do not do it without proper care.
- Women can also fall into eroticism; this is a general warning, not just for men.
- You need to understand yourself and the client well.
- Take it first to supervision!
- Make sure you are not misinterpreted!
- Keep on receiving your own personal therapy!
- Who am I?
- What are my tendencies?
- How might I hurt people during therapy, in my relationships?

―――

An image that may help when considering the receptive nature of any client is the little bird. There is a little bird and it is starving. It comes for counselling, and you know that what it needs is food. You are a good person, so you give it food. But the bird refuses it. You say, all right little bird, stay starving. But then you feel that, it is such a terrible thing that the bird stays starved when it really needs the food, that you put out food anyway. So who is serving whose purposes here? Somebody wants to feed but the other person isn't ready to eat yet. You must wait for the right moment and not offer sustenance until the little bird opens its beak. Then it can digest the food. In human terms, opening the beak is the equivalent of forming a working alliance! You have to form the beginnings of a working alliance before you can give. If you don't, you will just get your client turning away from you and saying to him/herself, "Well that counsellor never did understand me; the counsellor's always giving me empathy and understanding, but it doesn't mean a thing to me. After all that love I have received, I feel worse." If you discern this reaction, that is your signal that you are doing the wrong thing. Back off in the relationship and construct the working alliance again.

Satisfaction contract

I sometimes make something called a "Satisfaction Contract" when somebody asks me for something. This is an example; a female client says towards the end of a session, "Please, give me some feedback on how I am doing." I say that my job is not to give the client feedback. What is the point of that? "Tell me how well have I done in therapy!" It is like being at school and having a score-card. And I know that this person is thinking transferentially from school where they always had to perform well. "So if I tell you how well you are doing in therapy, all you are going to do is put it on your score card, and then you want to be a better client; that is not what I understand therapy to be about." "Yes, I know I am apt to behave like that, but I would like you at least to give me an indication of how I am doing." I then set up the satisfaction contract by asking, "If I tell you what you want to know, are you going to put it on your score card or are you going to use it to motivate yourself? You need to know that I will accept

189

you whether you do well or badly." And then she may say "Yes, I will use it to motivate myself". Then I may give her a very small piece of feedback e.g. "Well, I remember how at the beginning you used to be late all the time, and how for a long time now you have been on time. That really shows that you are committed to your therapy." Then I observe what she does. If she says, "Yes, that's right, I have changed", what have I learned? I have learned that I have got an open beak. If she comes back next week and she is late, what have I learned? Don't feed too readily. But when she returns on time, I might feed a small mouthful, then another and then another, while all the time checking to observe how well she digests the food. An alternative technique to use, when a client asks how s/he is doing in the counselling sessions, is to return the question: "How do you think you are doing?"

Don't ever feed when the mouth is shut: in such circumstances, it is your own need you are feeding, not the client's. That is why you must go back to the working alliance and make sure that the person actually wants the food you have to offer, wants it from you at the present time, and that there is an agreement about all this. Otherwise, don't start the feeding process, being as sure as possible that the bird will not just go elsewhere looking for food! The aim is to help the client avoid dependence.

SUMMARY:

Satisfaction contract

- Don't feed when the beak is shut! (Little Bird Metaphor)
- Feed first with small pieces.
- Check out during the next session what the client has done with the "food".
- Has the person digested the piece of food you offered?
- What has the person made of the small piece of food you offered?
- You might be satisfying your need to feed (proactive countertransference) rather than the client's need to eat.

Ask yourself the following questions
- Does the client want this food?
- Does the client want it from me?
- Does the client want it at this time, now?
- Check how you are using the working alliance. There needs to be an agreement.
- Then the small piece of food will probably be accepted and have a positive effect.
- Otherwise, keep the food in store.
- Am I helping the client to feed him/herself, or perpetuating a dependence?

———

11. Management and maintenance of the reparative relationship

What are the conditions necessary to manage and maintain a reparative relationship?

1. A solid working alliance in a relatively long-term psychotherapeutic relationship.

2. As already stated, there must be a temporary remission of the transference relationship. The reparative and transferential relationships are usually mutually exclusive. It may be that the client is in a transference relationship. It could be that the counsellor is in a pro-active or reactive countertransference. In either of these states, the counsellor is not fully available to provide intentionally what was omitted or committed during the client's childhood. It is essential to clear the transference dynamic first, and make sure that the working alliance or contract is sound and mutually understood.

3. Reasonable certainty in the counsellor that the client understands enough of the cognitive process to make good use of the planned experiment in relating.

4. Deficit replenishment takes many forms, from radical re-parenting, self-re-parenting to transmuting internalisations. The exposure to the new relationship in itself is a form of re-parenting. Sometimes, allowing a gratification is reparative for certain clients.

5. The availability of the counsellor only at a certain time

and place is reparative for most clients. This is particularly true for those clients for whom reliability, predictability and a holding environment are the kind of experience they have never enjoyed before. For others it can reinforce a defensive structure against spontaneity. For these clients the holding environment is just another destructive learning experience, and they need reparation in a different form.

6. The counsellor needs to be attuned and sensitive. For example, s/he needs to ascertain whether the original trauma consisted in over-stimulation by the environment or under-stimulation, and whether the trauma was followed by a lack of understanding and indifference by the people who caused it. The aims during therapy are:

    a. to help the client to regress to the traumatic experience,

    b. to watch carefully what degree of tension the client will be able to bear in this state,

    c. to see to it that the tension will remain at about the same level, by responding positively to the regressed client's longings, cravings or needs.

7. The counsellor needs to be receptive as well as responsive to opportunities for reparative experiences. Touch has the potential for a reparative experience, although, as we have said, it can be a two-edged tool. Some clients need challenge, control, constructive criticism, caring confrontation structure or set limits, for a reparative experience to take place.

SUMMARY:

The conditions necessary to manage and maintain a reparative relationship:

- A solid working alliance in a long-term therapeutic relationship.
- Temporary remission of the transference relationship.
- The client needs to have sufficient cognitive understanding of the process.
- Deficit replenishment takes many forms: radical re-parenting, transmuting internalisations, self-reparenting.
- Availability of the counsellor at a certain time and at a certain place is reparative for most clients.

- Allowing a gratification may be reparative for some clients.
- The counsellor needs to be finely attuned, sensitive, receptive and responsive for opportunities for reparative experiences.
- Touch has potential for reparative as well as for destructive experience.
- Some clients need structure, control, challenge, limits, etc.
- The counsellor needs to be receptive as well as responsive to opportunities for reparative experiences.

"Failures" which can become positive experiences, or create opportunities for breakthrough

It is important that we allow ourselves to fail with our clients. In the working through of these failures lies the potential for healing and growth. The counselling setting must not be an entirely artificial incubator. Clients must be exposed to the vicissitudes of real life. That means, there need to be disappointments, disillusionments. In this way, they can develop the robustness and resilience, which are necessary for the development of a sturdy self.

12. Jesus' death and God's forgiveness – a reparative experience

Jesus' death was not merely for individual sin, but for the sinfulness of the whole of creation. In therapy we are allowing that redeeming power of God to be focused on individual need. Both the suffering and the resurrection are part of the ministry of reconciliation. Many Christians know the theory that God forgives, but lack conviction about it. He was bearing our faults in his own body on the cross, so that we might die to our faults and live for holiness (1 Pt 2:4). Peter has in mind Isaiah chapter 53, v. 6:

> We had all gone astray like sheep,
> each taking his own way,
> and Yahweh burdened him
> with the sins of all of us.

13. Practical measures

Try the following illustration with a young person who needs to grasp the truth of forgiveness by Jesus. Have a rucksack, which the person carries in the left hand. This represents the individual, estranged from God by his sin. The right hand represents Jesus. "And the Lord has laid on him…" Move the rucksack from left hand to right. Now the left hand – the guilty person – is free; the right hand – Jesus – is carrying the weight. Think of Jesus on the Cross as the one who calls out, "My God, why have you forsaken me?" The answer is clearly shown in the hand exercise. "He bore my sins in his body on the tree."

With an adult, you might explore the example of Maximilian Kolbe, who changed places with the father of a family, as Jews were filing into the gas chamber at Auschwitz.

Many feelings of guilt have strong elements of false guilt. Often the fear of God the Judge is stronger then a sense of safety and being at home with God the lover. Such clients need reparative experiences. The psycho-spiritual therapists will model their behaviour on God's attributes of love, mercifulness and forgiveness

We can help the client to identify with a character from the Bible. This can be a useful tool for the client to bridge the gap between head and heart. Does any character from the Bible come to your mind? 1 John 1:8-9 may be useful. You could ask the client to read it aloud. Follow with some simple questions. "What does it say about God?" "What are some of the implications for you?" You could suggest that the client read it in the first person. "If I claim to be without sin, I deceive myself and the truth is not in me. If I confess my sin, he is faithful and just and will forgive my sin and cleanse me from all unrighteousness." This kind of identi-fication with Biblical passages can be a powerful healing agent (Green, 1991, 53).

The Bible is full of beautiful verses about God's for-giveness. Psalm 103:12 "He takes our sins farther away/than the east is from the west." This can be brought alive by imagining strongly being on top of a mountain looking into the far distant east. God has sent away my sins as far as my eye can see. Isaiah 43:28 brings home the completeness of His forgiveness. "I it is, I it is, who must blot out everything/ and not remember your sins." Micah 7:19 gives us a prayer: "Once more have pity on us;/tread down our faults,/to the bottom of the sea/throw all our sins." This conjures the picture of our sins being squashed into tiny fragments, which are then scattered over the water, where they sink without trace. Think of a word processor; you press the delete button, and it wipes everything out.

14. Exercises

1. God's forgiveness
Write down on a piece of paper the sins you have committed during your life, and then tear the paper to pieces and burn it. Lots of hymns speak of God's forgiveness. Why not sing such a hymn to yourself or recite it several times, so as to absorb its message.

2. Forgiving oneself
Write down all sinful things in your life, and then forgive yourself for each of these in turn. At the same time, become aware of the good things you have learned from your mistakes. This will remind you of the "O felix culpa" experience expressed in the exultet of Easter Vigil. "O happy fault, which has brought us such a redeemer." The experience of forgiveness often leads to change.

We pray the prayer our Lord taught us: "Forgive us our trespasses, as we forgive those who trespass against us." What does it mean – to forgive? When I feel others have done wrong, I choose not to hold it against them. This is a commitment of my will, although the feelings may pull me in the opposite direction. Jesus stressed the importance of forgiveness. "Yes, if you forgive others their failings, your heavenly Father will forgive you yours; but if you do not forgive others, your Father will not forgive your failings either" (Mt 6:14-15).

In Matthew 18, 21 Peter asks Jesus, "Lord, how often must I forgive my brother if he wrongs me? As often as seven times?" Jesus answered, "Not seven, I tell you, but seventy-seven times."

On the Cross he prayed: "Father, forgive them for they do not know what they are doing." This is astonishing empathy from one who was in such pain. Stephen, the first martyr, also prayed for forgiveness for those who stoned him (Acts 7:60).

SUMMARY:

Jesus' death and God's forgiveness – a reparative experience

- Jesus' death was not merely for individual sins, but for the sinfulness of the whole creation.
- In therapy we are allowing that redeeming power of God to be focused on the client's need.
- Many Christians lack the conviction of God's forgiveness. They need to go through a process of experiencing forgiveness, e.g. exercise with rucksack, or through a visualisation exercise.
- Feelings of guilt often interfere with experiencing God as loving Father.
- There is a need for reparative experience, for reparative relationship.
- The psycho-spiritual counsellor will use God's attributes of love, mercifulness and forgiveness as his/her model.
- We can help the client to identify with suitable Bible characters, for example The Prodigal Son, etc.
- Clients can be encouraged to read 1 John 1:8-9; Psalm 103:12; Isaiah 43:28; Micah 7:19 and other passages. Such reading, reflection, meditation may help our clients to learn to forgive themselves.
- The awareness that we can learn from mistakes or have learned from mistakes is an incentive to forgive ourselves.
- Jesus stressed the importance of forgiveness. He taught us to forgive and to pray for forgiveness.

- Jesus lived forgiveness: "Father, forgive them for they do not know what they are doing."

———

15. Anger and reparative experience

Anger is another area for the reparative relationship. Many clients consider anger to be bad and have therefore learned to suppress and repress it. They need to learn to express anger in a constructive way, neither exploding nor being passive-aggressive. Some may even think anger is sinful and therefore try to get rid of it. But what we do with anger may be reparative. To learn to use the energy of the anger in a constructive and productive way is probably a lifelong process. Let us think of Jesus. He was furious in the temple (Jn 2 13:16). He was angry with the Pharisees for their hypocrisy about Sabbath observance (Mk 3:5). There is anger against injustice and unholiness, and that is righteous anger. There is, however, also unrighteous anger (Eph 4:26). "Even if you are angry, you must not sin: never let the sun set on your anger or else you will give the devil a foothold."

There are several ways of dealing with anger:
1. The stiff upper lip: This is suppression. People keep it inside. It is seen as self-control. However, it leads often to depression or oozes out in criticism.
2. Splattering anger all over the place. As damage is caused by bricks which are thrown through the air, relationships are damaged by this kind of anger. It is easy to express anger inappropriately.
3. Anger can accumulate and lead to regular explosions.
4. Anger can lead to passive-aggressive behaviour.
5. Anger can lead to depression.
6. Anger can become psychosomatic.

We need to look for the real causal feelings underneath the anger, the feelings which cause us to have angry outbursts, e.g. anxiety or fear, and then deal with those. Once that is accomplished, the anger will usually disappear. Peter's angry expression, "I do not know the man!" came from his fear. He found it hard to forgive himself, but Jesus forgave him: he saw through the anger to the root cause.

How did Jesus deal with anger? As we have seen above, he could be very angry. We learn from what he did with his anger. He accepted the Cross. It is through the Cross that we find forgiveness for all our sins, including our sinful anger. It is through the Cross that we find the resources to forgive others for anything that has caused our angry reactions.

Can forgiveness start too soon? Forgiveness is a process. A prayer will not clear away all the feelings. But it is a help. What about anger against God? Even the anger against God needs to be expressed in a constructive way. Many of the psalms take us through the process of expressing anger, and end with a prayer. God will understand our anger. As we express it, we may become aware of many things, and may learn not to blame God for everything. Think of suffering for which we cannot blame any particular person. Our reasoning insists that it must be God's fault. But God created a good world. He put mankind in charge. Human disobedience led to the inherited sin, which we call original sin (a trait or tendency in human nature) and to disruption in the world. Human beings are responsible for it. Genesis 3:18 hints at this: Thorns and thistles would grow. Famine, war, abuse are part of the way the world has been spoilt; they are consequences of human irresponsibility and the misuse of God's gift of free will.

SUMMARY:

Anger and reparative relationship

Anger is another major area for reparative relationship.
Many clients consider anger to be bad or sinful and have learned to repress it.
There are many ways in which people deal with anger:
- Stiff upper lip.
- Splatter anger all over the place.
- Passive aggressive behaviour in its many forms.

- Anger collection and regular explosion.
- Anger may lead to depression.
- Anger may become psychosomatic.
- Anger is often the spontaneous expression of another underlying causal feeling which needs dealing with.

———

16. Exercise

Answer the following in your own words:
1. What can we learn from Jesus as far as dealing with anger is concerned?
2. Can forgiveness start too soon?

17. God's reparative relationship

God made us for a loving relationship with Him. In that relationship He bestows many gifts upon us. In return He looks for our trust and our obedience. Love does not force its own way. It is generous, and it leaves us free to choose. God is deeply aggrieved by sin. It evokes both His righteous anger and His profound compassion, but He has given us the gift of free will, and we are responsible for the way we use it We could ask, "Why does He not do something to intervene?" He has done so. He sent His Son to live and to die for us. This is how God showed His love among us. He sent His one and only Son into the world that we might live through him. "This is the love I mean: not our love for God, but God's love for us when He sent his only Son so that we could have life through him (1 Jn 4:9-10). Jesus died and rose again. Jesus has fully provided for our redemption. We can appropriate his redemption for ourselves by allowing his Spirit to work in us. The Cross is the supreme act of love in history. So what do we do with our anger against God? He does not actually deserve it. However, give Him a chance to respond. Jesus understands our struggle with anger. He struggled in the Garden of Gethsemane. On the Cross he could not understand where the Father was, when he needed Him most: "Why have you forsaken me?" He would have liked the situation to be different. However, at the end Jesus prayed, "Let it be as you not I would have it" (Mk 14:36).

18. The reparative effect of laughter

We can distinguish between different types of laughter:

The head laughter – This is based on the intellect, on wit. This is witty laughter, which is usually dependent on verbal or physical jokes. It is often experienced as cynical, sarcastic, in which case it is divisive. It separates. You understand it or you don't. You are either party to it or you are not. If used with informed discretion, it can be healing.

Hearty laughter comes from our emotional responses. When it is good, it is spontaneous, warm, understanding. However, it can also be cruel and malicious. It can be blue and obscene. It too can be divisive. It can be heartening or disheartening. However, this kind of laughter too can be healing if used with awareness and discretion.

Gut or **belly laughter** comes from the guts. It is wholesome and contagious. It is trusting, inclusive, There is nothing divisive in it. It is hospitable, liberating, healing. It binds people together, if used in the right context.

The great masters of the spiritual life recommend laughter. Did Jesus laugh? He was full of humour. It came out in a sense of the ridiculous, the fantastic, or the paradoxical. – in his proposition that a man might not be of more value than a sheep or a sparrow (Mt 10, 31) – Man being compared to a wandering fox, aimless and lost, that "decides" not to make a lair (Mt 8:20) – The idea of a mulberry tree being whisked into the centre of the sea to grow (Lk 17:6) – The contrast between the lily and Solomon.

What are some of the effects of healing laughter?

1. The functions of the mind are reinforced, because healthy laughter begins in the mind as a shared response.
2. The extra deep breaths induced by belly-laughter will increase the intake of oxygen. Fresh energy is spread throughout the body.
3. The parasympathetic nervous system releases endorphins and polypeptides responsible for feeling good and feeling loving.
4. Laughter dissipates negative emotions and enlarges optimism, even where problems seem insoluble.
5. The extra muscular activity speeds up the circulation of all fluids in the body; blood goes round more efficiently; digestion is improved, and the excretion of toxins is advanced.

Besides the purely physical effects which healthy laughter has on the body, there are numerous psychological reparative effects. Let us think of a very serious family, where laughter and smiles are experienced as threats and therefore not permitted. Members of such families have a deficit, which can be repaired through laughter in the therapeutic setting. From my experience with a co-therapist who has a gift of healthy laughter, I know how therapeutic laughter can be if used appropriately.

SUMMARY:

The reparative effect of laughter:
There are different types of laughter:
  • The head laughter
  • The hearty laughter
  • Gut or belly laughter

The great masters of the spiritual life recommend laughter. Did Jesus laugh?

Some effects of healing laughter:
  • Reinforcement of the functions of the mind.
  • Increase of oxygen.

- Release of endorphins and polypeptides with psychological effects of wellbeing.
- Dissipation of negative emotions.
- Speeding up of the circulation of all fluids in the body.
- Numerous psychological reparative effects.

———

19. Criteria for evaluating the effectiveness of the reparative relationship

The various components of reparative relationship are all intended to provide the client with a new beginning.

Balint (1989), using largely psychodynamic language, listed the following points, which he thought were characteristic for a new beginning:

1. During the increase of tension, that is before the gratification of the urge, most impressive and noisy symptoms appear. Then a sudden change sets in. This results in the feeling of a tranquil, quiet wellbeing which, if not carefully observed, may go unnoticed.

2. Intensity of gratification of the newly begun activities never reaches end-pleasure levels.

3. All new beginnings happen in the transference, that is, in an object relationship. They lead to a changed relationship to the patient's objects of love and hate and, in consequence, to a considerable diminution of anxiety.

4. Many new beginnings also lead to a character change, or to what would be clinically described nowadays as a change in the ego, for example the ego may become devoted to the service of other people.

And lastly, the most important:

5. New beginning means: a. going back to something "primitive", to a point before the faulty development started, which could be described as a regression, and b. at the same time, discovering a new, better-suited way

which amounts to a progression. In his book *Thrills and Regressions* (1959) Balint called the sum total of these two basic phenomena: regression for the sake of progression (Balint, 1989, 132).

Working within the transference relationship, and within the developmentally needed relationship cannot be done simultaneously. In the transference relationship we highlight or explicate a past pattern or relationship. In the developmentally needed relationship we introduce or explore a new interpersonal experience. Usually, the reparative or developmentally needed relationship can only be effective if the transference is either permanently resolved or temporarily in remission. For either of these relationships we need an intact working alliance. This working alliance needs to be capable of sustaining the crisis of confidence, fear, and potential satisfaction, which follows upon a renewed resolution of life's developmental and existential crises.

Some important questions arise: Can the client assume self-responsibility? Can the client generalise outside the therapeutic setting?

Here is a summary of criteria for the effectiveness of a reparative relationship: appropriateness, timeliness, intactness of the working alliance, neutralisation of transference/countertransference phenomena, generalisability and utility to other relationships, intrapsychic restructuring, increased adult effectiveness, enhanced stability under stress, establishment of intrapsychic nurturing, freedom and spontaneity in current relationships, enhanced capacity for imagination and creativity.

We need to watch out for an untherapeutic gratification of either the client's or the therapist's desire. We also need to ensure that we do not infantilise our clients. In all this, we need to keep in mind that there is no clear and established theory that affirms a linear or causal connection between childhood experiences and adult lives. Chaos and complexity theory put before us the possibility that a very small intervention can have unpredictable results.

SUMMARY:

Criteria for evaluating the effectiveness of the reparative relationship

Balint listed the following characteristic points for a new beginning:

- Tension, combined with impressive and noisy symptoms, changes to a feeling of tranquil, quiet well-being.
- Gratification of newly begun activities never reaches end-pleasure levels, because change takes place, often within the ego.
- All new beginnings happen in the transference and lead to a changed relationship, recognised by a diminution of anxiety.
- Many beginnings lead to character change.
- Regression for the sake of progression.

When is reparative work possible?
- When there is a good working alliance.
- We cannot work simultaneously within the transference relationship and within the developmentally needed relationship.

Clarkson summarises the criteria for an effective reparative relationship:

- Appropriateness
- Timeliness
- Intactness of the working alliance
- Neutralisation of the transference/countertransference phenomena
- Generalisibility to other relationships
- Utility to other relationships
- Intrapsychic restructuring
- Increased adult effectiveness
- Establishment of intrapsychic nurturing
- Enhanced stability under stress
- Freedom and spontaneity in current relationships
- Enhanced capacity for imagination and creativity

Watch out for:
- Untherapeutic gratification in the client
- Possible infantilisation of clients

———

20. Exercise

Make notes in response to these questions (then refer back to this chapter to discover what you have forgotten or not fully understood)

1. What is the difference between the reparative and the developmentally needed relationship?
2. How can we make sure that our provision of a reparative experience is not wasted?
3. What are some of the areas where you yourself need to work with the developmentally needed relationship?
4. In which areas do you need the reparative relationship?
5. How do you know whether the reparative work you do is successful and effective?
6. Why and when is there a need for reparative work?
7. What do you need to know to carry out reparative work with a client?
8. Give some criteria for evaluating the effectiveness of the reparative relationship.
9. What do you need to watch out for when you use the reparative relationship?
10. How can we do reparative work with the emotion of anger?
11. What is necessary to manage and maintain the reparative relationship?
12. What is it that you must not do, during reparative work, without proper care?
14. What is the heart of the reparative relationship?
15. What are some of the skills needed for the reparative relationship?

21. Three case studies of the reparative and the developmentally needed relationship

1. JOE is a Chinese priest, aged 55. He is a member of a religious congregation. He has been working in his own

country all his priestly life. In the first session the contract was discussed. He and his female trainee counsellor agreed to meet every week on Friday from 4.00 to 4.50 p.m. in the counsellor's house.

Three years ago Joe's mother had moved to Australia to live in her married son's house, which had a granny flat attached to it. Joe went to visit her for two months during his vacation. He noticed that her health had deteriorated. She mentioned repeatedly that this was the last time she would see him. He tried to distract her from this premonition, and would not talk about her death. Joe returned to China. A few months later, his mother died. It was impossible for him to go to the funeral. Joe now feels very guilty that he never said goodbye to her.

As Joe told his story, the counsellor listened empathically. She asked him how he would like to deal with his guilt. This was a question that betrayed some inexperience in the counsellor, because if Joe had known this, he would have done it without counselling. However, his reply was clear; he said that he would have liked to have allowed his mother to say what she wanted to say, and he wished he had said goodbye to her. The counsellor asked him how he would like to do that now. Again, it might have been better to draw this out of the client, rather than eliciting the answer through a direct question. He was not confused, but might have been. Joe chose to speak to his mother on her sickbed, imagining her to be on a couch. He placed a symbol of his mother on the couch. He shed many tears and told her that he regretted not giving her the opportunity to say what she wanted to say. His mother understood him and gave him her blessing. Joe then thanked his mother for all she had been and done for him. Joe then bade his mother goodbye and felt free in himself about letting her go. There were a few moments of silence after this. Then Joe said that he felt that a load had been lifted from his heart. The counsellor affirmed him for his courage in facing his pain.

There is a problem with this. Joe's suffering has been quickly bandaged. There is something of a "quick fix" about the trainee counsellor's methods. Joe has not really been

206

helped to face his pain, because the relationship has been left 'in the head'. It is almost certain to return. Working through presenting material, underlying feelings and forgiveness, is a process which takes time. This case study demonstrates a stage in the counsellor's training; the techniques are laudable, but they are applied without either counsellor or client having time to reflect or accumulate an understanding of Joe's material.

2. MARY is a 48-year-old Korean and has belonged to a religious congregation for nearly thirty years. She has been involved in various ministries in her Congregation including teaching, community co-ordination, youth ministry and Parish Catechesis.

In the first session the counsellor and client discussed the contract, and agreed that they would meet every Wednesday from 2.00 to 2.50 p.m. in the counsellor's office. Mary is an only child. When she was two years old her father was killed in war. She has no memory of him. Mary and her mother moved to the town where her mother found work in a factory run by Sisters. She took Mary to work with her. Mary was alone among the adults, some of whom were very kind to her, whilst others teased her, so that she felt frightened of them. Her mother was very strict with Mary. When she went to school, her mother never allowed her to visit her friends' homes. She fed and clothed her, but never showed any affection for her.

When she began her course of therapy, Mary was obviously very timid and feeling lonely. The counsellor was aware that a clear working alliance would help her feel accepted, understood and supported by the counsellor. She shed many tears as she related her story.

After working with Mary on her past experiences for a couple of sessions, the counsellor suggested that the lonely little child was still alive in her, and asked Mary what she would like to tell her inner child. Her spontaneous response was, "That I love her." The counsellor invited her to choose a symbol for her inner child from among the objects in her office. She chose a teddy bear. She held the teddy in both hands, as the counsellor asked her to tell her inner child whatever she wanted. She spoke very warmly saying: "I love you. You need not be afraid. I will cover you with love. I will not leave you on your own. I am your mother". When asked how the child felt, Mary replied, "Happier, but she does not trust much yet." She continued to hold the teddy in her arms for the remainder of the session. The counsellor encouraged her to find a symbol of her inner child, and to spend some time each day in the inner child's company, so that she could continue to be a mother to her; in this way, the counsellor said, her inner child would learn to trust her more. Towards the end of the session the counsellor invited her to return the teddy, which the counsellor held reassuringly in her own arms, until Mary had left the room. It was in this session that Mary connected with her inner child for the first time.

In the following sessions, and outside the sessions, Mary learned to be a nurturing parent for her inner child, whom she has begun to free. Mary is much less shy than she was, and feels much more at home with herself. She no longer feels the loneliness she experienced when she first came for counselling. She has learned to build up her trust, which she could not do as an infant.

3.   ELISABETH, a woman of 30, of African background, came to me for counselling because she felt that she did not want to live. These thoughts were frequently with her. She had no suicidal thoughts, but felt it was not worth going on living. I explored her childhood. She came from a very broken background. Her parents did not bother about her. There were six children. Her oldest sister gave her some attention, but suffered herself from the lack of care within the family. Alcohol was an enormous problem in the family. Elisabeth experienced much violence right from her early age. She never received any affirmation in the family or at school. She had to work hard at home, for she was looking for constant affirmation from her older sister. At school she was tired and could not concentrate. Elisabeth thought she was very stupid and blamed herself for everything that went wrong. She had learned to do that in the family. She had also learned from

her parents that she was to be blamed for many things that went wrong in the family.

I noticed that there was much work to be done with regard to the reparative relationship. Much damage done in the family needed to be repaired. There was a great lack of affirmation and as a consequence Elisabeth had developed an extremely low self-concept. She was very thin and, therefore, despised her body. Although she lived in England, she still had the cultural mentality that a girl should be fat. This body-concept affected her self-concept development. I focused her straight away on to how different cultures see and experience the body with regard to being fat or thin. Her body in the culture of Great Britain would be considered as beautiful, but her aunty had always referred to her as ugly as far back as she could remember and had shown that she did not like her. She had a great need to be liked by people, particularly by her aunty. I asked her to read about beautiful bodies in magazines.

Next time she came for her session, she smiled and said that actually her body would be considered as beautiful in this country. I affirmed her constantly on the beauty of her body. She could not take it at first, but after some time she accepted the compliments and became slowly proud of her figure. This showed itself the way she dressed. First she had tried to cover her body and make it look fat. Now she showed more and more of her figure. She started feeling better about herself generally. She was working in a big supermarket. Because she was becoming more self-confident, she was promoted after three months of counselling. I used every opportunity to affirm her in any way possible. Her confidence grew more and more.

After five months of counselling, I thought it was enough for her to carry on her own process and we terminated our counselling contract, since her life energy was growing more and more and she enjoyed life. She did not say any more that she did not want to live or that she was worthless. In fact, she enjoyed life, her work, her co-workers and even swimming. I encouraged her to go swimming. My idea was that she had to expose her body and could no longer hide it. This speeded up the process of counselling considerably. Once she realised how much her body image had affected her self-image she was prepared to undo the damage and use every opportunity to work on herself. She went for a swim as often as she could and enjoyed it more and more. Much reparative work was done. Obviously the work was not finished; however, she felt much better and was happy to terminate, because she knew how to carry on the process. One of my goals in counselling is to show clients a way forward into a happier future rather than finishing every aspect of the therapeutic work. My work as a counsellor consists in enabling my clients to carry on their own process.

CHAPTER SEVEN

The person-to-person *or* I–You relationship

1. What is the person-to-person relationship? 2. The destructive use of the person-to-person relationship 3. The constructive use of the person-to-person relationship 4. Discernment in the use of the person-to-person relationship 5. Self-disclosure 6. I–You relationship and object relationship 7. Further aspects of the I–You relationship 8. How to establish the person-to-person relationship 9. How to manage the person-to-person relationship? 10. When do we use the person-to-person relationship? 11. Distinction between person-to-person responses and countertransference responses 12. Failures as opportunities for breakthrough 13. Criteria for evaluating effectiveness of the person-to-person relationship 14. Exercise 15. Two case studies of the I–You relationship

1. What is the person-to-person relationship?

As we have described, there are at least five different kinds, or aspects, of therapeutic relationship. Sometimes, all these different aspects are required during a counselling session, but it is very rare that they will all be required simultaneously. While they are all potentially there at every session, and during every part of therapy, you can only pay particular attention to one or two aspects at any one time, just as you can only say one or two things at a time. During psychotherapy, you can usually tell which aspect of relationship is developing between you and the client. You can know from any two transactions which relationship is active. In this chapter, we explore the therapist as a person, relating to the client as a person.

The person-to-person relationship is sometimes referred to as a dialogic relationship. Sometimes it is called the existential relationship or the real relationship. It is also known as the core relationship, or as the I–You relationship, which in the deepest transcendent state becomes a "We" relationship. All these terms refer to the person-to-person aspect of the client/counsellor relationship. Here, we do not have a client asking for treatment, or a counsellor making a working alliance. We have two *persons* engaging in a relationship. The person-to-person relationship occurs within what are usually called "encounters".

SUMMARY:

What is the person-to-person relationship?
It is also called:
* Dialogic relationship
* Existential relationship
* Core relationship
* I–You relationship

———

2. The destructive use of the person-to-person relationship

For some people, having the therapist in a person-to-person relationship is very destructive. I will give you an example. Say a girl had grown up in a family where she had an over intimate relationship with her mother: the mother had told the child when she was only seven that the father was unsatisfactory in bed. This child has been used as a substitute for an adult listener, or even for the other parent. She has been burdened by someone in a parental position, who has abused her through over-intimacy.

What can we as counsellors do for such victims? Do we need to tell them all about ourselves? No! If we let them know all about ourselves, we are only going to traumatise them again, and we will not be able to give them any kind of new experience. Will they want to accept us without telling them our private history? No! They are under the impression that we have to tell them all about ourselves, so that they can feel that they are good children/clients. This presents the counsellor with a predicament.

Say this girl, now grown-up, comes to me for therapy. I warn her that I can imagine it will be very hard for us to form a working alliance. I might elaborate, as follows: "Unless you have reached the level of over-intimacy with me that you had with your mother, you probably won't feel that I really care about you. But our goal in therapy is for you to learn that it *is* possible for you to have an intimate relationship with another person, without its being sexual, and without its being over-intimate. Now, I know that it's going to be hard to reach that stage, and I know there are going to be times when you feel that I don't care about you. This will be partly because I am *not* giving you what your mother gave you. Are we going to decide to stick together in this, in order to arrive at a completely different way for you to approach close relationships?"

You can sense the nature of this different way. The young woman had to learn to tolerate intimacy, without being able to possess or colonise me, and without my needing to share my private life with her so that she could feel she was being a good client/child. Self-disclosure, knowing about my personal life, would be really very destructive, because it would inevitably repeat the transference trauma. So we began to create a completely different relationship.

SUMMARY:

The destructive use of the person-to-person relationship

- For some clients, the use of the person-to-person relationship can be destructive. Such clients were drawn into adult intimacy as children to support one parent over against the other. It may be difficult to establish a working alliance with such clients.
- "I, as a counsellor am not going to give you what your mother or father gave you." Self-disclosure of a counsellor in such situations is destructive.

———

3. The constructive use of the person-to-person relationship

Here is a typical case. The client's parents never seemed to be available, or they never shared anything with their children; when there was something important, they always went off into another room. They never fought or disagreed.

The child knew nothing of what was going on in the family, and felt completely excluded. I have met some adults who were so excluded from the parental pair that they have been really damaged by it, but this is not very common. A client with this background may want to know something about you. It may be very important for such a person that, when s/he comes in and says, "You look a little bit tired today", you do not say, "Now, we are not here to talk about me, we are here to talk about you." That may seem insulting; it will seem particularly so, if the client is coming from a child's perspective, which requires a real answer, with genuine information, to prove that the client is not mad or excluded. This is quite different from a client telling you that you look tired, so as to control you, because that is the way they controlled their parents. In such a case, you would not give them any self-disclosure. Self-disclosure is a very delicate thing that can be exactly right for one person or moment, but exactly wrong and destructive for another person or at a particular moment. In this instance of the client saying, "You look a bit tired", it is quite true that you are there "to talk about the client, not about yourself", but it is probably worth giving a very brief response to the comment, before moving on to: "And how are *you*?" Do not lay yourself open to role-reversal.

I told one client with this kind of child's perspective, that I had been burgled the night before, because that was just the kind of information that her parents had kept from her. We had the kind of working relationship that meant it was really important for her to know that about me. It counteracted her emotional memory of being called mad, when she called her father drunk – when he actually had been drunk, though everybody else said he wasn't. That is the kind of clinical rationale that I am talking about. If you watched such and such a game on TV last night and that comes out in your session, you will have a very good reason for mentioning it. Obviously, there is a difference between self-disclosure in terms of "I want to tell you about myself" and "I want to tell you about myself in order that it will be of benefit to you".

4. Discernment in the use of the person-to-person relationship

So, sometimes we would say something about ourselves, and at other times we wouldn't. The decision is not as simple as whether to self-disclose or not to self-disclose. It has to do with what that particular client needs at that moment in terms of relationship, the particular goal towards which s/he is working, and the stage in life that the client has reached. My own agenda is bound to be part of this. So we are looking at a person-to-person relationship, and its appropriate use.

It has to do with the way in which we are all subject to the pain, the confusion, the anguish and the frustration of life. All of us are wounded, and all of us are hurt, all of us become angry, all of us get confused, and all of us get despairing from time to time. I think that, to the extent that we are familiar with these very painful places of being human, to that same extent we can offer ourselves as enablers or facilitators for other people.

Some think that counsellors have everything, as it were, ready-made. Not so. We have our own particular, even peculiar ways of learning or enduring or sustaining, and of needing people to accompany us in existential difficulties; we are not being "better" than our clients. In this respect, there can be a great idealisation of the therapist: that s/he never gets confused, and has never really had to work through her/his issues. This is not true. It is to be hoped that every counsellor has worked on him/herself, and is aware of his/her woundedness. We have a certain relationship that is based on our humanness, which we can use either indirectly or overtly, and it is entirely dependent on what the client needs. At no point – and this is an absolute – do I think it is ethical for a counsellor to disclose anything at all about him or herself during therapy, unless it can be justified with a clinical rationale.

Counselling is the intentional use of relationship for the benefit of the client; unless I can see or hear this benefit being conferred, I think self-disclosure falls outside the ethical arena. Of course, this is a paradox. Although the counsellor and the client are different, they are on a more or less equal standing as human beings, and they share the same ambivalent and ambiguous legacy of existence. Do you really think that you can engage with any other human being for longer than two seconds without having disclosed yourself? You can't help it. There is an enormous amount of communication that we are presenting all the time to other people, e.g. treat me like this, this is my education, this is my background, this is where I come from, and this is my psychology. We have a certain way in which we deport ourselves, the way we hold our heads; we have the light in our eyes, the slope of our handwriting, our fingerprints, our hairstyles. All of this is in the public domain. We can't hide it.

SUMMARY:

Discernment in the use of the person-to-person relationship
- What does the client need at this moment?
- Being aware of our woundedness prepares us to become facilitators of other people's growth.
- At no time is it ethical for the counsellor to disclose anything about himself or herself, unless there is a clinical rationale.
- Counselling is an intentional relationship for the benefit of the client.
- We unavoidably self-disclose many things in many ways to our clients.

———

5. Self-disclosure

Scientifically, we have discovered that most of our communication occurs not so much through the words that we say, as through the way in which we say them, through what we see in the features of the person or people to whom we are talking, and through the atmosphere created by an encounter. We take in an enormous amount through our noses! The nose is the most primitive organ that we have, and it is directly related to our emotions, and it works far faster than other cognition or words. You know how a certain food or taste can take you right back. A hot day filled with the scent of eucalyptus, or a winter's day in town with the smell of roasting chestnuts, such smells can transport you back into the past.

When information about your personality, through touch, smell, and sight, is instantly available and in many cases undeniable, it may seem odd to say that you must not self-disclose. More accurately, what we would say is this. We communicate with each other much more than we realise. We can send contradictory messages, both verbally and non-verbally. You should be aware that you cannot help disclosing a great deal about yourself, but you must be careful how you describe this verbally, and how you choose which facts, stories, or anecdotes to relate about yourself. Only self-disclose verbally when it is in the client's best interests for you to do so.

Ambivalence of self-disclosure

The real or I–You relationship is that aspect of the therapeutic relationship, which focuses on the counsellor or formator's personal feelings, values, attitudes. It usually concerns private or undisclosed feelings, values and attitudes. This may involve such delight as that found in friends marrying, in discovering that water has been miraculously transformed into wine for the wedding celebration, or it might be a very private grief. Sometimes, judicious sharing of such person-to person feelings can be very beneficial to the counselling work, but sometimes it can be very damaging.

SUMMARY:
Ambivalence of self-disclosure

- The I–You relationship is that aspect of the therapeutic relationship which focuses on the counsellor or formator's feelings, values, attitudes.

- It usually concerns private, undisclosed feelings, values, attitudes.

- Sometimes, judicious sharing of such feelings may be beneficial to counselling or formation work, but at other times it can be very destructive.

—

Where in Kofler's personality model does the person-to-person relationship take place?

Always from the middle self of the counsellor to the middle self of the client. At the same time, it has to be remembered, as has been said several times in connection with these diagrams, that the three "selves" are not separate entities; integration is always the ultimate aim.

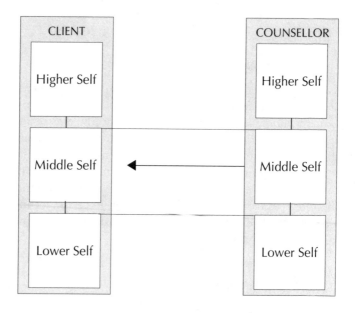

CLIENT	COUNSELLOR
Higher Self	Higher Self
Middle Self ←	Middle Self
Lower Self	Lower Self

6. I–You relationship and object relationship

The I–You relationship is also called the real relationship or the core relationship. Many people probably experience this relationship as being healing in normal human encounters.

Generally we are not aware how much healing happens in ordinary conversations and encounters between people. The I–You relationship is the opposite of an object relationship. For Buber (1970, 55) the other is a person, not an object:

> Whoever says You does not have something for his object. For wherever there is something there is also another something; every It borders on other Its. It is only by virtue of bordering on others. But where You is said, there is no something. You has no borders. Whoever says You does not have something; he has nothing. But he stands in relation.

In this relationship, then, counsellor and client stand in a kind of mutuality to each other, both stand as person-to-person. In the immediacy of the existential encounter, the mutuality is almost complete. The self of the therapist becomes the instrument through which healing evolves. For example, take an intuitive, introverted type of client, who has difficulty telling right from left. The female psychotherapist bends down to show the scar on her own left leg, which she used as a little girl to help her differentiate it from her right leg. This therapist has taken responsibility for self-disclosure. She has judged it appropriate and timely to trust the patient with a sense of shared personhood. The result is that the two have become "siblings" in the quest for wholeness.

SUMMARY:

The I–You relationship and object relationship

- The I–You relationship is the opposite of an object relationship.
- In this relationship counsellor and client stand in a kind of mutuality to each other.
- In the immediacy of the existential encounter, the mutuality is almost complete.
- The self of the therapist becomes the instrument through which healing evolves.

———

Self-disclosure must be done with care

Self-disclosure needs to be done with great care, otherwise it can become abusive. It could be an excuse for inauthentic acting-out of the psychotherapist's own need, in terms of display, hostility or seductiveness.

Genuine, well-judged use of the I–You relationship is probably one of the most difficult forms of therapeutic relating. It requires the most skill, the most self-knowledge and the greatest care. Its potential for careless or destructive use is great. There is always a danger of falling into a friendship, rather than maintaining a professional, therapeutic relationship.

The use of the I–You relationship in various counselling approaches

The I–You relationship is characterised by the here-and-now, existential encounter between two people. The process involves mutual participation. It involves recognition that each will be changed by the other. Its field is not object relations, but subject relations. The real person of the psychotherapist can never be totally excluded from the interaction between the client and him/herself. Existential psychotherapy (Boss, 1963) specifically includes the I–You genuine encounters as a major therapeutic modality.

Guntrip (1961) saw the real personal relationship between client and analyst as "the" psychotherapeutic factor, on which all other factors depend. For Guntrip, true psychotherapy only happens when the therapist and client find the person behind each other's defences.

Fairbairn (1952) points out that deep insight develops only inside a good therapeutic relationship. The "moment of real meeting" is therapeutic. This encounter is transforming for both psychotherapist and patient. It is a genuine experience of relationship centred in the here-and-now.

For Rogers, the establishment of a relationship of genuineness, respect and empathy becomes the central factor for facilitating human growth and development. The psychotherapist provides the client with a model of authentic being with which he can identify. Such authenticity may mean that the therapeutic relationship changes the therapist as much as the client. Psychotherapists must like their clients; prolonged dislike or lack of interest as well as too strong a love will interfere with therapy. Hence the need for supervision and counsellor's own therapy, and also the possibility of ultimate referral. Psychotherapists and counsellors, though, must wish to help and cure their clients; they must be concerned with the client's welfare. The kinship quality of the person-to-person relationship is similar to that of siblings – the shared empathic understanding from a similar, inherited frame of reference.

7. Further aspects of the I–You relationship

The person-to-person relationship may begin to emerge and deepen towards the end of the therapeutic process. The real relationship incorporates, on both sides, appropriate and realistic perceptions and interpretations of the other's behaviour. The feelings are genuine, the behaviour is congruent.

This relationship may have two aspects. One is "impersonal" or non-intimate and yet still real. The other is more intimate and personal. Both these aspects are important. They need to be attended to and used appropriately.

The "impersonal" aspect of the real relationship may include conversation about topics not directly related to the counselling process, yet of interest to the client or connected with the client's general welfare. The more "intimate" aspect includes personalised and feeling messages: "I feel sad when you talk about your mother's death." "I really enjoy counselling you." "I appreciate your open sharing." There are some comments of this kind that are open to misinterpretation or that may seem to invite a reversal of roles. For instance, a statement such as, "I get angry when you blame me" might come, or seem to come from the therapist's own problem. In such a case, it might be better to simply explore the "blame", so that the client does not have to deal with the counsellor's anger. Intimacy still requires professional caution.

Empathy and genuine congruence play an important part in the person-to-person relationship. It is a difficult transition to move from the developmentally needed or reparative relationship to the person-to-person relationship. This transition may happen between one transaction and another. It may happen early in the therapeutic process. It can happen in an emergency.

In some forms of therapy, the person-to-person relationship may be blocked. Some psychoanalysts and some formators in the past have tried to keep aloof and disclose nothing of themselves. The person of the psychoanalyst or formator was supposed to be hidden or at least to be obscured. Let alone that this is probably impossible to achieve, such therapists were probably unaware of one of the most potent factors in the healing process. "The therapist helps to heal by developing a genuine relationship with the client" (Yalom, 1980, 405). A client has the right to expect, as far as is reasonable, a person-to-person relationship, on a friendly basis. Part of the paradox of counselling, however, is that it is nevertheless a professional therapeutic relationship, so that, while in this relationship, "being friendly" must not become friendship.

We need to work through the expectation clients have, as far as their relationship with the therapist is concerned. It could be they hope for an intimate friend, a blank screen, or even a sexual love affair. It is important that the therapy session is an opportunity for the client to learn how to relate to the therapist or counsellor. S/he may learn from the manner, style, jokes, the unsaid, and from the atmosphere in the counselling room.

SUMMARY:
Some aspects of the I–You relationship
- It may emerge towards the end of the therapeutic process.
- The person-to-person relationship may have two aspects:

- One is "impersonal"
- The other is "personal"

- The "impersonal" may include conversation on topics not directly concerned with the counselling process.
- The "personal" includes personalised and feeling messages.
- Empathy and genuine congruence play an important part in the person-to-person relationship.
- Clients may expect too close a relationship with the counsellor.
- We need to work through the expectations that clients have with regard to the client/counsellor relationship.

———

8. How to establish the person-to-person relationship

There are several important factors:

1. There need to be appropriate expectations. The client may expect that the therapist will tell him what to do. The client may be under the impression that it is the job of the counsellor to heal him, whilst s/he is very passive.

2. The client's need to repair or replenish past deficits or injuries. This need has to be met in a way which will enhance future growth, development, and resilience to life's struggles.

3. The psychotherapist's own sense of him or herself as a person of authenticity and integrity. This must not be based only on self-assessment. It must also be based on the experience and feedback of significant others such as psychotherapists and supervisors.

4. Fears, training, supervision and limitations which the therapist brings to the session will influence the establishment of the person-to-person relationship.

How to establish the person-to-person relationship

Several factors are important:

1. Appropriate expectations.
2. The organismic need to repair or replenish past deficits or injuries.
3. The therapist's own self-awareness as a person of authenticity and integrity.
4. The fears, training, supervision and limitations which the counsellor brings to the session.

———

9. How to manage the person-to-person relationship

We make a clinical decision to have a person-to-person dialogue. It needs to be an authentic response to the client's need. The person-to-person relationship is often characterised by small exchanges. The therapist can set up person-to-person interventions by being authentically self-disclosing. S/he may do this at the beginning of therapy, when the client idealises the therapist or assumes unrealistic attitudes/qualities in the psychotherapist, who may respond with limited self-disclosure:

Client: "You are always punctual."
Therapist: "Most of the time!"

The psychotherapist replies with a small measure of self-disclosure and does not burden the client with details. Bugental (1987, 143-4) offers the following guidelines for therapist disclosure:

1. Strict honesty is required, and therefore therapists must not distort the information given to clients.
2. Therapists have a right to their own privacy.
3. Disclosure of process responses is usually suitable. This may include feelings and thoughts about the way the work is going.

4. Disclosure of hostile, resentful, punitive, erotic, seductive and competitive feelings in relation to the client – these are the therapist's "own stuff" to work through, and there is rarely any need to burden the client with them. The therapist must take time to examine as fully as possible his/her own needs, motives and intentions. If these feelings are very strong, the therapist should take the matter to supervision.

The therapist experiments with self-disclosure, and monitors the reactions of the client to the self-disclosure. The reaction can be understood as helping to diagnose the client's needs. For example, if the client ignores the counsellor's self-disclosure, this may indicate that at this point the person-to-person relationship is not what the client wants or needs: s/he needs an empathic, mirroring relationship, where attention is centred almost exclusively on him/her, to the extent that self-disclosure is a waste of effort. S/he may need repair work for a deficit of mirroring in early childhood.

Then again, if the client ignores self-disclosure, it might show that s/he has difficulties coping with the mutual exchange of intimacy. It may indicate an unhealthy kind of narcissism, especially if the ignoring of mutuality is persistent. It may also indicate extreme personal neediness. It is very important for the counsellor to keep remembering that self-disclosure needs to be there, only if it is helpful to the client. In any case, we are disclosing ourselves in all sorts of ways, through body language or tone of voice: this may be sufficient.

Any exchange regarding values must come from the person-to-person relationship. Potential clients should be able to get information about the therapist's values, because they need to be able to make a judgement about the appropriateness of the potential therapeutic relationship with the counsellor.

SUMMARY:

How can we use and manage the person-to-person relationship?

- We make a clinical decision to have a person-to-person relationship.
- The counsellor makes interventions, which are authentically and appropriately self-disclosing.
- This may be done at the beginning, to help the client not to idealise the counsellor.
- The counsellor should only use a small amount of self-disclosure, which does not burden the client with details. It needs to be used integratively and naturally.

Bugental (1987) gives the following guidelines for self-disclosure:

- Strict honesty.
- The counsellor has a right to privacy.
- Disclosure of process response is usually suitable.
- Disclosure of hostile, resentful, punitive, erotic, seductive and competitive feelings in relation to the client is very rarely necessary. When it does become so, the counsellor should first check with the supervisor.
- The counsellor experiments with self-disclosure and monitors the reactions of the client to self-disclosure.

————

10. When do we use the person-to-person relationship?

1. The decision to use the person-to-person relationship is geared to the diagnosed needs of the client.
2. It is geared to the stage of psychotherapy. Greater self-disclosure is possible as psychotherapy proceeds.
3. It is geared to fundamental existential experiences, like shock and pain after the death of a parent.
4. Some person-to-person relationship is very important at the beginning of therapy. The counsellor needs to establish

boundaries, particularly with clients who tend to "act out". It may be necessary to define specific boundaries. A counsellor might decide, for instance, to emphasise the element of time in the working alliance. There is no need for threats or warnings. Something like, "I shall always try to be punctual, and I'm sure that you will try to be so as well" meets the requirement of the person-to-person relationship, as well as of the working alliance, and indeed of the developmentally needed relationship. It seems to me that all three of these relationships already meet at such an early moment.

How can I know which relationship I am primarily working in, while aiming at integration?

Here is a checklist for recognising which relationship I am primarily working in, or which relationship I wish to work in:

1. What am I aiming for? Integration. What do I believe the client is aiming at?
2. What ego state am I aiming at for the client?
3. What kind of response am I receiving from the client?
4. What is the goal of therapy at this stage?
5. What is my organismic experience in the relationship at this moment? That is to say: Do I feel like a parent? Do I feel like myself? Do I feel as if someone is boxing me into a particular projection?
6. How is the client experiencing our relationship at the moment?
7. Which stage of treatment are we in now? Where are we in the therapeutic journey?
8. Am I repeating an interpersonal relationship from the client's past, or am I providing the exact opposite of a past relationship?
9. Am I authentically responding to the client as person-to-person?
10. Am I aware of any aspects of the transpersonal relationship that need attention?
11. What problems am I experiencing with the client?
12. What feelings are being expressed by the client's body language? Will body work be helpful at this stage?

SUMMARY:
When do we use the person-to-person relationship?
- When it is geared to the diagnosed needs of the client.
- When it is geared to a particular stage of counselling.
- When it is geared to the basic existential experiences like shock or pain after the death of a friend, etc.
- Some person-to-person relationship is important at the beginning of counselling.

———

11. Distinction between person-to-person and countertransference responses

How do you distinguish the person-to-person responses from proactive and reactive countertransference? When is it beneficial to share your personal reaction, and when is it counter-productive to do so? When should you provide the client with personal feedback about their behaviour, and when should you not do this?

The therapist's feelings and emotional responses can be of three primary kinds:

1. Proactive countertransference.
2. Reactive countertransference.
3. Autonomous, separate, independent here-and-now feelings and emotions.

What we are saying is that there are person-to-person responses, feelings, attitudes, and tastes, which are not basically countertransferential. For instance, a client may develop the habit of making sarcastic jokes about the counselling process; you go through the possible clinical options:

Is this how one of his/her parents responded?
Is this how s/he got attention in the family?
Is this a re-enactment of another relationship?
Is this how I feel – people don't take me seriously?

Is this his how I wanted to behave to people in my family?

You realise that some of these may be relevant. At an intuitive level, however, you discern that what is being called for, is a person-to-person response, because the client has never received an accurate reflection of his/her behaviour or personality. The client needs information about the way that s/he impacts other people. So, when the time seems ripe, you might be tempted to say, "Look here, I am irritated; I think your sarcasm in this situation amounts to inappropriate behaviour." This response, you hope, will begin to open the client's eyes to his/her impaired attitude. It is probable, however, that such directness will call up the client's defences. It might be better to suggest, rather than tell: "an we just look at your response for a moment. How were you feeling when you said that?" This should lead to a subjective exploration of the client's feelings behind the sarcasm. It might lead you to ask, "Is that how you sometimes respond to other people?" This in turn might allow you to ask, "So how do you think I might have felt, when you responded in that way?" This longer process should allow the client to deal with the cause of his/her behaviour and lead to the desire to change it.

To reiterate, person-to-person is an adult-to-adult, here-and-now relationship. Proactive countertransference is an invasion of the therapists' own past material into the therapeutic relationship. Reactive countertransference is the provocation of the client's past experiences into the psychotherapeutic relationship.

SUMMARY:

Distinction between person-to-person responses and proactive and reactive countertransferences

Given that there are three possible emotional responses which the counsellor may experience:

1. Proactive countertransference
2. Reactive countertransference

3. Person-to-person, autonomous, separate,
   independent here-and-now feelings.

How is s/he to distinguish between them?

First, you consider all the possible clinical options:
For example as above:

- Is this how one of his parents responded?
- Is this how he got attention in his family?
- Is this a re-enactment of another relationship?
- Is this how I feel towards some people?
- Is this how I wanted to behave towards people in my family?

Some of these may seem relevant. Your answers, together with your intuition, will lead you to the client's need, as long as you remain fully aware of the three possibilities:

1. Person-to-person is an adult-to-adult, here-and-now relationship.
2. Proactive countertransference is an invasion of the counsellor's past material into the therapeutic relationship.
3. Reactive countertransference is the provocation of the client's past experiences into the therapeutic relationship.

———

How long do you stay in the person-to-person relationship?

When is the person-to-person relationship *per se* reparative? Most people have suffered from lack of person-to-person intimacy. We talk about mature, affectionate, and intimate bonds. These are rarely met in our culture. We develop a deficit. We can differentiate between developmentally needed intimacy in the past and closeness in the present. Obviously, psychotherapy should help the client to establish mutually satisfying relationships outside the therapy room.

How long should the client stay primarily in the person-to-person relationship before terminating? I say primarily, because the counselling relationship never ceases to be person-to-person or, for that matter, transpersonal; it is simply that one particular facet of relationship is usually dominant. The questions you need to ask, when the person-to-person aspect is dominant are, "Is this benefiting the client – and *how* is it benefiting the client?" "Is this therapeutic or is it merely comfortable?" "Am I getting too much pleasure from this?" "Does the client indicate that s/he has had enough?" "Why would the client not want to terminate the counselling process?" "What could block me as counsellor from picking up the signs from the client that s/he is ready to terminate?" Well-judged answers to such questions will alert the counsellor to the distance or proximity of termination.

Petruska Clarkson (1995, 161-6) mentions the following recurrent themes in terminatory phases:

1. **Satisfaction and a sense of achievement**: This is to be welcomed. The client has worked on him/herself, with the counsellor's guidance, and is conscious that s/he has moved forward.

2. **Guilt and regrets**: We need to differentiate between person-to-person "sorry" feelings and what was needed for the inner child of the client during their psychotherapy.

3. **Anger and disappointment**: Clients may express their feelings of anger towards the therapist for terminating the work. While working through this issue of separation, clients will also deal with their disappointments about the therapeutic process. "I believed that you knew everything and now I discover you don't". "I expected at the end of my therapy never again to feel depressed, and the reality is that I do". Such comments may say something about the client's false expectations, but they may also alert the counsellor to a fault in the original working alliance.

4. **Sadness and nostalgia.** Clients may wish to return to an earlier stage of therapy, when they felt secure in the environment created by the counsellor.

5. **Fear and trepidation**: "What will I do if I have a problem?" "Will I be OK without you?" They also face the fear of separation. "Can I really tolerate the pain of ending this relationship?" The client may ask: "Can I come back and see you if I have problems?" The psychotherapist must not answer the question too soon. S/he needs to pay attention to the underlying emotion: is it the fear of "really ending"? The client needs to face the despairing position of being in the void and experiencing "aloneness". Therapists too may work just above this level in order not to face their own fear of really confronting endings.

6. **Envy and gratitude**: "I am very grateful for what I have received in therapy". The therapist needs to differentiate between pathological gratitude and genuine person- to-person gratitude. "I feel that I want to be able to lead the kind of life you lead." Such a statement can indicate current envy, or it may refer to past envy, which the client has experienced but not declared.

7. **Relief and release**: "I feel so relieved that I am no longer afraid of authority figures". Through expressing their relief they are released into allowing themselves to become more autonomous in the world. This release is both internal as well as external. They are internally released to be who they are. Because of the termination, they are experiencing themselves as being released from dependency into being interdependent autonomous human beings.

8. **Anticipation**: Clients talk and fantasise about what it will be like when they leave this relationship: "What will happen when we meet at a conference?" The client anticipates future ways of relating. It is an important issue to work through. This can be applied to many situations: a consultant and a junior doctor, a lawyer and his client, the rector and his students in a seminary, to the parish priest and his curate when the curate becomes a parish priest, or a businessman and a junior colleague

when one or other is about to leave the firm. The process involves active visualisation of how the client, student, curate sees himself in the future, without having the therapist, rector or office senior at his/her side. There is a difference between anticipation and fear. Anticipation is aspirational, while fear is more self-doubting.

9. **Past losses**: Terminating therapy often evokes the memory of past losses. There may still be feelings that need to be dealt with.

10. **Recycling**: Before clients terminate, they may benefit from recycling the earlier developmental stages of their therapy. The aim is to check what still needs to be addressed, and whether the reparative experience will really hold to be true.

11. **Existential**: the existential reality is that endings are part of life. Death is about ending. We live in the presence of our mortality. The avoidance of death detracts from the vitality of our lives. Here we are facing the despair of our aloneness and the void of nothingness.

12. **Archetypal or transpersonal themes**: These are the archetypal or transpersonal issues, images, dreams and experiences, which emerge towards the end of therapy. They indicate renewal, completion, death and rebirth.

The appearance of some of these themes in a client's responses or conversation may be a sign that it is time to terminate.

SUMMARY:

The "how long?" of the person-to-person relationship
Important questions to ask are:
- "Is this benefiting the client – and how is it doing so?"
- "Is this therapeutic or is it merely comfortable?"

Some of the themes encountered in terminatory phases are:
- Satisfaction and a sense of achievement
- Guilt and regrets

- Anger and disappointment
- Sadness and nostalgia
- Fear and trepidation
- Envy and gratitude
- Relief and release
- Anticipation
- Past losses
- Recycling
- Existential
- Archetypal or transpersonal themes

———

12. Failures as opportunities for breakthrough

Failures in establishing the person-to-person relationship are usually due to inadequacies or blind spots in the psychotherapist. They may also be due to mistiming, or misdiagnosing the client's ability, willingness or readiness to engage in such a relationship for its psychotherapeutic value.

We all suffer from blind spots, often as a result of improperly assimilated ideas from our training: we may blindly follow instructions, which we received as trainee counsellors. Through over-caution, we may fail to touch the client, when that is really needed.

It is a difficult transition from the developmentally needed or reparative relationship to the person-to-person relationship. This is where the integrative method is so necessary and effective, because it allows the different counselling approaches to be appropriately balanced within the therapeutic relationship.

Little (1986, 66) describes a case in which a breakthrough occurred only when she showed her pain at the distress of her client's "failure": "After five weeks her life was in evident danger, either from risk of suicide or from exhaustion – somehow I had to break through. At last I told her how painful her distress was, not only to herself and her family, but to me. I said that no one could be near her in that state without being deeply affected. I felt sorrow with her, and for her, in her loss. The effect was instantaneous and very great. Within the hour she became calmer, lay down on the couch, and cried ordinarily, sadly. She began to look after her family again…"

13. Criteria for evaluating effectiveness of the person-to-person relationship

It is an indication of success when the client says: "I am thinking of leaving", when this corresponds with the counsellor's unvoiced judgement. If the healing process is complete, the client will identify the final need: the need to leave. S/he may even say: "It would be nice to carry on the process, but I feel I am ready to leave." Healthy people are ready to terminate and move on.

Skills needed for establishing and maintaining the person-to-person relationship

All the skills mentioned in previous chapters are relevant to the establishment and maintenance of the person-to-person relationship. In addition to these, some further skills are important. One skill that is quite difficult for many people is the skill of introductory conversation. This is not really what is commonly known as "small talk", because it does have some bearing on the therapy, without being directly relevant. It helps the relationship to develop by lightening the burden of seriousness or introversion. It is conversation that is not too intimate, but that nevertheless draws personal interest from the client. Perhaps one can talk about the client's hobbies or what s/he has been doing during the time since the last session: about travel, a visit to the cinema, a television programme that attracted the client. Some people find it difficult because there was always serious talk going on in their family. They are not used to informal chat. Another skill is the skill to share intimately. For some people this is very easy, for others it needs considerable effort. All the skills which close friends use with each other are part of the reservoir of the skills needed for the person-to-person relationship. They listen to each other. They use open and closed questions. They mirror back what they have heard. They may summarise what they have said. They will challenge each other. They learn to be immediate, with regard to expressing their feelings with each other. They support each other. They affirm each other. I say that this is a reservoir of skills; the counsellor must never forget that the relationship with the client is a professional one.

14. Exercise

Respond as fully as possible to these questions:

1. What is the person-to-person or I–You relationship?

2. When is it appropriate to use this relationship in therapy?

3. When is it inappropriate to use it in therapy?

4. What is the difference between I–You relationship, proactive and reactive countertransference?

5. How do you know in what kind of relationship you are with a person?

6. Comment on the young employee who stresses mutuality in his relationship with his employers.

7. Comment on the leader who wants to be friends with everybody.

8. What re-adjustment is necessary when you move into a position of authority as far as the I–You relationship is concerned?

9. What happens when a person who moves into a position of authority does not adjust as far as the I–You relationship is concerned?

10. How do you ensure that the Person-to-Person Relationship is properly integrated with other facets of Relationship?

15. Two case studies of the I–You relationship

1. NTOMBI is an African Sister of 30 years of age. When she came for counselling, she shared that she had problems with her superior. We arranged to meet in my office every Friday from 5.00 to 5.50 p.m. We discussed the contract in detail, and signed it. The presenting problem centred on her relationship with her superior. Ntombi frequently felt angry with her, even over small things.

Together, we explored this relationship problem and found the root cause in Ntombi's early childhood. It emerged that the client felt abandoned and rejected by her mother. As we explored the issue of abandonment by her mother, I saw her clenching her fists; I asked her what she was feeling. She replied: "It is very painful – I feel angry with her. Why did she conceive me and then leave me alone?" I could see her anger in every bodily communication, facial expression, fists, body posture. I asked her what she wanted to do with her anger. She replied that she wanted to get rid of it. She asked whether she could speak to her mother. She was familiar with the chair exercise and wanted to do it. She placed the image of her mother on a cushion and with a racket she beat the image with all her strength, and she shouted at her mother as she beat and expressed how she felt. Then, all of a sudden, she sat down and cried bitterly.

After a few moments of silence, I asked her whether this outpouring of anger had helped. She said that she saw the image of her mother's face very clearly on the cushion when she began to express her anger. As she beat the image, her mother's face began to disappear. Now it is gone. When I asked how she felt now, she replied: "I feel better. I was able to express to my mother the anger I felt at her rejection. I could never do it as a child. Now I feel strong and there seems to be a new power within me. I am beginning to see that my anger towards my superior was really anger that I harboured towards my mother. Now I have forgiven her for what she did to me. Now I have forgiven her, and believe I can behave differently with my superior. I can now see who my superior really is, and I know she is not my mother!"

We had now reached the stage where we could move into the I–You relationship. The last few sessions of counselling were spent almost entirely in this person-to-person relationship. Since she had hardly related to her mother or her superior, or anyone else, as adult to adult, I was able to give her the opportunity to practise this relationship before terminating the counselling process.

2. MICHAEL came from a family with two children. His sister was ten years older. The parents had always wanted a boy. When he finally arrived they overprotected him and gave him no chance to develop his independence. They had great anxiety that they might lose him. Thus, they did everything for him and protected him from any sad or difficult news or situation. Even when he was twenty years old, they still treated him as a little boy. In many ways Michael enjoyed it and loved his parents, because "they loved him so much."

He came to me for counselling, because he did not know how to relate to grown-ups. He felt odd and inadequate in his working situation. Michael had not learned to initiate things and was always dependent on people who worked with him in the factory. Thus, his colleagues joked a lot about him and he did not know how to defend himself. They called him "the little baby", which infuriated him. He had never been aggressive at home. He found it very difficult to control his anger with the people in the factory, because they constantly teased him. He was very unhappy and wanted to leave the job. However, he did not think it would be good for his future to change his work so soon. His parents agreed with him and told him that he should try it out for at least a year. In many ways he was desperate. That is the reason why he came for counselling.

I realised that I had to use the I–You relationship frequently in my treatment plan. He needed to learn to relate as an adult to adult. I noticed that he was the little boy who tried to please me and do everything I would want him to do. Michael asked always for my opinion and wanted me to make small decisions for him. I explained to him what we needed to do in our sessions and how he could practice this during the week. He was still staying with his parents and only went out with them. He had no girl friend yet. I encouraged him to make small steps each day to become independent and to do things for himself. He had to learn to make decisions. I felt I had to see his parents and explain to them what the central aspects were in my treatment plan. He gladly gave me permission to do so, because only in this way could I speed up the process of counselling. This is what I did. Once they understood what needed to be done, they co-operated with me. Thus, they encouraged him to go out on his own, to make decisions for himself. He soon befriended a girl, who loved him, very much, because he was "such a gentle man". He shared with her what he needed to do. She encouraged him in their encounters.

In my six sessions I constantly helped him to make his own decisions and to talk to me as an adult. At the beginning it was rather heavy for me to be constantly alert to feed back to him, when he slipped into a child- parent relationship. He was so used to doing this. I rather like to use the social environment to speed up the process. Both his parents and his girl friend supported my therapeutic endeavours. The model of the therapeutic relationships focused me on the essential aspects which needed to be addressed with this client. After six sessions he had improved so much that he reported that his relationships with his colleagues had improved. We had also worked on an appropriate expression of his anger. I was convinced that he would manage now to carry on his process of growth with the support of his girl friend and his parents. He even mentioned that he was thinking of moving into a flat to prove to himself that he could be independent. His parents were happy with his decision. Thus, we agreed to terminate our counselling. I told him that he could always come back if he needed more support, particularly living on his own in a flat. I did some preparatory work with him so that he would not be surprised when he was on his own. I heard later that he married this girl and that they have established a happy marriage, supporting each other.

CHAPTER EIGHT

Relatedness to self

1. Low self-esteem 2. Improving our self-esteem 3. The destructive critic
4. How do I gain control over the destructive critic 5. Exercises
6. Body image and self-concept development 7. The influence of culture and
subculture on self-esteem. 8. The influence of family on self-esteem.
9. Support network 10. Exercise 11. Self-reliance and God-reliance
12. Training oneself for self-reliance and God-reliance 13. Exercise 14. How can
parents, teachers, counsellors and formators help children and others to develop a
healthy self-concept? 15. What are some of the signs of positive self-esteem?
16. How to improve the self-concept step by step. 17. Exercise
18. We are made in the image and likeness of God.

1. Low self-esteem

Finally, the most important relationship is the relationship that we have with ourselves. This will affect the whole counselling process and everything we do as people. The lectures I have given on Relationship have always had the relationship with self at their centre. This relationship with self applies to both client and counsellor. How the counsellor relates to him/herself, and how the client relates to him/herself, will affect the establishment of the working alliance. A counsellor or client with low self-esteem will bring much insecurity into the therapeutic relationship. Some low self-esteem issues may have to do with transferential matters. Parents may have "put down" children or not affirmed them, so that they learned to feel worthless, inadequate. When these children grow up, and are in the company of authority figures, they may experience themselves as inadequate. Low self-esteem, wherever it emerges, requires reparative work. Often the person-to-person relationship is difficult to establish, either because the client feels inferior to the counsellor, or vice versa. Low self-esteem can also interfere with the relationship with God. "God cannot love me knowing who I am." It is sometimes helpful to repeat, "God knows me fully, and loves who I am."

> The most important relationship is the relationship
> with oneself.
> This affects the whole of our life.
> It can also affect our relationship with God.

2. Improving our self-esteem

From my experience at the Institute of St Anselm, I have come to realise how fundamentally important it is to work with self-concept development. Many people suffer from low self-esteem. By testing participants at the beginning and end of their course, over several years, we have concluded that work with the self-concept has a good chance of succeeding. Some may have an inflated self-concept, which during the year becomes more realistic. More, however, suffer from low self-esteem. During the time they are at St Anselm's, with sound counselling, we have found that their self-esteem usually improves considerably. The same is true, perhaps even more so, of counselling situations outside the Institute. Many aspects of modern life can lead to people feeling as though they are not much more than a number or a statistic in the notebooks of those in power. While the recognition of powerlessness can sometimes lead to a kind of freedom, in other situations it can lead to deprivation and accompanying low esteem. Poverty, poor education, disability, social class can all lead to this affliction.

Self-confidence is the key to any enduring success. Many people do not value themselves properly. They often see themselves through a negative contrast with someone else. People with low self-esteem have developed a certain style of life, to which they have become accustomed. It is not comfortable, but the person is used to it. Such people cannot judge when their actions are worthy of praise. Say someone pays his friend, who does not properly prize himself, a compliment. Because this friend feels worthless, he will be unable to accept the compliment. A person who has high self-worth, on the other hand, will respond with pleasure and thank the compliment-giver.

Many people feel undeserving. They were brought up that way. "Be nice to others!" "Don't think well of yourself because it is selfish." People usually receive very little training in valuing themselves. Many of us have learned to be a doormat. However, we can learn to value ourselves. We can learn to develop high self-esteem. High self-esteem nourishes our talents and resources. Poor self-esteem is the root cause of many emotional and behavioural problems such as eating disorders, alcoholism, anxiety, and juvenile delinquency. Doctors, nurses and social workers often try to intervene in these problems, but because of the pressures of their professions, they only tangle with symptoms. We need to realise that to help people suffering from these life-crippling conditions, we have to treat at its root the more basic problem of low self-esteem. Counsellors, pastoral workers, formators, parents, teachers need to understand better how to improve the self-esteem of those in their charge. "Love your neighbour as yourself." This implies that one must have positive regard for oneself in order to love one's neighbour. Comb (1971, 39) says: "The self is the star of every performance, the central figure in every act." People see the world through the filter of self. Therefore, the view of self both colours and influences our experience of the world.

SUMMARY:

How does low self-esteem manifest itself?
- In being unable to accept praise.
- In regarding oneself as worthless.
- As the root cause of illnesses such as alcoholism and eating disorders.

The essence of God is love.
Since we are made in the image and likeness of God, we are loveable.
We are loveable, precious, beautiful.
Such thoughts as these can help combat low self-esteem.

---

3. The destructive critic

As people grow up, they acquire a destructive critic (McKay and Fanning, 1992) deep within themselves. It is that inner voice that attacks them and judges them, blames them for everything that goes wrong. It compares the beleaguered individual to others in terms of talents, abilities, achievements and successes. This destructive critic never reminds victims of their own successes, strengths, and abilities. It calls them names: "You are ugly." "You are selfish." "You are stupid." "You are weak." "You are incompetent." "You are a failure." This destructive critic inside one's mind exaggerates one's weaknesses. "You *always* say stupid things." "You *never* finish anything on time." "You *constantly* make a fool of yourself." "You have no right to exist." "You *always* mess up relationships." The accusations are generalised and seemingly irrefutable. This destructive critic undermines one's self-worth constantly, and in very subtle ways – so subtle that one grows to believe the critic's voice and tone; what the voice says sounds so natural and familiar. One never notices the devastating effects this critical voice has on one's self-esteem, because one is so used to listening to it. We need to learn to turn off the intruder's voice and refute its accusations, before it gets a chance to ruin our feelings of self-worth.

SUMMARY:
What is the destructive critic?
- An inner voice that accuses.
- It undermines our self-worth.
- We are used to listening to the destructive critic.

———

4. How do I gain control over the internal destructive critic?

I need to learn to recognise and resist the critic's words and tone

We communicate with ourselves in every conscious moment of our lives. Sometimes we interpret and evaluate our experiences: "I did not do well when I read aloud during the class". Sometimes we solve, and sometimes aggravate, problems through our communication with self. For instance, take a man who has a problem with speaking in large groups. He says, not only to himself, but to others, "I can't speak in a large group." This is eventually taken for granted, so that the person avoids ever speaking in a large group. Other members of the group may unwittingly increase the anxiety: "He doesn't read" is a cry too often heard in primary school. In our self-communication we are apt to speculate about the future: "Whatever I learn in counselling, it won't help me in my daily living situations." We review past events or instances, when we have failed in some respect, then when a similar challenge confronts us, we say to ourselves: "Here comes another failure experience. I can't cope." Communication with self is helpful, only when it is realistic and true. This means, above all, that we have to learn to turn a deaf ear to the destructive voice within us that so readily chimes in with: "Another failure." "You can't do it." "You are helpless." "You are bad at socialising." If we cannot silence the voice, then we need to alter what it says.

Let us take an extreme, but common example: "You never do anything right." We need to refute this. This is not true. This is an exaggeration. In my conscious self I dispute this statement. Of course, I do some things right. Admittedly, there are things that I have done wrong. I present both good and bad to the spiritual self, and thank God for the good things I have achieved. I also ask God for forgiveness for the wrong things I have done. At the same time I ask for God's grace that I may be able to forgive myself. I am now able to reshape the original accusation to: "Sometimes I do wrong things. Often I do right things." We all make mistakes, and will continue to do so, but we learn from them and grow as a result.

I need to become more aware of the destructive critic, who often abides in the lower self or unconscious

How can I get this overbearing critic out of my unconscious to look at him/her, and assess critically what s/he is saying? I need to watch for the critic's emergence whenever I am in a difficult situation.

a. It may happen where I risk failure or rejection.
b. It may happen when I face an authority figure.
c. It may happen when I feel criticised.
d. It may happen when I meet a stranger.
e. It may happen when I make a mistake.

These are all occasions when the destructive critic can come out of the unconscious and become very active.

We need to have ideals and high standards, but we must find intermediary goals that only demand small steps

It is important that we move towards these high standards by achieving small steps towards intermediary goals. It is important that we can celebrate the achievement of small steps on a daily basis. At St Anselm's we can celebrate these achievements in the Eucharistic celebration. Whatever our method, we need to celebrate small successes, which will encourage us to keep on moving in the direction of the ideal. We experience these successes in the conscious self and, by celebrating them, present them to the Higher or Spiritual Self, before storing the accompanying positive feelings as memories in the Lower Self. These small achievements, as they accumulate, will motivate me to continue my journey towards my high standards.

Blaming others can waste much energy

Nothing changes by blaming one's parents, the past, the novice master, the educational system, or superiors. Blaming is always negative, and gets us nowhere. We each need to take responsibility for our life, and for the development of our self-concept. Jesus said: "The kingdom of God is within you." Therefore it is my responsibility to allow God's kingdom to be rooted and established in areas of my life and personality that have been wounded through my own failings or those of other people. This is the way in which I can contribute towards more justice, freedom, love, and forgiveness in the world, since we are all interconnected. Any improvement I bring about in myself will influence others positively, and is a contribution towards a better world. If I start feeling better by taking more responsibility with regard to my life, and if my self-worth improves in this way, God's kingdom of love becomes more rooted in this world.

Some people perpetuate the miserable state of their existence, without necessarily realising it

They suffer from low self-esteem as a result. They may allow their Lower Self to dominate their life, and so experience many negative feelings and memories. These people need to develop their Middle Self, and live and act more in accordance with their conscious self. They need to learn to integrate their emotions, not allowing them to rule their thoughts and actions. By becoming aware how they generate in themselves negative feelings of anger, resentment or hatred and how these are linked with past events in their life, they can work through these events, so as to come to terms with their destructive emotions. As part of this process, they can also present these negative feelings to the Higher or Spiritual Self. In the presence of God they can be healed. Their negative feelings can become transformed into sources of energy, just as the wounds of Our Lord were transfigured in his risen state.

On the other hand, some people keep themselves miserable by just functioning from the Middle Self. They develop their intellect, using it to the detriment of other aspects of their personality. Their spiritual self and their unconscious self are being ignored and not integrated into their overall personality. Such people become one-sided and often experience themselves as unfulfilled. The task confronting them is to develop their unconscious self and their spiritual self. Dreamwork, meditation, reflection, celebrations and prayer may help them in this process.

Again, some people have given their life to God, yet feel totally dissatisfied, disappointed, let down by God. They have mainly functioned from their spiritual self and neglected their unconscious self, their conscious self and their embodiment. They may need to integrate their personal shadow (Jung), to develop their intellectual capacity, to undertake more physical exercise, so as to become more aware of what is going on inside them.

One way to improve our self-worth is to become aware of the language which we use in our self-talk

Do we often use phrases like "I have to", "I should", "I ought"? When we do so, we create certain heavy feelings in ourselves. We don't feel free, indeed we may feel as though we are enslaved. Of course, some "shoulds" and "oughts" make up a healthy conscience. The high self-esteemer has a healthy code of ethics. But what happens when he goes against his code of ethics? The high self-esteemer does not beat himself with never-ending guilt, but owns up to his transgressions, and apologises to people he may have hurt, to himself (as St Francis did), and to God. The high self-esteemer accepts responsibility for his/her behaviour. He may talk about lingering feelings of regret. He may go to confession. Then he lets the matter rest.

What happens when the person with low self-esteem goes against his code of ethics? He says: "I should have foreseen that", "I should have worked harder", "I should have been more sensitive", "Why did I do that?", "Why was I so stupid?", etc. After each pelting, he feels increased guilt. Who is making this man feel guilty? No one else. He keeps on pelting himself with negative remarks that produce more and more guilt. Nevertheless, others may have programmed the person in the past, by building unhelpful expectations: "you should", "you ought", "you must". Someone who suffers from low self-esteem may have acquired impossible standards of perfection, and needs to replace them with more realistic ones.

How can we give ourselves an instruction without damaging our self-worth? We can switch to alternative phrases such as "I want to do", "I choose to do", "I prefer to do", "I wish to do", "I desire to do". Thus we shift from the speech of slaves to the speech of choice and freedom; we reclaim power of choice, personal autonomy. We need to choose the right language in order to regain or increase our self-worth.

Having realistic expectations will help us to regain or increase our self-esteem

When we were children, many expectations came our way. Some of these were implicit, some were explicit, some were silent, while others were clearly expressed. Some of these expectations were reasonable, while others were not. The unreasonable expectations got us into trouble with our self-worth. If people asked far too much too soon, or conversely if too little was expected of us, we may well have concluded: "People think I can't do that." This leads insidiously to, "And they're right, I can't." This feeling or attitude may still be with us, insisting that we can't do many things, even though we know from experience that we can do them. Probably none of us grew up with expectations tailored exactly to our ability to handle them.

Let us make an honest inventory of our self-demands. We may suffer from perfectionism. Therefore, according to our own lights, we never succeed. Our self-expectations are too high. Our constant failures interfere with the healthy development of our self-worth. As long as excessive demands rule our thinking, we may constantly feel driven to meet them, or driven to rebel. Let us ask ourselves: "Am I a constant rebel, because my expectations of myself are too high?" or "Do I feel constantly driven and worn out, because what I achieve is never good enough?"

There is another whole cluster of subconscious memories, which may influence our self-concept. Our parents may have expected us to have only positive feelings. Negative feelings were not allowed. They were unacceptable. As a result, we may have learned that we have "parts" of ourselves that are not acceptable. We may have learned: "I am worth little or nothing, because of my 'bad' feelings." We may experience the feeling: "Something is wrong with me." These are symptoms of low-esteem learnt in childhood.

We need to learn to affirm ourselves

When we do this, we no longer need everyone's approval. We don't need to give others the power to manipulate us. Let us make an honest inventory of our self-demands, and of the expectations we impose on ourselves.

We need to learn to live with, and accept our imperfections

Imperfections are part of us. How many perfect people did Our Lord have round Him? If Peter was not perfect and the rest of the Apostles, can I not learn to accept my imperfections? How can I learn to live with my imperfections?

Some people put themselves down whenever they make mistakes

Making mistakes is human. Nobody likes making mistakes. But we can learn by trial and error. Powerful lessons can be learned from mistakes.

5. Exercises

Write short notes on the following:
1. Self-talk
   a. We talk to ourselves all the time. How much of it do we spend "ticking ourselves off"?
   b. Which kind of self-talk do you specialise in? Is it slave self-talk? Do you use a freedom vocabulary? Make some notes on how you talk to yourself.
   c. Make a list of "I can't" situations. Analyse them and see whether you can say instead: "I choose not to", or "I won't".

2. Mistakes
   – The biggest mistake is that we cling to our mistakes! We have to learn to forgive ourselves. For some people that is the most difficult thing to do. We can learn to be Christian with ourselves. Christ forgave us. He is our example and model. So I will learn to forgive myself for the mistakes that I have made.

– Look at ten mistakes you have made in your life. What have you learned from each mistake? Write the mistakes down, and forgive yourself for them!

3. Self-assessment
Choose one aspect of your life, and write down the various kinds of expectation you place on yourself with regard to them. How realistic are they? Re-write them where necessary.

SUMMARY:

How can you build your self-esteem?

- You need to learn to disregard the voice of the internal destructive critic.
- You need to become more aware of when the destructive critic is active.
- We need to have high ideals and standards, but we must find intermediary goals that only demand small steps.
- People often blame others and waste much energy in this way. Take responsibility for your life.
- Become more aware of the language you use in your self-talk.
- Having realistic expectations will help us to regain or increase our self-esteem.
- We must learn to affirm ourselves.
- We need to learn to accept and live with imperfections.
- Don't put yourself down when you make mistakes.

———

6. Body image and self-concept development

As I have observed in the clients I have counselled over the last thirty-six years, a person's self-concept development is closely linked with the image of his/her body's development. We all have ideas about the nature of our own body: whether it is beautiful or not, whether it is attractive or ugly, whether it is graceful or clumsy. This evaluation is closely linked with our culture. In some cultures a fat person is beautiful, in others ugly. Our own assessments do not necessarily agree with the more objective facts, or even with the opinions of others. However, these subjectively held beliefs are very important psychologically. Our reactions to these beliefs are likely to shape our strategies of social adjustment; for instance, one might try to lose weight because being slim seems a prerequisite for being considered beautiful; furthermore, our reactions to culturally held beliefs can reveal our feelings about ourselves to other people. Therefore, reactions to body image affect the development of self-esteem.

Self-esteem, however, is the outcome of much more than our physical attributes. As we grow older, self-concept development depends more on our social and psychological resources, though the assessment of our body will continue to interact with psychological and social factors. A person's physical size, muscularity or weakness often triggers notions of a social stereotype in others, as do subtle features of the face. Our body image is very much dependent on feedback from others, particularly from important people in our lives. Their remarks, praise or criticism will influence us as we construct a picture of ourselves. Parental approval is most influential during the first few years of our life; after that, the opinions of our peers and members of the opposite sex are likely to become paramount. Even small children are very acute in their perception of unusual features in others. They can be cruel in their ridicule and rejection of those singled out for teasing by some particular physical oddness. This can be psychologically very damaging: labels like "big face", "big ears", can prove harmful for a long time. One of my clients worked for a whole year on her "big nose" label – it had affected her whole self-concept development.

We have all passed through the changes associated with adolescence. The adolescent growth spurts can create very sorry creatures for some time: awkward and clumsy, with long arms and legs poking through outgrown clothes. These facts make it difficult to hold on to our earlier feelings of wellbeing and self-assurance. Pimples, fuzzy faces, breaking voices, menstruation, breasts or genitals that appear unexpectedly early or late, or do not seem right and normal, all lead to vulnerability and self-doubt. We must not forget that physical characteristics are the most visible aspects of the person: being unusually clumsy or uncoordinated; having a squint; having to wear thick glasses; ears that stick out; being unusually small, fat, weak; having a speech impediment. All these increase the chance that a minor physical problem can become a major psychological one. This happens through the rejection, ridicule and physical abuse which one person may receive from others. The abuse may shape fundamental attitudes that endure for the rest of a person's life.

In some people, the physical characteristics that produce a sense of inferiority might well prove to be their greatest asset. This is what Adler believes. He himself had been a very frail and sickly child. One of Adler's earliest recollections goes back to the age of about two. He was sitting on a bench, his limbs bandaged because of rickets. He was watching his elder brother jumping and running about. This created a sense of deprivation and inferiority, which in their turn drove him along the road towards aggressive physical competitiveness. This experience influenced much of his professional and personal life. The starting point of Adlerian Individual Psychology (1979) was very much connected with the sense of physical inferiority.

Psychological anguish and pain may be the fate of all of us we grow older and our bodies deteriorate. It will be our task to maintain our self-esteem as our body ages.

SUMMARY:

Body image and self-concept development

- Self-concept development is closely linked with our body image development.
- Self-esteem is the outcome of much more than physical attributes.

- Adolescence is a sensitive time for self-concept development.
- According to Adler, physical characteristics that produce a sense of inferiority can be our greatest asset.

———

7. The influence of culture and subculture on self-esteem

Capitalist culture stresses the accumulation of wealth, power and prestige. There is a lot of emphasis on upward mobility and productivity. Rapid transition in career, an unstable economy, the fear of unemployment, all create a precarious situation for many people. Therefore, we are likely to experience variability in the level of our self-esteem. Self-esteem may be lowered by many factors: poor housing, inadequate education, poverty, and inadequate job opportunities are among the major ones.

Membership of high-standing organisations such as the judiciary, company boards or university departments will influence people as to how they feel about themselves. Breaking the norms of society or the ethical code of the community results in disapproval, which erodes self-esteem. In negatively valued subcultures, self-esteem is almost bound to suffer.

8. The influence of family on self-esteem

Generally speaking, we can say that the more open the family system is, the higher is the self-esteem. The actual family climate is very influential for self-concept development. Is the family rigid, controlled and closed? Is the family open and growth-producing? Is the family cohesive and expressive? Is the family conflict-ridden? Is the family intellectual? Is the family religious? All these factors contribute towards the perception that a person has of him/herself and of the family as a whole. This perception will influence self-esteem. Positive perceptions will build up self-esteem, negative perceptions will lower it.

Family rules can influence self-esteem, depending on how they are perceived. Social skills, physical health and emotional health can all have an influence on the self-concept development. Self-esteem will also depend on the position one holds in the family. Recognition in the family plays an important factor. Is the sporting star appreciated in the family? Does the family support the educational achiever? Is being the eldest, most obedient child in the family properly recognised?

Family nicknames can fix the self-image: "Big mouth", "Sissy", "Baby", "Beauty" and of course, "Big nose" are some family nicknames that I have come across in my counselling experience. Sometimes these names are dropped after a few years, sometimes they are retained through adulthood. In such situations they tend to preserve earlier images. They inhibit growth and change and become "self-fulfilling prophesies".

SUMMARY:

The Influence of family on self-esteem
- Family rules can influence self-esteem.
- Family nicknames can fix a self-image.

———

9. Support network

We all need people. People with low self-esteem have an even greater need for help and approval than most. Often they have few friends to whom they can go for support, and have difficulty sustaining relationships. They may instinctively select friends who dump them. This makes them more wary of friendships. They may become very independent, even isolated.

The healthy person has a support network of several

people to whom they can go for support. Among these are family members, close friends, potential friends and acquaintances, clergy and members of the caring professions. Adequate support is a safety net for self-esteem.

10. Exercise

Support network
List the major people in your network. Describe each of them with a few adjectives! How is each person supportive of you? Adequate support is a safety net for self-esteem.

11. Self-reliance and God-reliance

We must learn to rely on the self that is made in the image and likeness of God. From our experience we know when we are relying on our true self, made in the image and likeness of God. If we rely on the wounded self, we can become destructive. So we need to learn to distinguish between these two selves. For this to be achieved, we need a great deal of self-awareness. Self-reliance and God-reliance are an insurance against future depression. Self-reliance and God-reliance are the means to bring out hidden potential. Self-reliance and God-reliance are the antidote to both dependency and isolation. The dependent person believes s/he can carry out activities only with the help of others. The isolated person does not look beyond him/herself for achievement. Both dependency and isolation, paradoxically, mean that we give too much power to other people. The solution to both isolation and dependency is to develop self-reliance and God-reliance. As a self-reliant and God-reliant person you will have confidence in your abilities, aided by God to handle new and difficult situations. This includes dealing with those people who contribute to the difficulties!

SUMMARY:

Self-reliance and God-reliance

- We must learn to rely on the self that is made in the image and likeness of God.
- When we rely on the wounded self, we become destructive.
- We need to learn to distinguish between the two: the true self and the wounded self.
- Self-reliance and God-reliance are the antidote to both dependency and isolation.

———

12. Training yourself for self-reliance and God-reliance

1. You must remove any blocks you have in order to be self-reliant and God-reliant. Some common doubts and nagging thoughts lead to dependency. "Bad things happen to me when I stand up for myself", "God is my father. He wants me to rely on Him." This last statement can be interpreted in the right way or in the wrong way. If I act as a child in front of God and not as an adult, I become too dependent on God and blame God for everything that goes wrong. Some other common fears lead to isolation. "Other people will let me down", "God will let me down." Such anxious forebodings as these will block me from establishing a relationship with other people and with God; the fearful apprehension needs to be uncovered and changed.

2. You already have a base for self-reliance and God-reliance, on which you can build. What skills need to be reactivated and sharpened? Find out where you lack self-reliance. Do I take care of my basic needs such as cooking, clothing, etc? Are my emotions dependent on other people's reactions and actions? Can I go out to social events by myself? Can I make decisions on my own, while relying on God's help? Do I

accept help from others and from God? Alternatively, you may find that you are over self-reliant at work. Do I make the effort to work as a member of a team? Your work may need to incorporate relationships with others, and with God.

13. Exercise over several weeks

Self-reliance and God-reliance

1. In answer to the questions above or similar questions that arise in your mind, make a list of self-reliant and God-reliant activities in which you are involved, and regard the list as a first act of self-reliance.

2. Based on this list, deliberately choose at least one situation a day in which to be self-reliant and God-reliant. Slowly you can increase the number of situations per day. Choose a situation that is challenging, but not so difficult that you won't try it out. Just concentrate on one day at a time and on the chosen situation, instead of vaguely worrying about how you're going to become more self-reliant and God-reliant.

3. Keep a detailed record of what you do, when you do it, and how you feel while you are doing it and after you finish. You might write down any concerns you may have had before trying it. Take notice whether your fears of a "bad" result came true. After several self-reliance experiences, take note of what they mean to you by describing them. Slowly you will get used to keeping detailed records. You might begin to rate your degree of self-reliance on a scale of 0 to 10 or 0 to 100. It might be useful also to have a rating of the level of anxiety linked to your action. The very act of keeping good records in itself shows self-reliance.

4. Slowly increase the number of self-reliance and God-reliance activities. Look at your inventory of activities and see whether you have left out any important ones. Avoidance is the greatest enemy of self-reliance and God-reliance. If there are any important activities you have left out, write them down and plan them as part your self-reliance programme.

5. The next step is to take on more complicated activities. For example, if you have never taken a trip or pilgrimage on your own, this can be broken down into separate tasks. Write down the various steps involved, such as deciding where to go, getting the information, and how you will get there. When you are ready for more complicated action, take some time, and become aware how you feel about yourself. When you move from helplessness to resourcefulness, you become motivated to aim at more difficult tasks.

It takes time to develop self-reliance and God-reliance skills. They can't be switched on to full power overnight. It may take six to twelve months for your self-reliance and God-reliance behaviour to become automatic. Be careful that you do not get discouraged by trying too much too soon. When we start acting with more self-reliance and God-reliance, we may feel strange. It is important that we do not back away from our strange feelings, or from our new way of acting. It *is* a new way and therefore, there are new, strange feelings. After some time we shall feel more natural. The time will come when we no longer need to make much effort to be self-reliant and God-reliant. For example, suppose you have a problem with being with people and tend to keep aloof from them. When you try to move towards people, you may feel "phoney", "strange". Many people go back to their old ways and habits rather than sit out this discomfort. You will be able to overcome this block if you accept your feelings.

To have models may help you increase your motivation to become more self-reliant and God-reliant. You might want to imitate the behaviour of someone you admire because of his/her self-reliance and God-reliance. Often people's self-change programmes fail, because they forget why they started them in the first place. It is important that we remind ourselves frequently why we want to be more self-reliant and God-reliant. Basically, it is part of the healing process. We should periodically review our motivation and progress.

There are various strategies for increasing self-reliance

and God-reliance. Some people try the "out-on-a-limb" method, to make sure that they carry out their intentions. They decide to divide a major task into many smaller ones. For example, a young woman decides to go on a pilgrimage by herself. She tries to ensure self-reliance and God-reliance by performing many small tasks to survive the pilgrimage: packing, listing stations and train times, preparing food for the journey, etc. Each task completed brings a measure of self-assurance. Another young woman may organise a party on her own for twenty people. She has to plan the meal, buy the food, cook it, tidy up, and clean the place, in order to live up to her expectations. She will list what she has to do, and tick each task she has accomplished.

Then there is the "commitment technique". This consists of telling others before you carry out your self-reliance and God-reliance plan. For example, an older lady plans a trip to Rome. She knows she is apt to be timid. She tells her friend beforehand about all the arrangements she is making: how she has booked a flight, and a hotel for a week, and how she is already making arrangements about what she will see in Rome. She also arranges to meet certain acquaintances in Rome. All this will help her to avoid the temptation of staying in her hotel room for the whole week.

Much dependency is linked with what people perceive as different roles of the sexes. Many men are dependent on women for taking care of the children, cleaning and cooking. Some women feel helpless about maintenance of the car, the house, financial arrangements, so-called "male jobs". Some sisters feel dependent on their community leaders for many things. How can we overcome this type of dependency? Some Sisters are afraid that the community leader or others will be angry, if they become too self-reliant and God-reliant. They are afraid that they may end up lonely instead of self-reliant and God-reliant. The best way is to test out how the community leader and other sisters feel about a sister becoming more self-reliant and God-reliant. On the whole, competency is more appreciated than helplessness. When you are self-reliant and God-reliant, people will be more relaxed with you because you don't want something from them. They will feel more comfortable and like being with you. When you are more self-reliant and God-reliant, you will also feel more comfortable with yourself. You don't need to please others. Your true self -how you really are, the God-likeness in you – is more attractive than the social façade. When you are self-reliant and God-reliant, you feel free to be yourself, and this makes you an easier person to be around.

Sometimes close friends and community leaders foster dependency by taking over responsibilities that should be yours. As you gain more self-reliance and God-reliance, you may find yourself in conflict with such people. Practice assertiveness by simply expressing what you consider to be your right. Explain that you need to develop your own abilities and initiatives. Explain that you don't want to miss any opportunities to practise self-reliance and God-reliance. It is important that, on the road to self-reliance and God-reliance, you discuss this issue with the significant people in your life.

If you feel anxiety over self-reliance and God-reliance activities, see this as a good sign. It is a signal that you are challenging yourself, demanding more of yourself, taking more risks or bigger risks. You can interpret this as confirmation that you are improving, changing, that something is happening. At the same time, as you make progress in becoming more self-reliant and God-reliant, expect some setbacks and some feelings of discouragement. All human progress is not linear, but more spiral and uneven. How can you overcome temporary difficulties? Make sure that you stick to your programme. Deprive yourself of a reward if you don't carry out your plan. For example, don't watch television until you have done your scheduled self-reliance and God-reliance activity.

SUMMARY:

Moving towards God-reliance and self-reliance
- You must remove any blocks you have to be self-reliant and God-reliant.
- You already have a base for self-reliance and God-reliance.

- Choose one situation a day in which to be self-reliant and God-reliant.
- Keep a detailed record.
- Increase the number of self-reliant and God-reliant activities.
- Take on more complicated activities.

———

There are several advantages to self-reliance and God-reliance

As you become more self-reliant and God-reliant:

1. **You will become less vulnerable to emotional disorders.** Your self-worth improves. You feel good about yourself. You are more in charge of your feelings. You cease to react to others' actions and events with extreme emotions.

2. **You will build up your self-esteem.** The more we move from helplessness to resourcefulness, the better we will feel about ourselves. What we think and feel about ourselves depends to some extent on what we do. We watch how we act and then we evaluate ourselves accordingly. This inner self-talk is going on all the time.

3. **You will become more efficient.** It is a fallacy to believe that it is easier to get someone else to do our work. Our life runs more smoothly and efficiently when we can take care of our own business. We may try for several hours to get somebody to type a report that we could type ourselves in one hour.

4. **You will be able to handle everyday stress more effectively.** The idea of the Paschal Mystery is a strong motivating force for us to deal positively with stress and suffering. Stress, suffering and pain are part of human existence. If I face them as Our Lord faced his suffering, it will help me to grow. The more we are able to believe that we can determine our own fate as Our Lord did, when he handed himself over to the soldiers, the better we will be able to deal with stress, suffering and pain. They become a challenge for us. When we decide to take control over our life as Jesus did, we increase our

resources for handling it, even in the most difficult situations.

5. **You will not be so easily intimidated by others**. The more dependent we are, the more intimidated we will be. We know in our hearts that we don't need the constant reassurance of those on whom we have become dependent, that we can take action ourselves by relying on God. We don't need human approval; God's approval is more than enough, and it is an enormous resource for us.

6. **Your relationships with others will improve**. Often, when people believe that they need others to support them, they drive them away. This leads to a vicious cycle. The more they move away from them, the more they try to hang on to them. The opposite happens when we are self-reliant and God-reliant. People will be more relaxed when we don't behave as if we want something from them. Because they will feel more comfortable, they will move towards us. When we are more self-reliant and God-reliant, we will be more comfortable with ourselves. We won't need to please them. We are free in ourselves. They will feel free with us.

7. **You will increase your freedom**. Depressed people are severely limited. Their feelings and modes of behaviour are constricted. They don't feel like doing anything. Self-reliance and God-reliance is on the other end of the continuum. Here your freedom is at its greatest. You can achieve many things. You will stay in a relationship because you want to. You will keep your job because you want to do it. These are not your only options. You feel free to make decisions. You have your own opinions. You make your own judgements. You follow your own direction rather than allowing yourself to be persuaded by others. You can yield to the truth, but you will not be devastated by it. In fact the truth will set you free.

SUMMARY:

Advantages of self-reliance and God-reliance
- You become less vulnerable to emotional disorders
- You build up your self-esteem

- You become more efficient
- You handle everyday stress more effectively
- You will not so easily be intimidated by others
- You will improve your relationships with others
- You will increase your freedom

———

14. How can parents, teachers, counsellors and formators help those in their charge to develop a healthy self-concept?

1. Parents, teachers, counsellors and formators need to listen to, acknowledge and accept the feelings of the children or adults entrusted to them.
2. They need to treat those entrusted to them with respect and acceptance.
3. They need to give specific praise and constructive criticism.
4. They need to be honest.
5. They should use "I" messages rather than "You" messages. For example, "I am annoyed because of the loud noise" rather than "You are so noisy".
6. Parents, teachers, counsellors and formators need to be consistent.
7. They need to give the children or adults in their charge space to manage their lives.
8. They need to give them responsibilities, independence and the freedom to make choices.
9. They need to involve them in opportunities to experiment and pursue interests.
10. They need to respect the uniqueness of each individual entrusted to them.
11. They need to be good models.
12. They need to avoid being judgemental.
13. They need to respect the judgements of those in their care, even when they may disagree with them.

15. What are some signs of positive self-esteem in people?

People with high self-esteem can be described as self-actualising. They have a fully functioning self. Maslow (1954, 327) postulates the following characteristics of such people:

1. They are reality-oriented.
2. They accept themselves, others, and the environment for what they are.
3. They have a great deal of spontaneity.
4. They are autonomous and independent.
5. They are problem-centred rather than self-centred.
6. They have an air of detachment and a need for privacy.
7. Their appreciation of people is fresh rather than stereotyped.
8. They identify with humankind.
9. Their relationships with a few specially loved people seem to be profound rather than superficial.
10. Their values and attitudes are democratic.
11. They do not confuse means with ends.
12. Their sense of humour is philosophical rather than hostile.
13. They are very creative.
14. They resist conformity to culture.
15. They may have mystical or spiritual experiences.

16. How to improve the self-concept step by step

Often, unfortunately, professional carers do not have a deep understanding of self-concept development. For formation programmes the self-concept development is very important. In any formation programme – pre-noviciate, noviciate, seminary, on-going formation – the development of the self-concept needs to have a central place. Many helpers focus on the development of strengths and do not follow a step by step approach. Diane Frey and Jesse Carlock (1984) stress four phases of intervention:

1. **First, the person needs to discover his/her identity**. Because of distorted perception, people with low self-esteem rarely have a clear picture of their identity. Such persons do not see their whole self. They may focus on the ideal self and how they do not match up to it. They may be viewing themselves as they were in the past, but ignore the present self. There are many ways and tools of finding out one's identity, for instance, background, talents, particularities of culture, tastes, ambitions, alterations in one's religious understanding and practice

2. **The next step is to discover one's strengths and weaknesses**. It is quite important to ask the question: "How do I use my strengths?" Everybody possesses both positive and negative qualities. In people with low self-esteem, the self is mostly seen as possessing negative qualities. The person needs to become aware of his/her strengths, and to deal with his/her weaknesses.

3. **The next step is to nurture this newly found identity**. A newly acquired positive self-esteem can be lost if it is not nurtured. It is important to teach people ways of nurturing their self-concept:

a. The person with low self-esteem needs to learn to transfer nurturing from positive environments to less positive environments. For example, the praise/criticism ratio may be high in the family, but low in the work environment. Such a person needs to draw strength from the positive home environment, so as to help nurture self in the workplace.

b. The low self-esteem person needs to learn to identify his/her nurturing needs, and how to ask others to help him/her to meet those needs.

c. People with low self-esteem need to learn to affirm themselves and others. The value of giving and receiving positive feedback cannot be underestimated.

d. The helper can assist the low self-esteem person with disrupting the self-fulfilling prophesy through the disputation of faulty reasoning. Faulty logic is the result of over-generalising, selective perception, taking excessive responsibility, dichotomous thinking and seeing catastrophes where they do not really exist.

4. **The low self-esteem person needs to learn how to maintain adequate self-esteem**. Self-esteem is a process. The low self-esteem person can be taught to:
  a. turn experiences into learning situations;
  b. practise facilitative risk-taking;
  c. set appropriate goals;
  d. publicly affirm goals.

This last is particularly helpful, because once a commitment is made in public, one is more likely to accomplish it. These four steps of intervention in enhancing self-esteem are best seen as a continuum. This approach of intervention is a stepwise progression from identity to maintenance. There is, however, some overlap between these steps. These steps are guidelines for a logical progression.

SUMMARY:

How to improve the self-concept step by step
  - First the person needs to discover his/her identity.
  - The person needs to discover her/his strengths and weaknesses.
  - The newly discovered identity with its strengths and weaknesses needs to be nurtured.
  - The person needs to sustain adequate self-esteem.

———

17. Exercise

Consider these questions as intuitively as possible
1. How would you describe your self-esteem?
    a. Do you believe in yourself and your self-worth?
    b. Do you put yourself down frequently?
    c. Do you love yourself?
    d. What does the Bible say about ourselves?

    e.   Is your self-esteem related to your feelings of success?

    f.   How do you feel as a person?

2. What kind of mask do you wear?

    a.   The nice guy/girl?

    b.   The trouble maker?

    c.   The poor me?

    d.   The workaholic?

    e.   The perfectionist?

    f.   The rescuer?

    g.   The saviour?

3. Who am I? Give a list of descriptions of yourself.

4. How did this description originate in your life? Who defined you that way?

5. Do you ever take reasonable risks?

6. Is your thinking mainly positive or negative?

7. How can you improve your self-talk?

8. How can you expand your support network?

9. What are your strengths?

10. What is your belief system?

11. What can you do about your weaknesses?

12. How self-reliant and God-reliant are you?

13. How do you see your body and various parts of your body?

14. Imagine what it means to be made in the image and likeness of God.

15. Visualise yourself becoming more self-accepting.

16. Visualise yourself becoming more self-loving.

17. Imagine what life will be like when you are more self-accepting, more accepting of others, more self-loving, more loving of others, more self- reliant and God-reliant?

18. We are made in the image and likeness of God

This has been a recurrent theme in this book, because it is at the heart of it. Where it is not evident, it is because the author is concentrating on a particular counselling approach or a facet of relationship. But we began with the transpersonal, and in a sense we have never left it. We are meant to be loveable, because as John the Evangelist expresses the essence of God, God is basically Love. Many people don't experience themselves as loveable. What went wrong? The way they grew up as children, the way they were treated by their parents or primary caretakers may be the reason why they feel worthless, ugly, inferior; some even feel evil. Possibly they did not receive enough love, or not the right kind of love. To be made in the image and likeness of God may mean many things. Perhaps the most important lesson we can learn from this fact is that we are loveable, precious, beautiful. This is possibly the deepest truth about the human being. One of the main goals of therapy, therefore, is to help clients to experience themselves once more as loveable. This is God's plan for us.

Conclusion

1. Summary 2. Recent work on the Spiritual dimension of counselling

1. Summary

Life is all about relationships. Relationships can heal us or destroy or wound us. Many people have been damaged in relationships. Many others have been healed through relationships. The knowledge and awareness of our different relationships is fundamental to our wellbeing and the wellbeing of others. The Institute of St Anselm has always put a strong emphasis on relationships and community building. Many people are craving for someone to whom they can relate. Very often, however, they are afraid to relate to people, because they have been hurt in relationships. In the Blessed Trinity we find perfect relationships, which supply us with models for our human relationships.

A constant awareness of the various kinds of relationship that exist, and an extensive knowledge of the appropriate use and response to these relationships, will improve the efficiency of our pastoral work, our community living, our counselling work, our work in formation and our daily encounters with other people. The five aspects of relationship, as defined and described in this book, are like a compass that tells us where we are in our relationships, and whether these relationships are appropriate in a given situation. If I am in therapy it is appropriate to be regressed and show my vulnerability and strong emotions. However, if I were leading a parish group on prayer this behaviour would interfere with the purpose of the group. As a person I may have a strong need to be cared for and listened to, however I must never use those entrusted to me to satisfy my needs. How can I make sure that my own needs are met? I look for a counsellor. If, as a carer or counsellor, I have a tendency to need to be reassured that my work is having the right results, it is inappropriate to use those entrusted to me for constant feedback. I need to do this with my supervisor.

To distinguish between the various relationships, and to

use them in the right way will help us to look after our own needs and the needs of others. We will become much better equipped truly to serve others. Part of our training needs to be in the proper use of the appropriate relationship. Normally, we will use these various relationships in the way we learned to use them in our own family. What we have learned may be a proper use or an abuse of relationship. For instance, if I learned to dump all my emotions on my mother or others in the family, I need to recognise that such dumping is abusive behaviour. I need to learn to contain my emotions in my working relationships and community living. The counsellor or therapist is there, so that I can express all these emotions and prevent them from doing further damage.

The more we learn to use the working alliance in our dealings with clients, the more effective we will be. Many mistakes are made, owing to the lack of a proper working alliance. Very often we assume things without checking them out. Frequently we don't express our expectations and feel let down by others who do not even know what we expected of them. As counsellors. it is important that we help our clients to express their expectations of us and to communicate how far they think we can fulfil their expectations or not. Many misunderstandings come about because of a faulty working alliance.

It is very important to be aware when transference and countertransference happen between two people. Although they can prove beneficial, they distort the real relationship, so that people do not encounter each other as they really are. Under the influence of transference, a client may see his/her counsellor as a punishing parent or a severe teacher. Clients can be enormously afraid of us. They may have all kinds of expectations of us, as if we were their mother or father. Some may hate us as they hated their mother. Others may resent us as they resented their father who was never available. You may not understand what is going on in the relationship and why a client is treating you in a certain way. This can lead to a great deal of frustration on both sides. An enlightened awareness of transference and countertransference helps us to deal with many problems in interpersonal relationships.

When you understand what is going on in a relationship you may avoid being drawn into countertransference. You may understand that this person has an authority problem, and is very angry with you who represent authority. This knowledge may help you not to be drawn into the person's anger. Alternatively, they may adore you as they adored their loving father, and so side-track you from being objective in your assessment of them.

From time to time, we are all in need of the reparative or developmentally needed relationship. A listening ear or an encouraging word helps us often to overcome hurt feelings. We have many opportunities to provide repair for what was damaged in childhood. Often an encouraging word can help a person tremendously if the person hardly ever experienced encouragement in the family or in the work situation. Saying sorry can be very healing if father and mother never said sorry. A smiling face may be very reparative if parents hardly ever smiled. Affirming a person can do wonderful work, if the person hardly ever received affirmation. We have hundreds and thousands of opportunities to do reparative work in our daily living situation and at work.

Awareness of the kind of relationship we are in will enable us to choose to go into person-to-person relationship. This is the relationship we are supposed to be in all our dealings in daily living situations. How often do people regress when they are supposed to be in a person-to-person relationship. Some people find it very difficult to be in a person-to-person relationship with others. They either regress to a child-parent relationship or they become parents telling everybody what to do.

From all this, we can see how useful the awareness of these relationships is to us as counsellors, pastoral workers, members of communities and in our daily working and living situation. It can help us enormously to improve the efficiency of our work and our relationships, because we can choose to be in an adult-to-adult relationship when this is expected of us. We can also help others to be in this relationship when they are with us. At the same time, when they regress, we will understand what is going on in our relationship with them.

If all the members of a community or family developed an awareness of these relationships and could monitor them, it would greatly improve the relationships between the various members of that community or family.

The first encyclical letter of Pope Benedict XVI (2006) starts with the following passage: "God is love, and he who abides in love abides in God, and God abides in him." (1 Jn 4:16). These words from the First Letter of John express with remarkable clarity the heart of the Christian faith: the Christian image of God and the resulting image of mankind and its destiny. In the same verse, St John also offers a kind of summary of the Christian life: "We have come to know and believe in the love God has for us." This love is the model and inspiration for our love for people. Thus our relationship with God is the foundation for all other relationships. We know about God's love from Jesus Christ. "God so loved the world that he gave his only Son, that whoever believes in him should... have eternal life" (3:16).

Jesus is the Way, the Truth and the Life. Therefore, He is supremely important for us as leaders, counsellors or employers. He has shown us the way to our ultimate goal, His Father and our Father. His fruitful suffering makes our suffering a success in our journey towards God. Therefore, He encouraged us: "Take up your cross and follow me." "Unless the seed falls into the ground and dies, it cannot bear fruit." Our relationship with Jesus Christ is central to our work, growth and meaning in life. He is the model for our personal spiritual journey, which is the basis of all we do and are.

2. Recent work on the spiritual dimension of counselling

The importance of the transpersonal relationship, the relationship with God, in our daily life, in community living, in counselling and pastoral work becomes clearer with new research (Schermer, 2003). In the last decade the awareness of the importance of spirituality has entered into counselling training as an important factor in the healing process. In their book *A Spiritual Strategy for Counselling and Psychotherapy* (1999), Scott Richards and Allen Bergin stress that when psychotherapists make a diagnosis of their clients, they should also assess the religious and spiritual dimensions of their clients' lives. This would help them to obtain a fuller and more accurate diagnostic picture. In *Integrating Spirituality into Treatment* (Ed. William R. Miller, 1999), the authors provide therapists with practical advice on including clients' spiritual aspects in the therapeutic relationship. Geri Miller in *Incorporating spirituality in counselling and Psychotherapy* (2003) offers expert guidance on how to handle issues of spirituality in furthering the therapeutic process. In her book *Integrating the spiritual dimension into the therapeutic practice: Psychotherapy and Spirituality*, Agneta Schreurs (2002) introduces psychotherapists to the subject of spirituality and the influence it may have in the therapeutic process.

As previously noted, Donah Zohar and Ian Marshall in their seminal book *SQ: Spiritual Intelligence the Ultimate Intelligence* (2000) show how to develop SQ (Spiritual Intelligence). This intelligence shows us how to balance meaning and value. It places our life in a wider context. They call it the ultimate intelligence, to contrast it with IQ (intelligence quotient), which is tested by psychological tests. Goleman pointed out that EQ (emotional intelligence) is also superior to IQ. In response to Michal Levin's *Spiritual Intelligence* (2000), Mike Thompson, Senior Lecturer in Environmental Studies, commented: "As a scientist I find the direction and content of Michal's work interesting, stimulating and very helpful." Books like *50 Self-help Classics*, by Tom Butler-Bowdon (2005), which includes inspirational works from various periods, show us how important spirituality has become in our time.

Petruska Clarkson (1995) demonstrated the importance of the transpersonal relationship for the psychotherapeutic process. Both spirituality and psychology are needed for healing to occur.

Mary Wolff-Salin in her book *No Other Light* (1989) had already outlined points of convergence in psychology

273

and spirituality. She concludes: "With this study of the 'sacred marriage' we have come to the end of the journey of this book which has attempted to compare some of the fundamental themes of psychology and spirituality and see where, sometimes surprisingly, they point in the same directions. Both agree, finally, in this aim of union in human life – whether that union is seen in terms of the conscious and unconscious, the latter including the domain of the One who lives beyond human consciousness, or whether it is formulated explicitly in terms of union with God – though it goes without saying that not all psychology speaks of this domain."

Jim McManus in his book *Healing in the Spirit* (2002, 5) quotes Dr. Arrun Sharma stating that "Spiritual healing is now one of the many complementary therapies that are now getting to the stage where they have to demonstrate their effectiveness and undergo the same scientific process that any treatment does in the health service." Jim McManus concludes: "This is a major development in a British university and the new Scottish Parliament in Edinburgh. It is recognition that those who undertake the medical care of the community should no longer ignore the spiritual dimension."

Victor Schermer (2003, 38) speaks of a new paradigm for psychology, psychoanalysis, and psychotherapy. He concludes: "Whereas previously spirituality was merely peripheral to the self and its treatment, now it becomes its centre." This has been my own theory and practice over the last forty years.

Glossary

Adult. An ego state oriented towards objective, autonomous data-processing and probability estimating.

Archetypes. Primordial images and thoughts. They provide instinctive patterns for mental activity.

Autonomy. Refers to the capacity for non-script behaviour which is reversible, with no particular time-schedule, developed later in life, and not under parental influence.

Awareness technique. A concentration technique, in which clients are asked to become aware of their body language, their breathing, their voice quality and their emotions, as much as of any pressing thoughts.

Child. The child ego state is a set of feelings, thoughts, attitudes and behavioural patterns, which are archaic relics of an individual's childhood.

Cognitive-behavioural theory. Describes therapies that extend behavioural therapy to have a major focus on changing covert thoughts as well as overt behaviour.

Complexes. Unconscious accumulations of associations, sometimes of a traumatic nature, that possess strong emotional content.

Congruence. Consistency between the thoughts and feelings the therapist experiences and his/her professional demeanour. Not putting on a professional façade.

Counselling. A relationship in which counsellors assist clients to understand themselves and their problems better. Then, where appropriate, counsellors use various interventions to assist clients to feel, think, communicate and act more effectively. The term is often used nowadays interchangeably with psychotherapy.

Defence Mechanisms. Infantilisms which operate unconsciously to protect the ego and may impede realistic behaviour long after they have outlived their usefulness. Examples include repression, reaction formation, projection, fixation and regression.

Developmentally teeded *or* **reparative relationship**. The intentional provision by the counsellor of correction or replenishment, where a previous relationship has suffered from abuse, deficiency or overprotection.

Dreamwork. Dreams are utterances or statements from the unconscious, not just unfinished business. The therapist has to discover how to read dreams. An understanding of myths and symbols is fundamental to this skill.

Eclecticism. The practice of drawing from different counselling and therapy approaches in formulating client problems and implementing treatment interventions.

Ego. The ego or "I" acts as an intermediary between the id and the external world and strives to

275

bring the reality principle to bear upon the id in substitution for the pleasure principle.

Empathy. The therapist's capacity to comprehend accurately the client's inner world or internal frame of reference and to communicate sensitively this understanding to the client. Not to be confused with sympathy.

Existential. These approaches to therapy are concerned with the science and processes of being.

Feminist therapy. Addresses women's problems and issues in the context of constricting gender role socialisation and power imbalances in society.

Id. Contains everything that is inherited and fixed in the constitution. Filled with energy from the instincts, the id strives to bring about the satisfaction of instinctual needs on the basis of the pleasure principle.

Integration. Blending together theoretical concepts and/or practical interventions drawn from different therapeutic approaches into coherent and integrated wholes.

Interpretation. Involves offering constructions or explanations of problems, states or dreams.

Irrational beliefs. Rigid, dogmatic, unhealthy beliefs that get in the way of people's efforts to achieve their goals. Such beliefs are characterised by demands, "musts" and "shoulds".

Openness. Allowing all significant sensory and visceral experience to be perceived; the capacity for realistic perception without defensiveness.

Organismic. Refers to a person's continuous weighing of experience, from which values are derived.

Parent State. The parent ego state is a set of feelings, thoughts, attitudes and behaviours which resemble those of parental figures. The Parent ego state may be seen in one of two forms: the controlling Parent or the nurturing Parent.

Person-to-person (I–You). That relationship which comes to exist between the adult self of the counsellor and that of the client.

Person-centred. The therapeutic approach which places the whole person of the client, rather than behaviour or analysis, at the centre of the counselling process.

Persona. A concept derived from the actor's mask in antiquity. At one level, the persona is the individual's system of adaptation or way of coping with the world. At another level, it is the mask of a collective psyche.

Psychotherapy. "Mind healing". It is often believed more accurate to speak of "psychotherapies", because of the many approaches.

Rational beliefs. Healthy, productive and adaptive beliefs that are consistent with social reality and are stated as preferences, desires and wants.

Script. A life plan based on a decision made in childhood, reinforced by parents, justified by subsequent events, and culminating in a chosen alternative. The purpose of script analysis is to get clients out of their script and thus to behave autonomously.

Self. The central archetype: the archetype of order. The self, which expresses the unity of the personality as a whole, encompasses both conscious and unconscious components.

Self-concept. The self as perceived by the individual, and the values attached to these perceptions, or what a person refers to as "I" or "me".

Self-transcendence. The human capacity to reach out beyond the boundaries of oneself by either fulfilling a meaning or encountering another person lovingly.

Tracking. Refers to the careful assessment of the "firing order", the ordering of the chain reaction of the different modalities, to assist therapists in selecting and prioritising treatment interventions.

Transpersonal. The relationship at the heart of therapy. It includes the supernatural or numinous, and goes beyond the personal. It provides the spiritual factor in relationship.

Transaction. In transactional analysis a stroke or unit of recognition is viewed as the fundamental unit of social interaction. An exchange of strokes constitutes a transaction. Transactions take place between ego states.

Transference. Clients perceive their counsellors or therapists as reincarnations of important figures from their childhood; they then transfer (or "carry over") emotions associated ith these figures onto the counsellors.

Countertransference. That material or unfinished business, which the counsellor projects onto the client in the therapeutic situation.

Unconditional positive regard. Consists of two dimensions: first, prizing and feeling positively towards clients and, second, non-judgemental acceptance of clients' experiencing and disclosures as their subjective reality.

Unconscious (The lower self). Consists of material that is inadmissible to consciousness through repression. The censorship of unconscious material coming into awareness is very strong indeed.

Working alliance. The contract made between the counsellor and the client. It relates initially to the time and place of sessions, the goals of therapy, and fees, but may come to contain other clauses to do with the client's own problems and personality. It is of fundamental importance to the counselling process that the working alliance should be made, with all due sensitivity, as clear and binding as possible.

Bibliography

Adams, Jay E. (1976) *What about Nouthetic Counselling?*
Grand Rapids, Mich.: Baker Book House

Adler, G. (1979) *Dynamics of the Self*. ((first published
1951) London: Coventure Adler,G. (1966) *Studies in
Analytical Psychology*. London: Hodder and Stoughton

Adler, A. (1969) *The Science of Living*. Anchor/Doubleday:
New York

Adler, A. (1954) *Understanding Human Nature*. Fawcatt
Premier: New York

Ajaya, Swami (1976) *Yoga and Psychology: the evolution of
consciousness*. (Eds. Swami Rama, Rudolph Ballentine &
Swami Ajaya). Honesdale, PA: Himalayan Institute

Ajaya, Swami (1983) *Psychotherapy, East and West: a
unifying paradigm*. Honesdale, PA.: Himalayan Institute

Archambeau, E. (1979) *Beyond Countertransference: The
Psychotherapist's Experience of Healing in the Therapeutic
Relationship*. Doctoral dissertation. San Diego:
California School of Professional Psychology

Becker, Gary S. (1964) *Other Side: Perspectives on Deviance*.
Glencoe: Collier-Macmillan

Becker, Howard S. (1973) *Outsiders: Studies in the Sociology
of Deviance*. New York: Free Press

Benedict XV1, Pope (2005) *God is Love* (1st Encyclical).
London: CTS

Berne, E. (1966) *Principles of Group Treatment*. New York:
Grove Press

Bordin,E.S. (1974) *Strategies in Psychotherapy*. London:
Wiley-Interscience

Bordin, E.S. (1979) 'The generalizability of the psychoanalytical concept of the working alliance' in
Psychotherapy: Theory, Research and Practice.

Boss, M. (1963) *Psychoanalysis and Daseinanalysis* (Trans.
Lefefre L.B.). New York: Basic Books

Buber, Martin (1937) *I and Thou* (trans. Ronald Gregor
Smith). Edinburgh:T. & T. Clark

Buber, Martin (1957) *Eclipse of God.* London: Harper & Row

Bugental, J.F.T. (1987) *The Art of the Psychotherapist.* New York: W.W. Norton

Carkhuff, Robert R. & Berenson, Bernard G. (1977) *Beyond Counselling and Therapy* (second edn). London: Holt, Rinehart & Winston

Cassidy, S. (1988) *Sharing the Darkness:The Spirituality of Counselling.* London: Darton, Longman & Todd

Combs, A. W. (1971) 'What can man become?' In *The helping relationship sourcebook* (ed.D. Avila, A. Combs, & W. Purkey) Boston: Allyn and Bacon

Clarkson, Petruska (1995). *The Therapeutic Relationship.* London. Whurr Publishers.

Clinebell, Howard (1979) *Growth Counselling.* Nasville,Tenn.: Abingdon

Dryden, W. (Ed) (1984) *Individual Therapy in Britain.* London: Harper and Row

DuPont, Robert (1984) *Phobias, a Comprehensive Summary of Modern Treatments.* New York: Brunner/Mazel

Egan, Gerard (1998) *The Skilled Helper: a problem-management approach to helping.* London: Brooks/Cole

Egan, Gerard (1985) *Exercises in Helping Skills.* Monterey, CA: Brooks/Cole

Erickson, Milton (1987) *Hypnotic and strategic interventions.* New York: Irvington Publishers

Erikson, Erik H. (1982) *The Life Cycle Completed.* London: W.W. Norton

Fairbairn, William Ronald Dodds (1952) *Psychoanalytic Studies of the Personality.* London: Tavistock Publications

Freud, Anna (1931) *Introduction to psycho-analysis for teachers.* London: Allen and Unwin

Freud, Anna (1937) *The Ego and the Mechanisms of Defence* (trans. Cecil Baines). London: Institute of Psycho-analysis

Freud, S. (1962) The Dynamics of Transference. In *The Complete Psychological Works,* ed. James Strachey (Standard edition Vol. 12). London: Hogarth Press

Freud, S. (1905) *Fragment of an Analysis of a Case of Hysteria*. (Standard Edition Vol. 7; 1953-74). London: Hogarth Press

Freud, S. (1910) *The Future Prospects of Psychoanalytic Therapy* (Standard Edn. Vol 11, ed. J. Strachey 1953-74) London: Hogarth Press

Freud, S. (1920) *Beyond the Pleasure Principle* (Standard Edition Vol.18; 1953-74) Edn.) London: Hogarth Press

Freud, S. (1937) *Analysis Terminable and Interminable* (Standard Edition. C.W. Vol 23; 953-74). London: Hogarth Press

Freud, S. (1973) Lecture XXV111 in *The Complete Introductory Lectures on Psychoanalysis* (trans.J. Strachey)

Frey,D. and Carlock, C. J. (1984) *Enhancing Self-Esteem*. Muncie, Indiana: Accelerated Development Inc.

Friedman, Howard S. (2006) *Personality* (third edn.) London: Allyn & Bacon

Friedman, John A. (1998) *The origins of self and identity: living and dying in Freud's psychoanalysis*. London: Jason Aronson

Galloway, K. (1988) *Imagining the Gospels*. London: SPCK

Gelso, C.J. and Carter, J.A. (1985) *The Counselling Psychologist*. Chichester: Wiley & Sons

Gelso, Charles J. (1998) *The Psychotherapy Relationship*. Chichester: Wiley & Sons

Gill, Martin (1982) *The Analysis of Transference* Vol.1. New York: International Universities Press

Green, Rosemary (1991) *God's Catalyst*. London: Hodder & Stoughton

Greenson, R.R. (1967). *The Technique and Practice of Psychoanalysis*, Vol. 1. New York: International Universities Press

Grof, S. (1979) *Realms of the Human Unconsciousness*. London: Souvenir Press

Grof, S. (1988). *The Adventure of Self-Discovery*. New York: State University of New York Press.

Guntrip, H. (1961*) Personality Structure and Human Interaction: The Developing Synthesis of Psychodynamic*

Theory. London: Hogarth Press and the Institute of
Psycho-Analysis.

Gurman, A.S. & Rice, D.C (1975) *Couples in Conflict: new
directions in marital therapy.* London: J. Aronson

Heimann, P. (1950). On Countertransference. In
International Journal of Psycho-Analysis, 31, 81-84

Horney,Karen (1993) *Feminine Psychology.* New York:
W.W. Norton

Hurding, R. (1992) The Bible & Counselling. London:
Hodder and Stoughton

Johnson, David (1991) *The subtle power of spiritual abuse.*
Minneapolis, Minn.: Bethany House

Jung, C.G. (1963) *Mysterium coniunctions.* (C.W. Ed.
Herbert Read, Michael Fordam, Gerhard Adler, trans.
R.F.C.Hull, Vol. 14). London: Routledge & Kegan
Paul

Jung, C.G. (1954) *The Practice of Psychotherapy* (C.W. Ed.
Herbert Read, Michael Fordam, Gerhard Adler, trans.
R.F.C. Hull, Vol. 16). London: Routledge & Kegan
Paul

Kahn, M.D. (1997) *Between the Therapist and the Client:
The New Relationship.* New York: W.H. Freeman

Keating, Thomas (2002) *Foundations for Centering Prayer
and the Christian Contemplative Life.* London:
Continuum

Keen, S. (1992) *Fire in the Belly: On being a Man.* London:
Piatkus

Kelsey, M. (1977) *The Other Side of Silence:A Guide to
Christian Meditation.* London: SPCK

Kirsch, I. (1990) *Changing Expectations: A Key to Effective
Psychotherapy.* Pacific Grove, C.A: Brooks/Cole

Levin, Michal (2001) *Spiritual Intelligence.* London:
Coronet

Liechty, D. (1995) *Transference and Transcendence.* London:
J. Aronson

Little, M. (1986). *Toward Basic Unity: Transference Neurosis
and Transference Psychosis.* London: Free Association

McKay, M. and Fanning, P. (1992) *Self-Esteem.* Inc.
Oakland, CA.: New Harbinger Publication

Marquet, Pierre Bernard (1971) *Rogers.* Paris: Editions Universitaires

Maslow, A.M. (1954) *Motivation and personality.* New York: Harper and Row

Maslow, A.M. (1967) Self-actualization and beyond. In J.F.T. Bugental (Ed.), *Challenges of Humanistic Psychology.* New York: McGraw Hill

Maslow, A.M. (1968) *Toward a Psychology of Being,* (second edn). New York: D. Van Nostrand

Miller, Geri (2003) I*ncorporating spirituality into counselling and psychotherapy.* London: Wiley and Sons

Miller, William R. (Ed.) (1999) *Integrating Spirituality into Treatment.* Washington: American Psychological Association

Peck, S. (1978) *The Road Less Travelled: A New Psychology of Love, Traditional Values and Spiritual Growth.* New York: Simon and Schuster.

Perls, F.S, Hefferline, R.F., and Goodman, P. (1951). *Gestalt Therapy: excitement and Growth in the Human Personality.* New York: Julian Press

Quinn, Susan (1987) *A Mind of Her Own: The Life of Karen Horney.* New York: Summit Books

Richards, P.Scott & Allen E. Bergin(1997) *A Spiritual Strategy for Counseling and Psychotherapy.* Washington: American Psychological Association

Rizzuto, A. M. (1976) 'Freud, God, the Devil and the Theory of Object Representation.' In *International Review of Psycho-Analysis,*Vol. 3, Part 2

Rizzuto, A. M. (1980). The Psychological Foundations of Belief in God. In *Towards Moral and Religious Maturity.* (The First International Conference on Moral and Religious Development.) Morristown, New Jersey: Silver Bundett Company

Rogers, Carl R. (1951). *Client-Centred Therapy.* Boston: Houghton Mifflin.

Rogers, Carl R. (1961) *On becoming a person: A therapist's view of psychotherapy.* London: Constable & Co.

Rogers, Carl R. (1990) *The Carl Rogers Reader.* London: Constable & Co.

Samuels, A. (1985). *Jung and the Post-Jungians.* London: Routledge and Kegan Paul.

Schreurs, Agneta (2002) *psychotherapy and spirituality: integrating the spiritual dimension into the therapeutic practice.* London: J. Kingsley Publishers

Shermer, Victor L. (2003)*How We Believe: Science, Skepticism and the Search for God.* New York: Henry Holt

Stern, Max M. (1988) *Repetition and Trauma.* Hillsdale,NJ: Analytic Press

Stewart, I and Joines, V. (1987) *TA Today.* Nottingham: Lifespace.

Tanquerey, Adolphe (1930) *The Spiritual Life. A treatise on ascetical and mystical theology* (trans. Herman Branderis). Tournai: Desclée & Co.

Wilber, K. (1998) *The Essential Ken Wilber.* Boston: Shambhala

Winnicott, D.W. (1975) Hate in the countertransference. In *Through Paediatrics to Psyhoanalysis,* (pp. 194- 203). London: Hogarth Press and the Institute of Psycho Analysis

Wolff-Salin, Mary (1988) *No Other Light: Convergence in Psychology and Spirituality.* New York: Crossroad

Wolpe, Joseph (1973) *The Practice of Behavior Therapy.* New York: Pergamon

Zeig, Jeffrey K. & Munion, Michael W. (1999) *Milton H. Erickson* London: Sage

Yalom, Irvin D. (1980). *Existential Psychotherapy.* New York: Basic

Yalom, Irvin D. and Sophia Vinogradov(1989) *Concise Guide to Group Psychotherapy.* American Psychiatric Press

Zohar, Danah and Marshall, Ian (2001). *SQ: Spiritual Intelligence: The Ultimate Intelligence.* London: Cygnus Books.

Index

A

abuse
  financial 77
  of Bible in counselling 53,
    54, 58
  physical 252
  sexual 24, 27, 184, 185, 198,
    212
adolescent 96, 135, 174, 251
Africa 98, 100, 167, 208
alcohol addiction 96, 210, 242
anger 33, 104, 127, 149, 198,
  199, 222, 231, 237, 238
  and reparative experience 197,
    198, 205
anticipation 122, 123, 152, 167,
  232, 233, 234
anxiety 38, 197, 202, 238, 242,
  244, 257, 260

B

belief
  systems 9, 12, 142
bereavement and grief 97, 99,
  129, 149, 217
betrayal 78, 147
Bible in counselling 30, 53, 58
bishop 23, 65, 117, 131
body 15, 17, 36, 132, 145, 171,
  182, 193, 194, 201, 209, 210,
  240, 250, 251, 252, 275
boundaries 22, 48, 68, 71, 75,
  76, 77, 79, 81, 100, 101, 102,
  176, 179, 227, 277
"burnout" experiences 92

C

case studies
  person-to-person 211, 237
  reparative/developmentally
    needed 205

transference 139
  countertransference 167
transpersonal 59
working alliance 98
child
  and God-representation 133,
    134, 136
  in regressive state 180
  in transference 103, 104,
    106, 108, 109
  inner 207, 208, 231
childhood experience 24, 52,
  96, 104, 108, 109, 110, 133,
  163, 173, 174, 176, 183, 184,
  187, 191, 203, 208, 225, 237,
  271
  and self-esteem 248
cognitive-behavioural
  therapy 53, 54, 82, 127, 150,
  275
Confession 27, 247
creativity 16, 174, 203
  regression and 172
crying/tears 134, 206, 207

D

danger in counselling
  situation 11, 75, 78, 99, 116,
  185, 220, 234
death/dying 41, 61, 96, 106,
  233
  and rebirth 61, 62, 233
  of a parent 167, 168, 206,
    221, 226
defensiveness 88, 114, 276
despair 233
destructive critic 240, 243, 244,
  245, 250
developmentally needed or
  reparative relationship 23, 26,

45, **169–205**, 230, 234, 271
devil 134, 138, 197, 282
dream/fantasy 111, 124, 132,
    149, 172, 233
    dreamwork 246

E
education 21, 22, 116, 131, 135,
    136, 139, 175, 177, 241, 245,
    253, 254
empathy 22, 64, 67, 68, 69, 70,
    82, 83, 89, 92, 93, 112, 128,
    130, 131, 145, 156, 157, 187,
    189, 196, 220, 222
evil 34, 138, 268

F
failure 75, 162, 175, 234, 243,
    244, 245
    and breakthrough 193, 211,
    234
faith 25, 43, 44, 45, 49, 51, 53,
    135, 136, 169, 272
    and spiritual unfolding 30,
    49, 50, 52
    and suffering 34
father 23, 53, 56, 57, 61, 62, 69,
    104, 107
    God-prepresentation 49
    Prodigal Son 57
fear 16, 38, 49, 121, 124, 129,
    140, 144, 151, 152, 156, 162,
    184, 194, 197, 203, 232, 233
    of blood 98
    of death 61
    of separation 232
    of spiders 78
    of the unknown 135
    of unemployment 253
fees
    in working alliance 22, 76,
    79, 93, 94, 96, 97, 99, 277
forgiveness
    The Trinity and reparative
    relationship 87, 169, 170,

193, 194, 195, 196, 198,
    199, 207, 244, 245

G
God in the counselling
    relationship 12, 31, 32, 33,
    36, 37, 39, 40, 41, 43, 44, 47,
    49, 51, 53, 55, 60, 61, 62, 86,
    87, 132, 194, 195, 246, 272
God-representation 103, 131,
    132, 133, 134, 135, 136, 137
Gospel 56
guilt 96, 105, 108, 194, 206,
    231, 247

H
happiness 17, 18, 31, 61, 92
    counsellor's personal 92
hate/hatred 66, 86, 87, 104,
    113, 246, 270, 283
health(y)
    laughter 169, 200, 201
    physical 52, 60, 254
    self-esteem 19, 248, 254,
    263
    unhealthy relationship 104,
    124, 150, 171, 225
Holy Spirit 19, 32, 56
hope 41, 49, 102, 125, 222
hypnosis 121, 165

I
illusion 124, 162, 170
imagination 56, 57, 58, 132,
    150, 172, 203
    in the use of the Bible 56

J
Jesus Christ
    Gospel contemplation 133
    suffering and death 34, 169,
    193, 196, 199
    the Healer 32, 95

K
kenosis 30, 36, 37, 39, 40, 41, 47

L

late(ness)
  counsellor's 122, 163
  in attending sessions 96, 176, 190
laughter
  reparative effect of 169, 200, 201
love
  Divine 22, 31, 34, 55, 61, 86, 133, 144, 199, 242, 268, 272
  for clients 22, 41, 189
  higher self and 36, 60
  in transference 34, 63, 104

M

memory 17, 167, 207, 214, 233
mother in client relationships
  and case studies 30, 101, 108, 109, 118, 122, 133, 134, 140, 141, 142, 143, 144, 150, 153, 156, 167, 168, 182, 206, 207, 208, 212, 213, 237, 238, 270, 271

N

note-taking 11
numinous 35, 44, 45, 47, 277

P

pain and suffering 108, 110, 169, 198, 261
  and the Cross 31, 169, 170, 193, 272
  client's and case studies 34, 41, 206, 242
  in rejection/deprivation 153, 237
person-to-person relationship 45, 99, 121, 130, **211–236**, 238, 240, 271
personality 9, 123, 130, 136, 217, 279, 280, 282
  and middle self 246

client's 58, 149, 229, 245, 277
client's changing 83
counsellor's 42, 79, 83, 104, 149, 150
Kofler's Personality Model 15, 17, 20, 23, 24, 26, 29, 48, 64, 65, 139, 159, 218
poverty and deprivation 184, 185, 241, 253
prayer 10, 17, 18, 19, 32, 49, 51, 52, 59, 132, 137, 144, 195, 198, 246, 269, 281
preparation by counsellor 43, 92, 93, 137, 146
priests and religious 13, 95, 115, 117, 118, 123, 136, 137, 149, 205, 232
psychiatry (ist) 72, 79, 93, 96, 121
psychosis 96, 97, 281

R

regression 25, 121, 171, 172, 180, 181, 182, 202, 203, 275
  and reparative work 169, 171
resistance of client 35, 64, 103, 114, 120, 121

S

self-disclosure 88, 211, 213, 214, 215, 216, 217, 219, 220, 224, 225, 226
self-esteem 28, 149, 179, 240, 241, 242, 243, 246, 247, 248, 251, 252, 253, 254, 255, 261, 264, 265, 266, 267, 280, 281
sexual 16, 35, 52, 92, 96, 102, 155, 156, 162, 185, 213, 222
  homo- 19
spiritual(ity) 9, 10, 12, 15, 16, 17, 18, 19, 20, 21, 25, 30, 32, 34, 35, 36, 41, 44, 45, 46, 48, 49, 50, 51, 52, 53, 56, 57, 58, 59,

286

60, 62, 137, 160, 194, 196, 200,
201, 244, 245, 246, 264, 269,
272, 273, 274, 279, 281
intelligence 18, 19, 20, 32,
49, 273, 281, 283
psycho- 9, 15, 21, 25, 49,
137, 194
suicide 96, 97, 147, 234
supervision 67, 71, 76, 80, 81,
86, 92, 99, 145, 161, 164, 165,
166, 168, 173, 186, 188, 221,
223, 224, 225

T

teach(er) 10, 11, 43, 52, 53, 54,
78, 94, 95, 101, 104, 116, 118,
131, 136, 142, 144, 147, 153,
187, 207, 240, 242, 263, 265,
270, 279
terminaton, transference 6, 11,
22, 23, 25, 83, **103–139**, 141,
142, 143, 144, 145, 146, 148,
149, 151, 152, 153, 154, 156,
158, 159, 160, 161, 162, 163,
164, 165, 172, 173, 191, 202,
203, 270, 277, 279, 280, 281
countertransference 11, 23,

25, 33, 37, 38, 103, 117,
118, 119, 123, 127, 128,
131, 137, **145–167**, 168,
173, 191, 203, 211, 228,
229, 270, 271, 277, 278,
281, 283
proactive and reactive 37, 38,
41, 148, 149, 151, 154, 161,
162, 164, 168, 228, 229
transpersonal 15, 21, 24, 25,
30–59, 62, 63, 227, 231, 233,
234, 267, 272, 273
trauma 24, 121, 169, 171, 177,
178, 184, 192, 213, 283

V

violence 45, 72, 73, 75, 96, 208

W

war 72, 184, 198, 207
working alliance 21, 22, 23, 45,
49, **64–98**, 99, 100, 101, 103,
104, 123, 128, 129, 131, 155,
157, 162, 163, 164, 166, 181,
183, 189, 190, 191, 192, 203,
204, 207, 211, 212, 213, 227,
231, 240, 270, 277